Send For[illegible] You[illegible] Light

Also by Willard M. Swartley:

Slavery, Sabbath, War & Women: Case Issues in Biblical Interpretation

Homosexuality: Biblical Interpretation and Moral Discernment

Building Communities of Compassion: Mennonite Mutual Aid in Theory and Practice (editor with Donald B. Kraybill)

Violence Renounced: René Girard, Biblical Studies, and Peacemaking (editor)

Send Forth Your Light

A Vision for Peace, Mission, and Worship

WILLARD M. SWARTLEY

Herald Press
Scottdale, Pennsylvania
Waterloo, Ontario

Library of Congress Cataloging-in-Publication Data

Swartley, Willard M., 1936-
Send forth your light : a vision for peace, mission, and worship / Willard M. Swartley.
p. cm.
Includes bibliographical references and index.
ISBN 978-0-8361-9384-8 (pbk. : alk. paper)
1. Peace—Biblical teaching. 2. Peace—Religious aspects—Christianity. 3. War—Religious aspects—Christianity. 4. United States—Relations—Israel. I. Title.
BS680.P4S93 2007
261.8'73—dc22

2007016853

Library of Congress Catalog Card Number: 2007016853
International Standard Book Number: 978-0-8361-9384-8
Printed in the United States of America
Book design by Sandra Johnson
Cover by Sans Serif

16 15 14 13 12 11 10 09 08 07   10 9 8 7 6 5 4 3 2 1

To order or request information, please call 1-800-245-7894, or visit www.heraldpress.com.

To Mary,
to celebrate our
Golden Anniversary
of marital covenant

August 2008

CONTENTS

ABBREVIATIONS

AMBS	Associated Mennonite Biblical Seminary
BCBC	Believers Church Bible Commentary
cf.	compare
esp.	especially
ET	English translation
FS	Festschrift (for)
GNB	Good News Bible = Today's English Version
HWB	*Hymnal: A Worship Book*. Edited by Rebecca Slough for the Hymnal Project. Scottdale, PA: Mennonite Publishing House (et al.), 1992.
IMS	Institute of Mennonite Studies, Elkhart, Ind.
JBL	*Journal of Biblical Literature*
JSNT	*Journal for the Study of the New Testament*
JSNTSup	Journal for the Study of the New Testament: Supplement Series
lit. trans.	literal translation
LXX	Ancient Greek version of the OT
MQR	*Mennonite Quarterly Review*
NEB	New English Bible
NICNT	New International Commentary on the New Testament
NISBCO	National Interreligious Service Board for Conscientious Objectors
NT	New Testament
NTS	*New Testament Studies*
OT	Old Testament
RSV	Revised Standard Version
SBL	Society of Biblical Literature
SNTSMS	Society for New Testament Studies Monograph Series

SPS	Studies in Peace and Scripture
TDNT	*Theological Dictionary of the New Testament.* Edited by G. Kittel and G. Friedrich. Translated by G. W. Bromiley. 10 vols. Grand Rapids, 1964-76
WCC	World Council of Churches
YHWH	Yahweh = LORD in English OT

FOREWORD

One would expect a book like this from Willard Swartley!

Swartley is a superb scholar—dedicated, astute, extremely competent. But he is also a great man—gracious, gentle, generous, and godly. Both his calling and his character shine throughout these pages.

This book is written to urge the historic peace churches to reclaim their heritage with renewed zeal, but it also stimulates all Christians to discover that peace is the center of the New Testament message. As Swartley declares in a previous book subtitle, every Christian needs to be awakened to "the missing peace in New Testament theology and ethics."

I have admired Willard Swartley ever since I first met him and read his work many years ago, but my respect for him is heightened because this book presents his case so thoroughly and faithfully. Each part of the volume fulfills its purpose exceptionally well, and we rejoice to receive the benefits of Swartley's four decades of discipleship and teaching.

Part 1 lays the book's groundwork by thoroughly demonstrating the biblical accent on peace in the First Testament, in Jesus, and in Paul. This section is so rigorous and comprehensive that no one can doubt that peacemaking is an essential, and not optional, dimension of the gospel message. Members of those mainline and evangelical churches who have not emphasized the ministry of reconciliation that God has entrusted to us all will wonder how such a crucial component of Christ's being and teaching has been lost.

Part 2 deals with prominent issues for a peace witness today. Here Swartley is extremely prescient, for he answers our questions before we ask them. Especially noteworthy are his explication of Romans 13 and his finding a third way to handle the problem of the biblical promises given to Israel. I am particularly grateful for Swartley's personal example of what to do about paying taxes when one doesn't condone the government's use of those monies to perpetrate war and violence.

The third part of this book weaves an unbreakable cord as it laces together the three themes of the subtitle—peace, mission, and worship. All along, Swartley had invited us to think about worship by ending each chapter with an example of resources that knit us to the God of peace, but now he makes explicit the core truth that ardent worship will form us into Jesus' character, which will inevitably lead to both mission and peacemaking.

Why have churches so often split evangelism from social action? We need a larger story—the metanarrative of God's reconciliation of the cosmos and our participation in it.

Swartley helps us learn that story more earnestly and woos us to engage in it more deeply. For his masterful teaching I am forever grateful. I pray that this book will have a vast impact—to nourish those churches that have historically lived and died to give a peace witness and to challenge those Christians who have not previously recognized their vocation to do so.

Marva J. Dawn
author, *Unfettered Hope* and *Joy in Divine Wisdom*

PREFACE

Over the four decades of my teaching career, the biblical foundations for peacemaking and peace theology have been a sustained interest. My students over the years have engaged me in ways that contributed to my ongoing learning. I express appreciation to the many people who have assisted me in this pilgrimage. For some years I teamed with Old Testament [OT] colleagues Millard C. Lind and later Ben C. Ollenburger to teach the course "War and Peace in the Bible." I value the memories and invigoration of those co-teaching experiences.

This book complements my extensive study of peace and peacemaking: *Covenant of Peace: The Missing Peace in New Testament Theology and Ethics* (Eerdmans, 2006). *Covenant of Peace* exposits peace and related themes in the entire New Testament (NT) canon. It is designed as a (supplementary) text for courses in NT Theology and/or Ethics. *Send Forth Your Light: A Vision for Peace, Mission, and Worship* has a broader focus, intended for wider readership. The middle section focuses on three issues, on which disagreements exist even in historic peace churches.

Many of the chapters have had their origins in specific speaking or writing invitations within the last five years. Chapters 2 and 3, for example, originate from a 2004 Symposium in Sacramento, at which I represented the Christian voice among Jewish and Muslim voices on "The Influence of Religious Texts on Peace and Violence." Each religion was represented by one scholar. I was pleased that a "pacifist" perspective was invited. I introduced my speech by stating that I do not represent the "just-war" position held by most Christians, but that the pacifist tradition represents more directly the teachings of Jesus, Christianity's founder. Chapters 4 and 5 are new but draw on previously published articles: my article in John A. Lapp's edited *Peacemakers in a Broken World* (Herald Press, 1968) and an article I coauthored with Alan Kreider, published in *War and Pacifism*, edited by Oliver Barclay (Leicester, UK: Inter-Varsity Press, 1984). I am indebted to Alan for a section in chapter 5, represented in the discussion supported by footnotes 22-27. For chapter 7, I explain at the outset its origin: leading a Mideast study tour in 1975. It addresses a problem that is as thorny today as it was then. Chapter 8 is an adaptation of a 1980 *Mission Focus* article on mission expansion, based mostly on the book of Acts. Chapter 9, drawing on chapter 1 in *Covenant of Peace*, is an article I wrote recently for a *Festschrift* for Wilbert Shenk upon his retirement from Fuller Theological Seminary. Chapter 10 is new, a cutting edge in my thinking. It most directly develops the thesis embedded in this book's subtitle, that *Peace, Mission, and Worship* are intertwined. It also opens up the important topic of the relation between worship and politics. Chapter 11 makes available what I have occasionally used in congregations over the past two decades. It had its origin in congregational Bible studies on Revelation, first at Lombard Mennonite Church in 1984.

I am indebted to Richard A. Kauffman for his "Compiled" quotations, in his "Reflection" column in *Christianity Today*, to introduce chapters 2, 3, 4, 5, and 6 (Yancey [chap. 2] from Nov. 2004, 76; Meier and Willimon/Hauerwas [chap. 3] from May 2003, 60; Nouwen [chap. 5] from March 2005, 74; Bonhoeffer [chap. 4] and Fénelon [chap. 6] from Jan. 7, 2002, 62). I thank Richard for this much appreciated monthly contribution, for many years now.

I am grateful also to Mary for efficiently assisting me in the preparation of the indexes, and to Michael Degan of Herald Press for his careful editorial work, which has improved the manuscript.

The book's purpose is to strengthen commitment to peace and mission among Christian believers, for those in the historic peace churches and in other traditions as well. It invites the wider Christian family to embrace these understandings and commitments. Further, the book seeks to show the inextricable relationship between peacemaking, mission, and worship. The Christian life is one whole in its many facets of experience. Each of the legs of the peace-mission-worship tripod infuses the others with clarity and passion. The epistle of James addresses the issue of faith without works. This book addresses the issue of peace without mission and worship, mission without peace and worship, and worship without peace and mission. Each empowers the other two from a NT theological perspective. Let us "pursue those things that make for peace" (cf. Rom 14:19), engaging in the gospel's peace-mission, and uniting with fellow brothers and sisters in worship of God and Jesus Christ, in the power of the Spirit.

To the praise of God's glory!

INTRODUCTION

In spring 2005 I heard Tom Oliver, member of Pasadena (Calif.) Mennonite Church, present to his Sunday school class the story of how through Bible study he and Patricia, his wife, came to the belief that participation in war is wrong. This conclusion was costly: Tom would have to quit his military career, seeking a discharge from the army. He connected to the military first through ROTC in high school and enlisted in the army at age seventeen. Beginning as a private, he advanced to noncommissioned officer and then to lieutenant. His goal was to retire from the Reserves, after a military career.

During his fifth year he and Patricia committed themselves to reading the Bible to determine God's desires for their lives. They discussed especially its moral teachings and sought to know what Jesus means for their lives. They came to the conviction that as Christian believers committing themselves to the gospel of Jesus Christ, Tom must quit the military. What they then felt and saw ahead was a lonely future in taking such a "ridiculous" and costly stand. They knew nothing of the historic peace churches. But then from travels in Pennsylvania they discovered they were not alone. An entire group of people, the Amish, they learned, also did not believe in participating in war. A few weeks later in Plain City, Ohio, on a Choice Books rack they picked up literature on the Amish and also learned of the Mennonites. For about a year they lived mostly on the road, making connections with Amish and Mennonites. At Asheville (NC) Mennonite Church the pastor told them about NISBCO (National Interreligious Service Board for Conscientious Objectors) and the organization's *Manual* outlining steps to appeal for release from the military on religious, conscientious grounds.

Upon return to Los Angeles, they looked for a church and found Faith Mennonite, with Stanley Green then as pastor. Tom's next step, in 1991, was the daunting and courageous task of applying for discharge from the army on the basis of his religious belief. It was a soul-wrenching time for him, for he knew he might be faced with a prison sentence (though this was just before the mandatory prison sentence was set for such appeal). He filed the necessary papers requesting a discharge. The process took six months, involving a drug test, undergoing psychiatric and medical testing, and then appearing for a series of interviews before several military officials. Stanley Green supported and on occasion accompanied Tom in this process.

On hearing his story of how he came to this conviction, one of the interviewing officials said, "None of us here likes war, but in some cases it is necessary, and it's the duty of citizens to participate." The 1991 Persian Gulf War was imminent, and this last interview took place just a few days before President George H. W. Bush made his memorable "line in the sand" statement. But it would be another six months until Tom heard anything. Becoming anxious about the delay, Tom anticipated a negative response, denial of the request, or a jail sentence. While in the military Tom had often heard, "If you seek a discharge, you'll have to go to jail." Service personnel were never told about a way out. Thanks to the NISBCO Manual, Tom knew more, but he couldn't guess what the outcome for him would be. In light of his religious convictions and the manner in which he developed and presented his convictions, as well as his affiliation with a peace-church body, the military after six months of silence granted him an honorable discharge! Tom, Patricia, and Stanley were amazed and most grateful.

After hearing that story I pondered: How many young men and women in the Mennonite Church, as well as the wider historic peace churches, have really thought through the biblical basis for conscientious objection to war? To what extent have they studied the biblical teachings, as did Tom and Patricia?[1] Have we been faithful as churches in our teaching and counseling? Do we historic peace church members realize the legacy given to us in this church body, which has objected to participating in war for nearly five hundred years thus far, often suffering and migrating for such convictions? Do we appreciate the government's recognition of this historic peace church stance, which together with personal belief has during times of universal conscription formed the basis for granting exemption to military service? This is a rich inheritance, a treasure to be cherished and passed on to future generations. In this context I contribute these essays.

Part 1 of this book sets forth biblical teaching that anchors our identity in Scripture as God's covenant people committed to Jesus' way of peace. It presents peacemaking as an essential, not optional, aspect of the church's mission. Peace and peacemaking are linked inherently to the mission of the church. This book also focuses on mission because the two topics are not independent of each other, but intrinsically related.

Part 2 takes up issues that challenge the peace and mission commitments of the church: Christian witness to government, payment of taxes used for war, and what the Bible teaches about Israel (and God's promise of the land).

Part 3 focuses first on biblical foundations for the mission of the church. Both Acts and Paul's writings narrate the extraordinary Spirit-driven missionary work of the early church. Paul spent his life witnessing to Christ, beginning new church fellowships, and guiding the churches into worship—worship of God and of Jesus Christ, the focus of chapter 10. We shall see how these three emphases of peace, mission, and worship merge into a cord of three strands. The cord connects us to the "God of peace," to God's mission (*missio Dei*), and to worship of God and Jesus Christ in spirit and truth.

The main title of the book is from Psalm 43:3, with

expanded portions of the verse coming with each new division heading in this book. The translation here is a mix of KJV, RSV, and NRSV. Verse 4 is an appropriate ending complementing the Sending.

Some may wish to use this book as a study resource for small groups. For a quarter of study, I suggest using the first session to introduce the book and have participants identify their key biblical and theological questions on peace, mission, and worship. Depending on the group's interest, either chapter 7 or 10 could merit two sessions (thus a total of thirteen). The final session would be a worship service, done either by and for the study group or by the study group for the congregation.

Part 1

Biblical Foundations for Peace Witness

Send forth your light

CHAPTER ONE

Shalom-Jubilee: Biblical Call to Peacemaking

Let me hear what God the Lord will speak,
for he will speak peace to his people. . . .
Righteousness and peace will kiss each other.
—Psalm 85:8-10

Blessed are the peacemakers,
for they will be called children of God.
—Matthew 5:9

The kingdom of God is . . . righteousness and peace
and joy in the Holy Spirit. . . .
Let us then pursue what makes for peace and mutual upbuilding.
—Romans 14:17, 19

[Christ] is our peace; in his flesh he has made
both groups into one, . . .
that he might create in himself one new humanity
in place of the two, thus making peace, and might reconcile
both groups to God in one body through the cross.
—Ephesians 2:14-16

A harvest of righteousness is sown in peace . . . [by] those
who make peace.
—James 3:18

The Bible brims full with the language and vision of peace. In many cases it is language of inspiration and hope, sometimes language of judgment, promise, or command.

Shalom is the Hebrew word for *peace* (occurring more than 250 times in the OT). It has many dimensions of meaning: wholeness, well-being, harmony, peace, salvation, and justice. It includes covenant faithfulness. Its Greek counterpart, *eirēnē* embraces Christian community, the fruits of the Spirit, and the hope of the life to come. *Shalom* often occurs when one is inquiring about another's *welfare* (Gen 29:6; 37:14; 43:27; Exod 18:7; 1 Sam 10:4; 17:18, 22; 25:5; 30:21; Jer 15:5 for shalom of Jerusalem; 38:4). Inquiry about one's "welfare includes everything necessary to healthful living: good health, a sense of well-being, good fortune, the cohesiveness of the community, relationship to relatives and their state of being, and anything else deemed necessary for everything to be in order."[1]

English versions may translate *shalom* as prosperity (Ps 30:6; Isa 54:13). *Shalom* also has moral connotations: it is opposed to deceit (Ps 34:13-14; Jer 8:22–9:6). *Shalom* assumes relationship with God and relationships of integrity with fellow humans. Cheating others, hurting others in any way, violating covenants, and living selfishly deprive the community of shalom. As humans in covenant relation to God, we are called to seek and pursue peace (Ps 34:14; 1 Pet 3:11), but at the same time regard peace as God's gift, a treasure we experience through God's grace. *Shalom* is God's will and *gift* for God's people.

A Christian epistle rightly begins, as Paul's do, with "Grace and peace to you." The Greek greeting "grace" (*charis*) and the Hebrew greeting "peace" (*shalom*) are fitting umbrellas under which all discussion of the Christian life takes place.

I present the biblical calling to peacemaking under three headings:

1. The biblical call *gives* us a *vision* of *shalom*—from God.
2. The biblical call *gives* us a *passion* for *shalom*—from

God's Spirit.

3. The biblical call *gives* us a *strategy* for *shalom*—from Jesus, the Servant-Messiah.

In each case note the verb *gives*. Shalom is a gift from God—a gift that in the biblical drama is also a calling and task for God's people.[2] Shalom is *Gabe* and *Aufgabe*, a gift to and a task for God's people. This task is our call.

The Biblical Vision of Shalom—from God

Humanity is made in the "divine image" (Gen 1:26-27). Each person potentially reflects God, the divine presence over all creation. When each person regards every other person as a potential mirror of God's presence, then creation's vision of shalom is fulfilled. How we treat other people is how we treat God, says the Son of man in his judgment (Matt 25:31-46). All human life is sacred, for it potentially images God's presence on earth.

Interlude. Men and women, created as humanity in God's image, refuse the role of *image* and seek to become "as God." Arrogance and disobedience (in short, sin) bursts the shalom of God's good creation. Humanity strives to be "as God," replacing God's dominion with our own dominion, refusing the image and "playing God" according to our own machinations. We puncture and destroy God's shalom—God's Eden.

We hate and kill our Abels. We build our Babel; the five letters are five sides, like the Pentagon. Like Lamech of old, we kill without cause and plead no mercy, for like him our civilization provides our defense—armies, bombs, submarines, guided missiles, nuclear warheads, and so forth.

So, like Lamech of old, we make a hit tune out of murder: "Lamech said to his wives: 'Adah and Zillah, hear my voice; you wives of Lamech, listen to what I say: I have killed a man for wounding me, a young man for striking me. If Cain is avenged sevenfold, truly Lamech seventy-sevenfold'" (Gen 4:23-24). Lamech is secure with his civilization: cities, metallurgy, and music to entertain. And like Cain *we* say, what do I care—with nuclear warheads stocked in pairs?

Humans continue in the way of Adam, Cain, Lamech, and Babel. Through sin's arrogance, the world is engulfed in its own potential destruction. Playing God has produced humanity's own portending genocide. At any one time in contemporary history, forty wars or more go on.

Interlude Consequence. Abraham, the father of Israel, is called to become a channel of God's blessing to all nations. But what is that blessing? Is it not God's righteousness that God gives Abraham on the basis of his obeying faith? Righteousness is the means to shalom, and both are gifts of God to be expressed in life. Abraham's righteousness stands in the service of shalom as his payment of tithe and homage to Melchizedek, king of Salem, witnesses (Gen 14:18). *Melek-tsedek*—king of righteousness, headquartered in Jerusalem—is the *cornerstone* (Jerus) of *peace* (shalom). Abraham, the father of the faithful, bows before and toward the archetype of *righteousness* and *shalom.* The goal of the life-made-righteous-by-faith is shalom for the world. Who was *Melek-tsedek* anyway? To whom did Abraham bow? In Hebrews, Jesus Christ is linked with the priestly order of Melchizedek precisely in his perfection *through* his godly fear, his learning obedience through his suffering (Heb 5). Jesus Christ thus qualifies as priest forever after the order of the "king of righteousness" who is "the cornerstone of peace" (Heb 7).

Shalom is the *fruit* of God's steadfast love, faithfulness, righteousness, and justice. The semantic field of shalom comprises:

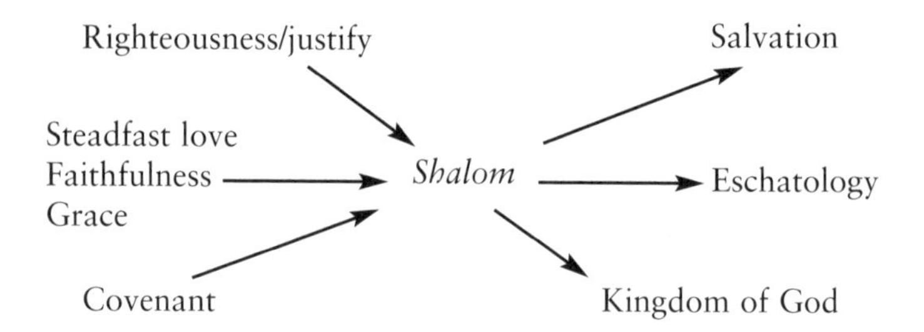

Key OT texts are: "Steadfast love and faithfulness will meet; righteousness and peace will kiss each other" (Ps 85:10); "Righteousness and justice are the foundation of your throne; steadfast love and faithfulness go before you" (89:14). Based in God's own moral attributes and rooted in covenant relationship, shalom promises salvation and hopes for a future in which God's kingdom will fully come. The prophetic burden is the establishment of shalom through justice. Justice is the practice of righteousness. Prophets Micah and Isaiah expect God's people *to learn to do justice*—to live out God's righteousness in life. Isaiah 2:1-4 sets forth the torah as the basis of justice, and Mic 6:8 specifies justice as what the Lord God requires. Without justice, kindness, and humility, the best *worship* ritual is of no account (6:6-7). So also Deut 16:20: "Justice, and only justice, you shall pursue, so that you may live."

The semantic field for justice in the OT and NT compared to that of shalom appears as follows:[3]

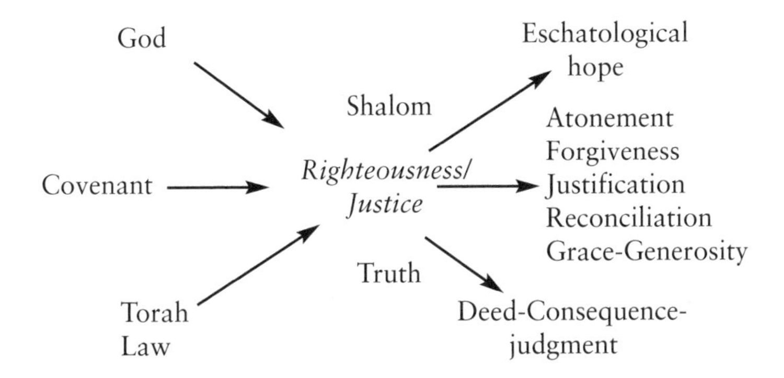

The three designates on the left (shalom, covenant, Torah) are the foundation of justice and righteousness in the OT. Shalom and truth are indispensably close to justice: above and beneath. The three on the right (eschatological hope, various images for salvation, and deed-consequence/ judgment) are the out-workings of those on the left, in canonical trajectory, within the OT and culminating in the NT. Without this foundation and context, justice readily becomes a will o' the wisp, an elusive goal.

The Jubilee provisions guarantee justice in practical life. The Sabbath, sabbatical system, and Jubilee all enact the justice of God's righteous shalom. In its basic form the entire system of Sabbath, sabbatical, and Jubilee are expressions of God's justice. The humanitarian purpose of the Sabbath enables the servants to rest as well as the masters (Deut 5:12-14). The sabbatical provisions give servants freedom to choose anew their masters (Exod 21:1-6) and cancel debts in order to ensure economic equality (Deut 15:1-6). The most fundamental guarantee of justice is the Jubilean redistribution of property. In addition to these specific provisions, the social legislation for Israel's life repeatedly protects the rights of the poor and the community's responsibility for the poor, the widow, orphan, and stranger (Exod 22:21-24; 23:9-11; Lev 19:9-10; 25:25-28, 35-55; Deut 15:4-11; 23:24-25; 24:19-22). The second tithe, to be paid every three years, is for the dispossessed Levite, the fatherless, the widow, and the sojourner (Deut 14:28-29; 26:13). Further, these responsibilities are all rooted in Israel's covenant relationship with God (Lev 25:17, 38; Exod 23:9b, 13).

The Bible is a story about humanitarian eschatology. Faith and love ever hope for and live toward righteousness and justice. Jesus proclaims that the kingdom has come near. God's shalom has come near in Christ Jesus. Faith produces righteousness, love produces justice, and righteousness-justice produces shalom.

The biblical call to be peacemakers gives us a vision of shalom—from God.

The Biblical Call to Peacemaking Gives Us a *Passion* for Shalom—from God's Spirit

Observe Luke's introduction of Jesus' prophetic ministry:

"The Spirit of the Lord is upon me,
because he has anointed me
to bring good news to the poor.
He has sent me to proclaim release to the captives
and recovery of sight to the blind,
to let the oppressed go free,
to proclaim the year of the Lord's favor." . . .
Then he began to say to them,
"Today this Scripture has been fulfilled in your hearing."
(4:19, 21)

Numerous emphases in Luke's Gospel, found also in Mark and Matt, coincide with the Jubilean emphases, most notably Mary's Magnificat, in which the lowly are exalted and the hungry fed (1:52-53), the call to kingly servanthood at Jesus' baptism (3:22), Jesus' resistance of the temptations to kingship on worldly sociopolitical terms (4:1-13), Jesus' call to costly discipleship (12:49–14:35) and rejecting the sword (22:25-46), and the Lord's Prayer itself (11:3-4), which uses a word for "forgiveness" of sins and debts regularly used in the debt-cancellation contract of Jubilee.[4]

Luke emphasizes Jesus' blessings upon the poor and woes for the rich (6:20, 24). Luke-Acts sets forth a Jubilean understanding of Jesus (see Luke 12; 16; 18:18-30; 19:1-10). Jesus' followers practice community of goods so that there is "not a needy person among them" (Acts 2:43-46; 4:32-34), widows' material needs are met (6:1-6), and the church at Antioch sends a relief gift to the poor in Jerusalem (11:27-30; Gal 2:10). Jesus and the early church thus continue aid to the poor and needy, as commanded in the Torah and the Prophets.

Luke's Gospel stresses other points that also fit well with a Christian vision of the Jubilean justice: the prominent role of women: Elizabeth, Mary, Anna, the women from Galilee among Jesus' disciples (8:1-3), Martha and Mary, and the women at the tomb; Jesus' accepting outsiders and outcasts so that the forgiven prostitute and prodigal come into Jesus' messianic community (7:36-50; 15); and Jesus' welcoming Samaritans and Gentiles into God's kingdom.

Hence the OT vision and prophetic ethic of Jubilee justice and righteousness find fulfillment in Jesus' teachings and actions. The poor inherit the kingdom, the blind see, the lame walk, and the prisoners are released. Through Jesus' faithful expression of God's love, the poor and the outcasts find welcome and justice in God's kingdom.[5] In the OT the passion of the prophet for shalom-justice comes from the call of God and the anointing of the Spirit. The kings are "the anointed." What is the king's task and call in the power of the Spirit? On this matter see Pss 72 and 82. Psalm 72 calls the king, God's royal son, to do justice: to "defend the cause of the poor of the people, give deliverance to the needy, and crush the oppressor" (72:1-4). Psalm 82 condemns the gods-kings of the earth for failing to do precisely this. Isaiah 11:1-5 outlines the work of the messianic "shoot from the stump of Jesse" upon whom the Spirit of the Lord shall rest: through "the spirit of wisdom and understanding, the spirit of counsel and might, the spirit of knowledge and the fear of the Lord, . . . he shall not judge by what his eyes see, or decide by what his ears hear; but with righteousness he shall judge the poor, and decide with equity for the meek of the earth. . . . Righteousness shall be the belt around his waist, and faithfulness the belt around his loins" (Isa 11:1-5).

Similarly, the key text of Isa 32 makes shalom-peace the fruit of righteousness, and Isa 42 makes "justice in the earth" the work of the Spirit-anointed Servant of the Lord:

> See, a king will reign in righteousness,
> and princes will rule with justice, . . .
> until a spirit [RSV: 'the Spirit'] from on high is poured out on us,
> and the wilderness becomes a fruitful field,
> and the fruitful field is deemed a forest.
> Then justice will dwell in the wilderness,

and righteousness abide in the fruitful field.
The effect of righteousness will be peace,
and the result of righteousness,
quietness and trust forever.

(32:1, 15-17)

I have put my spirit [RSV: 'Spirit'] upon him;
he will bring forth justice to the nations. . . .
He will not grow faint or be crushed
until he has established justice in the earth;
and the coastlands wait for his teaching.

(42:1b, 4)

The call and task to bring justice and peace to those both near *and far* (57:19) launches a new vision and phase in God's salvation for humanity. The past "warfare is ended" (Isa 40:2 RSV), and the beautiful gospel of peace is at hand (52:7). The mission is comprehensive and radical (61:1-2), and it requires suffering (Isa 53).

The *passion* for shalom comes from God himself, from his Spirit. Whenever we seek the renewal of the Spirit, there is a pressing need to test the renewal against the prophetic standard: the spirit of justice, which Matthew describes Jesus the Servant as bringing (12:19-20 NEB; quoting Isa 42:2-4a):

He will not strive, he will not shout,
Nor will his voice be heard in the streets.
He will not snap off the broken reed,
Nor snuff out the smouldering wick,
Until he leads justice to victory.

Shalom without justice mocks the Lord's servant of Isa 40-55, and indeed Jesus also.

The prophetic passion for justice is the *social face of righteousness*. It is part and parcel of God's concern for the poor. As José Miranda points out in his insightful and disturbing book, *Marx and the Bible*, the OT terms for *justice* (*mishpat*) and *right*(eousness) (*tsedaqah*) are used synonymously. In addition to appearing together in synonymous parallelism thirty-four times (e.g., Ps 33:5; 72:1-2; Prov 2:9; 8:20; Isa 5:7b; 32:16; 33:5-6; 54:17; 60:17b; often in Zech), the two roots (*shpt* and *tsdk*) are paired together in thirty-two other instances.[6]

In the "golden text" of the prophetic ethic, Amos declares, "Let justice roll down like waters, and righteousness like an everflowing stream" (5:24). Micah's classic summary is similar:

> He has told you, O mortal, what is good;
> and what does the Lord require of you
> but to do justice,
> and to love kindness,
> and to walk humbly with your God? (6:8)

Isaiah also, lamenting Israel's perversion of values, enunciates the same divine standard with striking puns and antithetic poetic parallelism:

> [God] expected justice [*mishpat*],
> but saw bloodshed [*mispah*];
> righteousness [*tsedaqah*],
> but heard a cry [*tse'aqah*]! (5:7b)

The prophetic passion for justice is summed up well by Abraham Heschel:

> Instead of dealing with the timeless issues of being and becoming, of matter and form, of definitions and demonstrations, [the reader of the prophets] is thrown into orations about widows and orphans, about the corruption of judges and affairs of the marketplace. Instead of showing us a way through the elegant mansions of the

> mind, the prophets take us to the slums. The world is a proud place, full of beauty, but the prophets are scandalized, and rave as if the whole world were a slum. . . . To us a single act of injustice—cheating in business, exploitation of the poor—is slight; to the prophets, a disaster. To us injustice is injurious to the welfare of the people; to the prophets it is a deathblow to existence; to us, an episode; to them, a catastrophe, a threat to the world.[7]

The Biblical Call to Peacemaking Gives Us a Strategy for Shalom—in Jesus Christ

Jesus Christ is the historical enfleshing of God's passion for shalom upon earth: *Peace* on *Earth*! (Luke 2:14).[8] Anointed by the Spirit, Jesus as Messiah begins his ministry of good news to the poor, release to the captives, sight to the blind, and liberty for the oppressed (Luke 4:18-19). The vast stream of prophetic justice is now focalized in his proclaiming and doing Jubilean justice. The prophetic vision is *incarnated* in Jesus.

He denounces substituting laws of religion for love of humanity.

He cleanses the temple, defending the rights of the Gentiles.

He rebukes Peter for identifying messiahship with oppressive power.

He calls his followers to take up a cross, not a sword.

He sets before his disciples the images of cross, child, and servant.

> So Jesus called them and said to them, "You know that among the Gentiles those whom they recognize as their rulers lord it over them, and their great ones are tyrants over them. But it is not so among you; but whoever wishes to become great among you must be your servant, and whoever wishes to be first among you must be slave of all. For the Son of Man came not to be served but to serve, and to give his life a ransom for many." (Mark 10:42-45)

Jesus weeps over Jerusalem (cornerstone of peace) because it rejected the things that make for *shalom*. He then takes upon himself the jealous, selfish hate and evil of both the religious and military powers, is crucified, and said: "Father, forgive them; for they do not know what they are doing" (Luke 23:34). Paul declares that in Jesus' death "he [God or Christ] disarmed the principalities and powers, making a public example of them, triumphing over them" (Col 2:15 RSV). The cross thus exposes sin as sin. It exposes what evil does when confronted by Jesus, servant of justice and righteousness.

But God's strategy does not stop with the cross. *God* through Jesus, the holy servant, has not only disarmed and made a public example of the principalities and powers through the cross and resurrection of Jesus; God has also vindicated his faithful *servant* (Acts 3:13-15, 26). God's strategy continues in creating a new community, the church, the *life* and *body* of *Christ* in the world.

God's strategy includes both servanthood and resurrection power. Our call and task is to serve in justice; God's gift is to raise in power.

Shalom and *Eirēnē* in Concert with Messianic Hope

Eirēnē (Greek for "peace") also has a wide semantic field:[9]

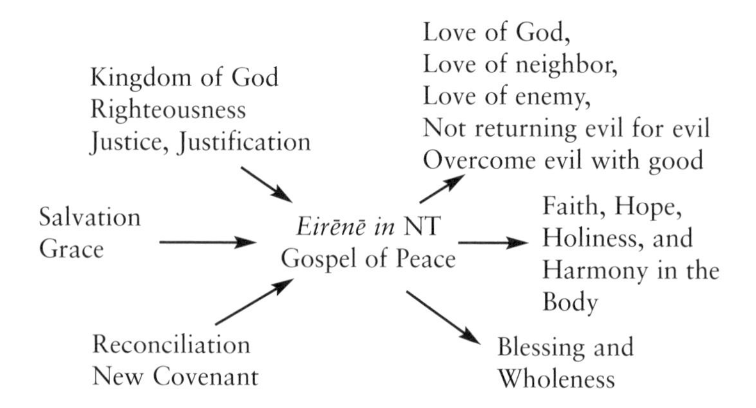

Numerous key prophetic texts anticipate the coming of a messiah who will bring justice and peace on earth. Some well-known ones occur in the *Messiah* oratorio, such as Isa 9:1-7; 11:1-9; 40:1-11 (cf. Zech 9:9-11; Mic 4:1-5; Isa 52:7). Isaiah 52:7, not as well known, is most important since it is quoted in the NT to sum up Jesus' ministry. I put the two texts (Isa 52:7, 10 and Acts 10:34-36) side by side:

How beautiful upon the mountains
are the feet of the messenger
who announces peace,
who brings good news,
who announces salvation,
who says to Zion, "Your God reigns." . . .
The Lord has bared his holy arm
before the eyes of all the nations;
and all the ends of the earth shall see
the salvation of our God.

Then Peter began to speak to them:
"I truly understand that God shows no partiality,
but in every nation anyone who fears him
and does what is right is acceptable to him.
You know the message he sent to the people of Israel,
preaching peace by Jesus Christ—
he is Lord of all."

Most significant, the phrase "announcing/preaching peace" is similar in the Greek version of Isa 52:7 and Acts 10:36. In Greek, both are a form of *euangelizisthai eirēnēn*. The noun *gospel* is already in the verb as well as the verbal act of proclaiming or preaching. *Eirēnē* then is the object, which is preached. Chapter 9, in part 3 on mission (below), shows this connection in more detail and its significance. The point we must not miss is that both testaments inextricably link *peace* and *mission*. The Isaiah oracle concludes with "all the ends of the earth shall see the salvation of our God." This is the fruit of mission, and the phrase implies worship as well. In its context the Acts text is Peter's "Gettysburg Address" for the founding of a new nation of peace, in which alienated peoples become one in the Messiah Jesus, surpassing—even subverting—warring nations.

Peter is declaring the basis on which Cornelius, a Gentile military official, is legitimately included in the kingdom of

God, inaugurated by Jesus. The point here is not to approve the morality of the Roman military, but to recognize that this person, the hated Roman presence, is "bending his knee" to worship Peter (cf. Acts 10:25), which Peter refuses (10:26). The enemy is saved! Jew and Gentile bend together into the lordship of Christ: "[Jesus] is Lord of all!" (10:36). Just as the Messiah's gospel is the "end of the law" (Rom 10:4), so it is also the end of the military might—with all the fascinating interpretations of just what "end" (*telos*) means for both. On the political side, it certainly means *end* in terms of consummation. Just as Abraham bowed down to Melchizedek, so Cornelius—representing Rome's might—bows down to Jesus.

The subsequent chapters of this book build the new messianic "temple of God," in which true worship means commitment to both mission and peacemaking.

Conclusion

For he is our peace;
  in his flesh he has made both groups into one
and has broken down the dividing wall,
  that is, the hostility between us.

(Eph 2:14)

There is no longer Jew or Greek,
  there is no longer slave or free,
there is no longer male and female;
  for all of you are one in Christ Jesus.

(Gal 3:28)

The biblical *strategy* for shalom is (1) servant living inspired by the justice of God's righteous love; (2) costly discipleship inspired by faithfulness to Jesus, the perfect servant; and (3) vindication by God's resurrection power.

To this you have been called,
because Christ also suffered for you,
leaving you an example,
so that you should follow in his steps.
"He committed no sin,
and no deceit was found in his mouth."
(1 Pet 2:21-22)

The biblical strategy *calls* us to follow Jesus—to be servants of justice and peace, in mission that unites all in Jesus Messiah. Neither imperial power with all its intimidation nor the horrible sinfulness of the people excuses us from this unique witness. Rather, the *incarnation* teaches us that following Jesus leads us to give our lives for God's shalom work in Jesus Christ. We are called to continue the incarnation, witnessing to Christ's making peace through the cross.

We have this treasure in earthen vessels,
to show that the transcendent power belongs to God and not to us.
We are afflicted in every way, but not crushed;
perplexed, but not driven to despair;
persecuted, but not forsaken;
struck down, but not destroyed;
always carrying in the body the death of Jesus,
so that the life of Jesus may also be manifested in our bodies.
For while we live we are always being given up to death for Jesus' sake,
so that the life of Jesus may be manifested in our mortal flesh.
(2 Cor 4:7-11 RSV)

Through this *vision*, *passion*, and *strategy* of shalom, the justice and righteousness of God's shalom-Jubilee will be established throughout the earth, as the link between Isaiah

52:7, 10 and Acts 10:36 demonstrates. In chapter 9 (below) we further explore this link and its significance as Jesus fulfills the Isa 52:7-10 vision: mission, gospel, peace, and the kingdom of God.[10]

Affirmation of Faith

Leader: We believe that peace is the will of God. God created the world in peace, and God's peace is most fully revealed in Jesus Christ, who is our peace and the peace of the whole world.

All: Led by the Holy Spirit, we follow Christ in the way of peace, doing justice, bringing reconciliation, and practicing nonresistance even in the face of violence and warfare.

Leader: As followers of Jesus, we participate in his ministry of peace and justice. He has called us to find our blessing in making peace and seeking justice.

Side 1: We do so in a spirit of gentleness, willing to be persecuted for righteousness' sake.

Side 2: As disciples of Christ, we do not prepare for war, or participate in war or military service.

Leader: The same Spirit that empowered Jesus also empowers us

Side 1: to love enemies,
Side 2: to forgive rather than to seek revenge,
Side 1: to practice right relationships,
Side 2: to rely on the community of faith to settle disputes,
Side 1: and to resist evil without violence.

Leader: We give our ultimate loyalty to the God of grace and peace, who guides the church daily in overcoming evil with good, who empowers us to do justice, and who sustains us in the glorious hope of the peaceable reign of God.

From a Mennonite Church USA church bulletin insert, March 23, 2003, from Mennonite Mission Network (Newton, Kan., and Elkhart, Ind.), as excerpted from article 22 of *Confession of Faith in a Mennonite Perspective*.[11] Used with permission.

CHAPTER TWO

Jesus on Peace and Violence

When Jesus prayed to the one who could save him from death,
he did not get that salvation;
he got instead the salvation of the world.
—*Philip Yancey in* Christianity Today

Most Christians regard war under certain conditions as acceptable.* I am a pacifist, a minority voice in the Christian tradition. The historic peace church tradition, shared by Amish, Brethren, Hutterites, Mennonites, and Quakers, has variety in beliefs, but a commitment to peace and resisting violence is common to all. Though not all individual church members choose the position of the church, participation in war is forbidden in the denominations' teaching and practice.

Most of these groups (except Quakers) trace their origins to the sixteenth-century Anabaptists, the Radical Reformers who broke with the state church and, true of most but not all of them, renounced war and participation in it. Hence I draw on this peace church tradition, but my citations are not limited to writers in these Christian groups. A vast number

* The content of this chapter was first presented in a 2004 fall Symposium in Sacramento exploring Christian, Jewish, and Muslim perspectives on how their founding religious texts promote peace and/or violence.

of contemporary Christian scholars interpret the NT texts in harmony with a peace church perspective.

The founding document for Christian faith is the NT. Scripture for Christian believers, however, includes the OT, also called the Hebrew Bible or Tanak (Torah, Nevi'im, and Kethuvim = Law, Prophets, and Writings). This chapter is grounded on the faith's founder, Jesus Christ. Although limiting itself mostly to the NT part of Christian Scripture, its declarations often appeal to the OT for grounding authority. A notable example is 1 Pet 3:9-12. Echoing the words of Jesus, "Do not return evil for evil, or reviling for reviling; but on the contrary bless" (RSV). Here 1 Pet quotes Ps 34:12-16a (Ps 33:13-17 LXX) to substantiate, authorize, and intensify his admonition. These verses read:

> Those who desire life and desire to see good days,
> let them keep their tongues from evil
> and their lips from speaking deceit;
> let them turn away from evil and do good;
> let them seek peace and pursue it.
> For the eyes of the Lord are on the righteous,
> and his ears are open to their prayer.
> But the face of the Lord is against those who do evil.
> (1 Pet 3:10-12)

Indeed, the NT is in debt to the OT, in quotations, theology, and even structural form.[1]

In appealing to the founder of the Christian faith, I distinguish between the four Gospels (Matthew, Mark, Luke, John) and the remaining twenty-three NT books, of which Paul wrote seven to thirteen (scholarly judgment varies). Christians regard all twenty-seven books as canonical and authoritative for faith and life, accepted by the church as bearing the authority of divine revelation (defined differently among Christian adherents). Factors of apostolicity (written in the first century with connection to one of the apostles), widespread use and acceptance over the next two centuries, defense of the faith against heresies, and the survival of books amid persecution—all played important roles in determining which books came to be recognized as canonical.[2]

This chapter is oriented to what Jesus taught according to the four Gospels. Chapter 3 focuses on the teachings of Paul and other NT writers. One crucial point often overlooked by critical NT scholars who emphasize the NT's diversity is that on the issue of peace/peacemaking, the NT as a whole is quite consistent.[3]

To understand Jesus' teachings in context, we must consider that Jesus lived and taught within a sociopolitical setting in which his actions and words would *not* have been heard as theological or moral abstractions. Rather, the Gospel narratives, when read against first-century world realities, reflect the political character of Jesus' life, death, and resurrection.

Jesus: Political King. According to the Gospels' portraits, Jesus is born "king of the Jews" (Matt 2:2), the one who "will put down the mighty from their thrones" (Luke 1:52 RSV). His baptism calls him to kingship (Mark 1:11b echoes Ps 2:7, a royal psalm). The temptations pose alternate ways to kingship (Matt 4:1-10). Jesus preaches the imminent arrival of the kingdom of God, a political conception (Mark 1:15), and the Jubilean ethic of social justice, subverting prevailing social order (Luke 4:18-19). He chooses disciples who are Zealots: Simon (Acts 1:13), most likely Judas, and possibly also Peter, James, and John. He accepts Peter's confession, "You are the Messiah" (Mark 8:29), a truth Jesus himself does not deny before the chief priests at his trial (Mark 14:61-62; cf. 15:25-26).

The Jewish leaders turn Jesus over to Pilate on the charges that he is a political subversive who tells people not to pay their taxes and claims himself to be a king (Luke 23:2). He dies the Zealot's death of crucifixion. His cross bears the inscription, "The King of the Jews" (Luke 23:38). And upon his resurrection, he is acclaimed royal Messiah and imperial Lord (Acts 2:29, 36).

Jesus: Prince of Peace. Jesus' birth prompts the angelic chorus, "On earth peace among those whom he favors!" (Luke 2:14). His baptism calls him to the vocation of the prophetic suffering servant (Mark 1:11c echoes Isa 42:1, a suffering servant song). In his temptations he refuses the popular Jewish expectations of political messiahship. Among his disciples is also Matthew, the tax collector, a Roman collaborationist (Matt 9:9; Acts 1:13). His kingdom preaching keynoted by its Jubilean platform (Luke 4:16-19) says nothing of military conquest but affirms the merciful strand of Jewish messianic hopes.

He thus welcomes the outcasts, even Samaritans and Gentiles, into God's love and grace (Luke 15; John 4). He teaches his disciples to love not only their neighbors, but also their enemies (Matt 5:43-44). He recognizes Peter's political-power view of messiahship and calls it satanic, because the Messiah-Son of Man must suffer and die (Mark 8:31-37). During Jesus' trial, Pilate declares three times that he finds no sustainable charge against Jesus (Luke 23:4, 14, 22). On the cross, Jesus says: "Father, forgive them; for they do not know what they are doing" (Luke 23:34). Upon his resurrection, Jesus is acclaimed to be saving Messiah and Lord, who forgives the sins of the people (Acts 2:36-38).

In light of this dual lens to perceive Jesus, it is wrong to regard Jesus as nonpolitical, or to count him as "political" in the usual sense of the word. John Howard Yoder's well-known book *The Politics of Jesus* contends that Jesus birthed a *new politics*, which Donald B. Kraybill has described as *The Upside-Down Kingdom*.[4]

The Beatitudes

Jesus said, "Blessed are the peacemakers, for they will be called children of God" (Matt 5:9). And Jesus commands, "Love your enemies," for this will mark you as "children of your Father in heaven" (5:44).

The Beatitudes promise God's blessing for lowly people.

Blessing is God's word of grace and hope. The entire Sermon on the Mount is *gospel*, a present and future gift from the heart of God for the people of the covenant (*diathēkē*),[5] whose lives are characterized by being poor in spirit, mourning, meek; by hungering and thirsting for righteousness; by being merciful, pure in heart, peacemakers, persecuted for righteousness' sake. The Beatitudes (Matt 5:3-12) promise *blessedness* precisely where it does not exist in this world, for people who are meek, lowly of heart, humbly trusting in God. Such people fear the Lord and are friends of God (Ps 25:14).

Jesus' blessing on the peacemakers connotes positive action. It speaks not of merely thinking peace or avoiding evil, but of a proactive *making of peace*. The current dominant use of the term *nonviolence* to denote the work of peacemakers merits reconsideration, since the word, like *nonresistance*, suggests what one does *not* do. Rather, peacemaking, loving the enemy, overcoming evil with good, and reconciliation are the biblical moral imperatives.

This seventh Beatitude is linked to one of Jesus' most distinctive teachings, his command to love enemies:

> I say to you, Love your enemies
> and pray for those who persecute you,
>   so that you may be children of your Father in heaven;
> for he makes his sun rise on the evil and on the good,
>   and sends rain on the righteous and on the unrighteous.
> For if you love those who love you,
> what reward do you have?
>   Do not even the tax collectors do the same?
> And if you greet only your brothers and sisters,
> what more are you doing than others?
>   Do not even the Gentiles do the same?
> Be perfect, therefore, as your heavenly Father is perfect.
> (Matt 5:44-48)

The two texts are linked by an identity claim: *children of God*. In the Beatitude, peacemakers will be called "children of God." In the love-of-enemy-command, similarly, those who love enemies do so because "your Father in heaven" does so. From him come both the sun and the rain on both the just and unjust alike.[6] Here Jesus links peacemaking to God's moral character. Children bear the image of the parent. Being children of peace is the gospel's identity mark for those who follow Jesus. Here is the Christian's vocational charter, to reflect the character of being God's children. Jesus calls disciples to train them in this new radical thought and action. The Gospel narratives are Jesus' catechism for the disciples.

We thus see a strikingly similar emphasis between the seventh Beatitudes (for the peacemakers) and the eighth (for those persecuted) and in Jesus' command to love enemies even when they persecute you. The seventh and eighth blessings in Matthew's form of the Beatitudes show strong verbal and thematic affinities to his wording of Jesus' command to love enemies. "Blessed are the peacemakers, for they will be called children of God. Blessed are those who are persecuted for righteousness' sake, for theirs is the kingdom of heaven" (5:9-10). These blessings are analogous to "Love your enemies and pray for those who persecute you, so that you may be children of your Father in heaven" (5:44-45a).[8]

Jesus' blessing the peacemakers and commanding his followers to love enemies call his disciples to do the unthinkable. To love enemies is beyond human capacity, for the natural human response to enemies is at best toleration; or on an average level to retaliate in kind; or with our basest instinct, to wipe them out if possible. Rarely does one think of responding in such manner that might convert the enemy into a friend! But this is at the core of Jesus' gospel. Its uniqueness shines![7]

How do we know we are children of the heavenly Father? From the sixteenth-century origins of the Christian tradition known as Anabaptism, the etching of Dirk Willems saving his enemy's life has become an icon inspiring like action on the part of those who seek to emulate the way of Jesus. The art depicts the story: pursued by a "thief catcher," Willems ran for his life over ice. When his pursuer broke through the ice, Willems turned back to help and save his persecutor's life. Willems was then captured, imprisoned, and burned at the stake.[9]

Is Jesus' Command to Love Enemies Unique Among the Religions?

Jesus' command contrasts sharply with the emphasis in Qumran literature, in which the sons of righteousness will mete out vengeance upon the sons of darkness. It contrasts also with the Maccabean patriotism that converts zeal for the law into battle against foreign political oppressors.

Is Jesus' command to love the enemy unique? Does it have parallels in pre-Christian Judaism? William Klassen says it testifies to the "deepest union of Judaism and Christianity, . . . a view of God's love . . . fundamental to both religions, . . . and a view of what God's people are called upon to be and to do to the stranger, the outsider, and the enemy."[10] Rather, the novel part is that Jesus acts to create a people of peace. Jesus' gathering together "children of peace" and designating his followers as such (Matt 5:9; Luke 10:5-6) is the novel expression of the love command."[11]

Others take a different view, considering Jesus' commandment unique. Jewish scholar David Flusser says that while Rabbi Hanina taught his audience to love the righteous and not to hate the sinner, Jesus' "commandment to love one's enemies is so much his definitive characteristic that his are the only lips from which we hear the commandment in the whole of the New Testament."[12] Elsewhere, mutual love is commanded, extending the Torah's double love command to love God and neighbor (Deut 6:5; Lev 19:18). Indeed, this double love command, especially the second part, is pervasive in the NT (Gospels, Paul, James).[13] While Flusser is technically correct, Paul's moral commands in Rom 12:14-21, especially verse 20—"If your enemies are hungry, feed them; if they are thirsty, give them something to drink"—demonstrate action consistent with love of enemies.

Both the Greek and Jewish ethical traditions concur in showing that Jesus' command is unique. In both traditions one can find injunctions not to retaliate in kind (Plutarch; Musonius Rufus; Prov 25:21; Exod 23:4-5); yet the explicit positive initiative to love *enemies* is unique to Jesus. He was the first to interpret the sequence of three terse commands in Lev 19:17-18 as extending love for neighbor to include love for enemy.[14] After examining numerous Jewish writings from between 200 BC and AD 100, Gordon Zerbe says: "There is no evidence in early Judaism of an explicit exhortation to love one's enemies," though there are many "exhortations to good will or kind actions in response to adversaries or abuse. The theme of 'love' toward injurers, however, applies only to local, personal conflict (*Testaments of the Twelve Patriarchs*), not to situations of socio-political oppression by outsiders."[15] Considering Jesus' love of enemies command from a social-scientific analysis of reciprocity in the ancient world, Alan Kirk concludes similarly. Jesus' command fits no existing reciprocity model; it is novel.[16]

Only if one regards exhortation to extend kind responses toward enemies as the same as the command "Love your enemies" can one say that Jesus' love-of-enemy command is not novel. But kind responses may be simply prudential, as an effort to pacify the enemy's anger. This is not the same as positive action motivated by love, seeking the welfare of the enemy.[17] Regarding Islam, the same distinction applies. In several places Islamic texts speak of kindness toward enemies, but they do not exhort love for enemy.

Jesus' command to love the enemy is fleshed out with positive response (pray for your persecutors, do good to those who hate you), with concrete motivation (be children of the Father, be perfect in love, follow the golden rule), and with specific examples (turn the other cheek, go the second mile).[18]

Nonresistance

Jesus teaches his followers to not resist one who does evil, but to overcome evil with good. The key Jesus sayings, reverberated by later NT authors, are these:

> I say to you, Do not resist an evildoer. But if anyone strikes you on the right cheek, turn the other also; and if anyone wants to sue you and take your coat, give your cloak as well; and if anyone forces you to go one mile, go also the second mile. (Matt 5:39-41)

> Do not repay anyone evil for evil. . . . Never avenge yourselves. . . . "If your enemies are hungry, feed them." . . . Do not be overcome by evil, but overcome evil with good. (Rom 12:17, 19-21)

> Do not repay evil for evil or abuse for abuse; but, on the contrary, repay with a blessing. (1 Pet 3:9: cf. 1 Thess 5:15, virtually the same)

These verses form the foundation for the nonresistant/ pacifist view held by the tradition of historic peace churches. The Quaker John Ferguson notes that it is not clear how we should translate Matt 5:39: "Do not make a stand against (resist) the evil one" (Who? The devil? This hardly fits), or "Do not make a stand against (resist) by evil means." The latter, totally faithful to the Greek text, concurs with Rom 12:21: "Do not use evil means in the endeavor to overcome evil with good."[19] These verses are integral to Jesus' teaching on love, peace, and forgiveness. They provide the basis for Christian refusal to exercise power in governmental justice and for Christian refusal to participate in war. Nonresistance is intrinsic to the doctrine of salvation (1 Pet 2:21-23; Phil 2:5-11, 14-15).[20]

One of the exegetical challenges of Jesus' teaching on not resisting evil is to understand his five shocking examples in Matt

5:39-42: turn the other cheek, go the second mile, give your cloak as well, loan and don't expect return, give to one who begs. Those in the Galilean multitude who hear Jesus' Beatitudes and these commands to do what seems impossible have good reason to hate those in the Roman-controlled domination system, and thus to "share a rankling hatred for a system that subjects them to humiliation by stripping them of their lands, their goods, finally even their outer garment."[21] Addressing those under Roman occupation, all five "focal instances" point Jesus' hearers to an unexpected response that disarms the enmity.

Walter Wink holds that "do not resist" (*antistēnai*) means to not resist violently. The examples show a form of *nonviolent* resistance whereby the poor or oppressed claim their dignity and open the door to a new relationship between the oppressor and oppressed. Jesus commands a nonviolent shock tactic that exposes the indignity of the oppression. The enemy is disarmed by a "surprise" response: turn the *other* (*left*) cheek to one who insultingly hits you with a backhanded slap on your *right* cheek; when sued for your coat in court, give your *undergarment* also, and thus stand there naked; and offer to go a *second* mile when a Roman soldier compels you to carry his load *one* mile (*milion*). Such response throws the opponent off balance, introducing a third way instead of flight or fight, and thus radically redefining the situation. This approach of nonviolent resistance does not guarantee that the other side will refrain from violence or that there will be no casualties. It rather creates a new paradigm by using "moral jujitsu" to disarm the enemy.[22] Wink's approach is insightful and helpful, but any "tactical" action must be evaluated against the criterion of "loving the enemy."[23]

Luise Schottroff, in her extensive study of Jesus' teaching, perceptively connects *not resisting evil* with *love of enemy*:

> Matthew 5:38-41 . . . commands the refusal to retaliate as well as prophetic judgment of violent persons. . . . As

> imitators of God, Christians are supposed to confront the enemies of God with his mercies. . . . Loving one's enemy is the attempt to change the violent person into a child of God through a confrontation with the love of God. That is, love of one's enemy can be concretely presented as the prophetic proclamation of the approaching sovereignty of God.[24]

Especially persuasive is her interconnection of both these commands to another important strand of NT teaching: God alone in sovereign justice and mercy judges those who do evil. We do not know how vengeance and judgment transforms the heart of the evildoer through mercy. Our human task is peacemaking, a daunting but life-giving challenge. John Paul Lederach has had numerous experiences of peacemaking in Nicaragua, Somalia, and other settings of dangerous and violent conflicts that threaten and produce violence and death. Such interventions do not promise *happiness*—a poor translation of the *blessing* of the Beatitudes. John Paul writes about reconciliation, the fruit of the meek, broken-in-spirit approach to horrendous evil and violence through painstaking, patient mediation.[25] This is the peacemaking that disarms the violence and effects reconciliation.

Jesus' teaching on love of enemies and not resisting evil are two sides of the same coin. Both are foundational to the task of being peacemakers. Luke's Gospel account of Jesus' sermon makes their indissoluble relationship clear:

> I say to you that listen, Love your enemies,
> do good to those who hate you,
> bless those who curse you,
> pray for those who abuse you.
> If anyone strikes you on the cheek, offer the other also;
> and from anyone who takes away your coat
> do not withhold even your shirt.
> Give to everyone who begs from you;

and if anyone takes away your goods,
do not ask for them again.
Do to others as you would have them do to you.

If you love those who love you, what credit is that to you?
For even sinners love those who love them.
If you do good to those who do good to you,
what credit is that to you?
For even sinners do the same.
If you lend to those from whom you hope to receive,
what credit is that to you?
Even sinners lend to sinners, to receive as much again.
But love your enemies, do good, and lend,
expecting nothing in return.
Your reward will be great,
and you will be children of the Most High;
for he is kind to the ungrateful and the wicked.
Be merciful, just as your Father is merciful.

(Luke 6:27-36)

This teaching distinguishes the disciple of Jesus from those who love only those who love them. It portrays the nature of God. To be perfect in love is to be like God, indiscriminate in love.[26] Ronald Sider similarly says: "One fundamental aspect of the holiness and perfection of God is that He loves His enemies. Those who by His grace seek to reflect His holiness will likewise love their enemies—even when it involves a cross."[27]

In stressing the positive, active aspect of love, an important complement to Jesus' teaching on nonresistance in Matt 5:39, Sider says that Jesus is not "advocating a passive, resigned attitude toward oppressors." His command to love the enemy is a "specific political response to centuries of violence and to the contemporary Zealots' call for violent revolution."[28] Indeed, the sequence of Matt 5:38-42 and 5:43-48 makes an essential connection that precludes a negative, passive nonresistance. Nonresistance is put into the service of the all-embracing, positive commandment to love: "The pacifism of Jesus . . . is never 'passivism.'"[29]

Further, genuine love does not allow one to withdraw from evil but "goes into the very heart of an evil situation and attempts to rectify it. . . . It is in the midst of sinful situations that love must be found working, if it is love at all" (Matt 11:19; Luke 7:34). Gordon Kaufman identifies three expressions of love: witnessing to the truth, accepting the neighbor or enemy in their sinfulness, and not forsaking a person or society even when it chooses what we consider wrong and sinful (Matt 5:46-47; Rom 5:10; 2 Cor 5:21; 1 John 4:10, 19). Apparent contradictions may ensue, such as refusing to participate in war but continuing to love and accept an individual or a group of people who choose to participate in war. Loving responsibility will lead, through letter writing or voting, to responsible counsel that recommends the best alternative on political issues, even though nonresistant pacifists cannot fully endorse or participate in such political or military action because of their religious commitment.[30]

Live in Peace

As followers of Jesus, we need to learn to live at peace with one another and with all people insofar as this is possible. Jesus urges this of his disciples when they are quarreling with one another over who is greatest among them. In Mark this command comes in the middle of Jesus' extended teaching on the nature of his messiahship and discipleship (in 9:50). Mark carefully crafts a structural design in 8:27–10:52 that correlates Jesus as suffering Messiah with shock-teaching to convert his disciples from a military-conquest view of the Messiah to that of a Son-of-Man view, one who will suffer and die. The focal images for character formation here are "taking up the cross," valuing a "child," and living as a "servant," in contrast to seeking power, prestige, and position. Concluding this block of teaching in chapter 9, Jesus commands us "to make peace with one another."

Drawing on the imagery of well-prepared salted sacrifices (Mark 9:49-50c evokes Lev 2:13), Jesus calls for the self to be purified of evil and ambitious desires, and for his followers to live peaceably with one another (*eirēneuete en allēlois*, v. 50d). To live peaceably with one another contrasts with the segment's initial portrait of the disciples disputing with one another over who is the greatest. To walk in Jesus' way means denouncing rivalry, seeking not to offend "the little one," and striving to live peaceably with one another.[31]

The Sword

Jesus teaches against the use of the sword:

> Jesus said to him, "Put your sword back into its place; for all who take the sword will perish by the sword. Do you think that I cannot appeal to my Father, and he will at once send me more than twelve legions of angels?"
> (Matt 26:52-53)

> When those who were around him saw what was coming, they asked, "Lord, should we strike with the sword?" Then one of them struck the slave of the high priest and cut off his right ear. But Jesus said, "No more of this!" And he touched his ear and healed him. Then Jesus said to the chief priests, the officers of the temple police, and the elders who had come for him, "Have you come out with swords and clubs as if I were a bandit?"
> (Luke 22:49-52)

In his third temptation (Matt 4:8-10) at the beginning of his ministry, Jesus resists the devil's offer to give him the kingdoms of the world. At his arrest he similarly refuses to call twelve legions of angels to defend himself against the Romans who arrested him.[32] During his final instruction to his disciples before his arrest, Jesus speaks a word in Luke's Gospel that has led some to say Jesus condoned violence: "The one who has no sword must sell his cloak and buy one" (22:36b). This word is "grimly ironic," expressing metaphorically the intensity of opposition the disciples are about to face. It does not condone use of violence, as later verses make clear. The next verse (22:37) explicitly gives the reason for this saying: to fulfill Scripture, citing, "He was counted with the lawless" (Isa 53:12). When Peter later uses a sword to cut off the high priest's servant's ear, defending Jesus, Jesus' response is clear and definitive: "No more of this!" (22:49-51). Further, Jesus' healing the cutoff ear clearly indicates that Jesus will have nothing to do with violent self-defense.[33]

In his arrest, trial, and hanging on the cross, Jesus, though crucified as a rebel criminal, models defenselessness (Luke 23:35). This reinforces his saying that denounces use of the sword and accords with similar teaching to renounce hatred in order to make peace (Matt 5:21-22; 15:18-20; 1 John 3:15).[34] On these occasions, and others, Jesus refuses a sword-type response,[35] thus renouncing violence. As Messiah he stands not for war and military victory but for nonviolence and peace.[36] Matthew 26:52 is a "definite and unambiguous" text forbidding even the defensive sword.[37]

Two additional texts are related to Jesus' refusal to use the sword. In his trial before Pilate in John 18:36, he answers Pilate:

> My kingdom is not from this world. If my kingdom were from this world, my followers would be fighting to keep me from being handed over to the Jews. But as it is, my kingdom is not from here.

Paul declares: "The weapons of our warfare are not worldly but have divine power to destroy strongholds" (2 Cor 10:4 RSV).

In both these texts it is clear that Jesus and his follower Paul speak of a kingdom and a fight against evil that are of a different species than military power. The same is true of Paul's call for believers to be clothed with God's armor and thus to stand against all the wiles of the devil (Eph 6:10-18).

To enter Jerusalem, the royal capital of his people, Jesus chooses to ride on a donkey as a humble king (Mark 11:1-10; cf. 1 Kings 1:38). In Matthew, this event is interpreted by a peace text from the Hebrew prophet Zechariah (9:9-10):

> Rejoice greatly, O daughter Zion!
> Shout aloud, O daughter Jerusalem!
> Lo, your king comes to you;
> triumphant and victorious is he,
> humble and riding on a donkey,
> on a colt, the foal of a donkey.
> He will cut off the chariot from Ephraim
> and the war horse from Jerusalem;
> and the battle bow shall be cut off,
> and he shall command peace to the nations;
> his dominion shall be from sea to sea,
> and from the River to the ends of the earth.

By quoting this text, Matthew portrays Jesus repudiating the view of the Davidic Messiah as a military conqueror forcefully freeing Israel from political oppression, crushing the Gentiles. In his portrayal of Jesus' triumphal entry (21:1-16), Matthew transforms the messianic "Son of David" hopes of political triumph that crush Israel's enemies. Jesus is nonmilitant Messiah.

Entering Jerusalem, Jesus goes to the temple and takes prophetic action against its defilement from commercial transactions in its sacred precincts. Jesus directs his action[38] against two injustices: the economic exploitation (overcharging) in the selling of sacrificial animals (note that pigeons, the sacrifice of the poor, are especially mentioned), and the injustice of infringing on the worship of the Gentiles (note that 'He would not allow any one to carry anything through the temple [court]'). Decrying this misuse of the temple, Jesus says, "Is it not written,

'My house shall be called a house of prayer *for all the nations*'? But you have made it a den [hangout] of robbers'" (Mark 11:17, emphasis added; quoting from Isa 56:7; Jer 7:11). Jesus acts prophetically to stand against cheating the poor and crowding the Gentile worship space with commercial greed. Though some have argued that Jesus here uses violence,[39] it is more correct to emphasize his prophetic confrontation.

Another consideration, sometimes identified as contradicting what Jesus teaches, is Matt 23, what appears as Jesus' condemnation of the Pharisees. This has led to the question: Does Jesus love his enemies? The majority understanding among Matthew scholars is that we must see Jesus' condemnation of the Pharisees' actions as intra-Jewish critique, akin to that of all the Hebrew prophets (Isaiah to Malachi). Donald Senior sums up the point well: "Sharp and inflated language roundly condemning what are judged to be failures or excesses on the part of one's opponents was characteristic of such intra-Jewish debate and has precedents in the Bible and in extracanonical Jewish texts of this epoch."[40] The danger arises when Christians lift such rhetoric from its context and use it against Jews; that indeed violates the love command and is an enemy-making action. Read as intra-Jewish polemic, Matt 23 does not sanction ethnic hatred, and, specifically, not discrimination against Jews. The "woes" of Matt 23 fall under the rubric of Jesus' prophetic word as judgment on his *own* people, and specifically on the leaders, not on all Israel. As long as Matt 23 is understood as intra-Jewish critique, it fits into the stream of prophetic critique against religious leaders. It is not exceptional.[41]

These aspects of Jesus' ministry require us to assess the role of prophetic critique as an essential expression of love. In our Western culture, love has come to mean "being nice." But that falls short of what Jesus means by love of God, neighbor, and enemy. Both Jesus and Paul speak and act in ways that "sting," but also that correct and transform us. At the heart of these seemingly harsh encounters is both the plea for change and the readiness to forgive (for Jesus, Matt 6:12-15; Luke 7:36-50; 23:34; 24:47; John 8:1-11; for Paul, 2 Cor 2:1-11; 7:2-16).

To summarize Jesus' key emphases:

- instead of vengeance—forgiveness (Matt 6:14-15; Luke 17:3-4; 23:34)[42]
- instead of violence—readiness to suffer (Matt 5:38-39)
- instead of greed—sharing (Luke 12:33-34; 18:22)
- instead of domination—service (Luke 22:24-27; even sharper, Mark 10:42-45)
- instead of hatred—love (Matt 5:43-45; Luke 6:27-31)[43]

A most authentic demonstration of these Jesus-type actions—forgiveness, suffering, sharing, service, love—is the Amish community's response to the tragic shooting of ten Amish schoolgirls, by a neighbor, Charles Carl Roberts, on October 2, 2006, in Lancaster County, Pennsylvania. Columnist Diana Butler Bass details how the Amish practice of forgiveness leads to peacemaking.

> [It] unfolded in four public acts over the course of a week. First, some elders visited Marie Roberts, the wife of the murderer, to offer forgiveness. Then, the families of the slain girls invited the widow to their own children's funerals. Next, they requested that all relief monies intended for Amish families be shared with Roberts and her children. And, finally, in an astonishing act of reconciliation, more than 30 members of the Amish community attended the funeral of the killer. As my husband and I talked about the spiritual power of these actions, I commented in an offhanded way, "It is an amazing witness to the peace tradition." He looked at me and said passionately, "a witness? I don't think so. This went well past witnessing. They weren't witnessing to anything. They were actively *making* peace."

This is the peacemaking to which Jesus calls us. Yes, it takes a community commitment to make such response possible. It also requires personal commitment of the members of the community to this way of life. The interest that this forgiving response stirred throughout the English speaking world testifies to the power of the gospel, the way of the upside-down kingdom, which Mary's song enunciates at the birth of the Son of the most High, the Savior, Emmanuel.

Come, join in Mary's prophet song*

Come, join in Mary's prophet song
  of justice for the earth,
for right outgrows the fiercest wrong,
  revealing human worth—
bound not within the wealth we crave
  or in the arms we bear,
but in the holy reign God gave—
  the image that we share.

The "Peace on Earth" which shepherds heard
  is not some fantasy.
The angels sang to greet the Word,
  whose birth is victory.
The maiden Mary, not so mild,
  bore into death's domain
true God, and yet an infant child,
  who over death would reign.

Emmanuel, God-with-us here,
  grows peace where we would dare
to act despite our tremb'ling fear
  and bring God's holy care.
The image God made "Us" to be
  is also borne on "Them."
Christ bids us join our enemy
  to sing war's requiem.

*CMD Suggested tunes: SALVATION, RESIGNATION, KINGSFOLD

Dedicated to Tom Fox (1951-2006), Norman Kember, James Loney, and Harmeet Singh Sooden, Christian Peacemaker Team hostages held in Iraq, November 2005—March 2006.

CHAPTER THREE

Paul on Peace and Violence

A Christian cannot win God's forgiveness,
but he/she can lose it by refusing to extend it
to a brother/sister.
—*John P. Meier,* The Vision of Matthew

In the [Los Angeles] riots following the first
Rodney King verdict,
Reginald Denny was dragged from his truck
and viciously beaten by a raging gang.
After his painful recovery, he met face to face
with his attackers,
shook hands with them, and forgave them.
A reporter, commenting on the scene, wrote,
"It is said that Mr. Denny is suffering from brain damage."
—*William Willimon and Stanley Hauerwas,*
Lord Teach Us: The Lord's Prayer and the Christian Life

New Testament writings continue Jesus' exhortation to be at peace with one another and with all people, if possible. Believers are admonished to be at peace with one another and to seek/pursue peace (Rom 12:18; 14:19; 2 Cor 13:11; 1 Thess 5:13; 2 Tim 2:22; 1 Pet 3:11; Heb 12:14). William Klassen has studied the "pursuit of peace" texts in the New Testament and has grouped the texts by categories:[1]

Source of peace

God of peace	*Christ as our peace*	*The peace of God*
Rom 15:33; 16:20; 1 Cor 14:33; 2 Cor 13:11; 1 Thess 5:23; Phil 4:9; Heb 13:20	Eph 2:14; *Peace of Christ*: Col 3:15	Phil 4:7; *Peace from God*: 1 Tim 1:2; 2 John 3

Ethical admonition

Let us have peace with God.	*Let us have peace with each other.*	*Live at peace with all.*
Rom 5:1	Mark 9:50c; 1 Thess 5:13; Rom 14:19; 2 Cor 13:11; *Keep the bond of peace*: Eph 4:3; *Pursue peace*: 2 Tim 2:22; 1 Pet 3:11; Heb 12:14; Rom 14:19	Rom 12:18; Heb 12:14

Believers are called to peace (1 Cor 7:15), and as members of one body are to make "every effort to maintain the unity of the Spirit in the bond of peace" (Eph 4:3-6).

God of Peace: Paul's Distinctive Contribution

Paul, as apostle of the gospel of Jesus Christ, introduces us to God as "God of Peace," a God who loves humans even while they were at enmity with him. Paul frequently employs the phrase "God of peace." Several writers have observed this virtually unique phenomenon and have made brief, insightful contributions.[2] The phrase occurs seven times in Paul, once in Hebrews, and only once outside the NT, in *T. Dan.* 5:2.[3] Four occurrences are in benedictions:[4]

- Rom 15:33: The God of peace be with all of you. Amen.
- Phil 4:9: Keep on doing the things that you have learned and received and heard and seen in me, and the God of peace will be with you.
- 1 Thess 5:23: May the God of peace himself sanctify you entirely; and may your spirit and soul and body be kept sound and blameless at the coming of our Lord Jesus Christ.
- 2 Thess 3:16: Now may the Lord of peace himself give you peace at all times in all ways. The Lord be with all of you.

Two more are in assurances or promises:

- Rom 16:20: The God of peace will shortly crush Satan under your feet. The grace of our Lord Jesus Christ be with you.
- 2 Cor 13:11: Finally, brothers and sisters, farewell. Put things in order, listen to my appeal, agree with one another, live in peace; and the God of love and peace will be with you.

The seventh is a moral pronouncement:

- 1 Cor 14:33: God is a God not of disorder but of peace.

Another "God of peace" benediction occurs in Hebrews, likely a Paul-related epistle:

- Heb 13:20-21: Now may the God of peace, who brought back from the dead our Lord Jesus, the great shepherd of the sheep, by the blood of the eternal covenant, make you complete in everything good so that you may do his will, working among us that which is pleasing in his sight, through Jesus Christ, to whom be the glory forever and ever. Amen.

Paul's frequent use of the title "God of peace" is significant. "God of hope" occurs only once (Rom 15:13) and "God of love" only once—in conjunction with "God of peace" (2 Cor 13:11). Other similar phrases emphasizing divine attributes are absent in Paul but occur in Jewish Literature: "the God of faithfulness" (Deut 32:4, lit. trans.), "the God of truth" (Isa 65:16, lit. trans.), and "the God of glory" (Ps 29:3).[5] Mauser rightly observes that Paul's choice of "God of peace" likely reflects Jewish piety expressed in the *shalom* benediction.[6] Other characteristics of God's activity are not so privileged. Nowhere does "God of wrath" or "God of judgment" occur as titles for God in Paul.[7] In light of the prominence of "God as warrior" in the OT (Exod 15:3), it is striking that no such terms for God are found in Paul or any other NT writer. The favored status of "God of peace" for Paul is a key to his larger theology, for his central doctrinal emphases are much associated with peacemaking.

Paul's gospel (*euangelion*) indeed proclaims that God's work in Jesus Christ has wrought peace with God (Rom 5:1),[8] even when humans were God's enemies (5:10). Salvation makes peace between previously hostile peoples: Jews and Gentiles. Peace with God and peace with fellow humans, even enemies, are twin gifts of Jesus Christ. In Colossians *peace* takes on a cosmic dimension in which all creation is recipient through the blood of the cross (1:20).

What Paul affirms is a twofold gospel reality: that *all*, both Jews and Gentiles, are recipients of God's saving righteousness manifest in Jesus Christ, and that by God's grace those who receive this gift will be transformed and liberated from enslaving sin. Peace is the fruit of this all-encompassing regeneration, both personally and corporately. Most of Paul's writings reflect this peacemaking breakthrough, peace with God through Christ and peace between former enemies.

Accordingly, it is not surprising that *apostolic mission* is at the center of Paul's vocational self-consciousness. Paul's *call* to be an apostle for peacemaking between Jews and Gentiles forged his doctrine of justification by faith.[9] Justification is a "social event." The "works of the law" separated peoples, erecting "the dividing wall, that is, the hostility between us [Jew and Gentiles]" (Eph 2:14-15). The social meaning of justification, sociopolitical to the core, inherently links this key emphasis in Pauline thought to peace and peacemaking. Its logical consequence is to refuse to take another human's life. John Howard Yoder says, "It is the Good News that I and my enemy are united, through no merit or work of my own, in a new humanity that forbids henceforth my ever taking his life in my hands."[10] Aware of the negative emphasis much Protestant interpretation has put on law for the sake of justification by grace through faith, Perry Yoder in a study of shalom, put a chapter on law after one on atonement. Law has a positive function, as the instrument of justice. It maintains the justice of God's justifying, atoning work, in the service of shalom.[11]

If justification were based upon human achievement of any type, it would be a division-creating doctrine. But because it is, first and foremost, founded on the faithfulness of Jesus Christ (*extra nos*) and then upon our receiving by faith his salvation work for us (the numerous *hyper* statements for atonement formulas), the ground is level, and all come to salvation in the same way, the very way in which Abraham too was counted righteous: "He believed the Lord; and the Lord reckoned it to him as righteousness" (Gen 15:6).[12]

Peace and reconciliation are linked to Jesus Christ, anchored in Jesus' death on the cross. Likewise, no separable distinction can be made between establishing peace with God and peace uniting formerly alienated Jews and Gentiles.

Ron Sider's perceptive commentary on the moral significance of Jesus' death for humans while they were sinners, in enmity relation to God, is especially pertinent:

> Jesus' vicarious death for sinful enemies of God lies at the very heart of our commitment to nonviolence. It was because the Incarnate One knew that God was loving and merciful even toward the worst of sinners that He associated with sinners, forgave their sins, and completed His mission of dying for the sins of the world. And it was precisely the same understanding of God that prompted Him to command His followers to love their enemies. . . .
>
> It is a tragedy of our time that many of those who

> appropriate the biblical understanding of Christ's vicarious cross fail to see its direct implications for the problem of war and violence. And it is equally tragic that some of those who most emphasize pacifism and nonviolence fail to ground it in Christ's vicarious atonement. It is a serious heresy of the atonement to base one's nonviolence in the weak sentimentality of the lowly Nazarene viewed merely as a noble martyr to truth and peace rather than in the vicarious cross of the Word who became flesh. The cross is much more than "Christ's witness to the weakness and folly of the sword" although it certainly is that. In fact, . . . death for our sins is the ultimate demonstration that the Sovereign of the universe is a merciful Father who reconciles His enemies through self-sacrificial love.[13]

The "God of peace" commissions followers of Jesus to be ambassadors of reconciliation, to follow the path of suffering for the gospel, and to imitate Jesus' way of making peace.

The task of believers to be agents of reconciliation is initiated by, grounded in, and empowered by God's own initiative of reconciliation in Christ Jesus. This is highlighted in the following chiastic analysis of 2 Cor 5:17-21:

a In Christ, *new creation* (old passed away; all become new)
  b All this is from God, who reconciled us to himself through Christ,
    c and has given us the ministry of reconciliation;
      d that is, in Christ God was reconciling the world to himself,
      not counting their trespasses against them and
    c´ entrusting the message of reconciliation to us.
        So we are ambassadors for Christ,
        since God is making his appeal through us;
  b´ we entreat you on behalf of Christ, be reconciled to God
a´ that we might become the righteousness of God.[14]

Each unit of the chiasm includes some form of the word "reconcile" (*katallassō*). This analysis makes it clear that reconciliation is God's initiative. It specifies—first, middle, and last—that *God's* act in Christ reconciles humans to God (not God to humans by pacifying divine wrath) and that humans reconciled-to-God are then enlisted into the ministry of reconciliation. As such, humans are ambassadors *for* or *in behalf of* (*hyper*) *Christ's* work of reconciliation, and God makes his appeal through us humans. Again, the appeal itself, "be reconciled to God," is grounded in "on behalf of [*hyper*] Christ." The task is firmly rooted in God's initiative in Christ. All Christian peacemaking efforts must never lose sight of this important feature for their identity and long-term empowerment.

Believers are called to take up the task of reconciliation with their commitment to follow Jesus' way and imitate the way of suffering servanthood. Discipleship means identifying with/following/imitating Jesus Christ. Virtually all pacifist writers emphasize this theme. John Howard Yoder, after relating these images of discipleship to God's nature and to Jesus' life, devotes one section to "The Disciple/Participant and the Death of Christ." He includes the following dimensions:

1. Suffering with Christ as the definition of apostolic existence (2 Cor 4:10; Col 1:24; 1 Thess 1:6).
2. Sharing in divine condescension (Phil 2:3-14).
3. Give your life as he did (Eph 5:1-2; 1 John 3:16).
4. Suffering servanthood in place of dominion (Matt 20:25-28; Mark 10:42-45; John 13:1-15).
5. Accept innocent suffering without complaints as he did (1 Pet 2:20-21; 3:14-18; 4:12-16).
6. Suffer with or like Christ the hostility of the world, as bearers of the kingdom cause (Matt 10:37-42; Mark 8:34-38; Luke 14:27-33; John 15:20-21; Phil 1:29; 2 Tim 3:12; Heb 11:1–12:5; 1 Pet 4:13).
7. Death is liberation from the power of sin (Gal 5:24; 1 Pet 4:1-2).

8. Death is the fate of the prophets; Jesus, whom we follow, was already following them (Matt 23:34; Mark 12:1-9; Luke 24:19-20; Acts 2:36; 4:10; 7:52; 23:14; 1 Thess 2:15-18).
9. Death is victory (1 Cor 1:22-24; Col 2:14; Rev 12:10-11; cf. 5:9-14; 17:14).[15]

We are told to follow or copy one aspect of Jesus' life:

> There is thus but one realm in which the concept of imitation holds, but there it holds in every strand of the New Testament literature and all the more strikingly by virtue of the absence of parallels to other realms: this is at the point of the concrete social meaning of the cross and its relation to enmity and power. Servanthood replaces dominion, forgiveness absorbs hostility. Thus—and only thus—are we bound by New Testament thought to "be like Jesus."[16]

Discipleship relates to the atoning work of Christ. Christians identify with Christ (Rom 6:5, 10-11; 1 Cor 4:9-13; Col 2:12), and Paul's life and ours are not "to be understood as a *duplication* of Jesus but a witness to him.[17] Gospel texts (Matt 5–7; 10:34-39) proclaim King Jesus' call, "Follow me."[18] Revelation also unites discipleship with atonement because the triumph of believers through their faithful witness-death (*martyria-martys*) is assured because of King Jesus' own triumph in his witness and death.[19]

Witness to the Powers

Jesus Christ's victory over the powers is the theological basis for Christian witness to the powers. Jesus' own pattern of speaking truth to power in his trial before Pilate is a basis for this emphasis in Paul's writings. From Eph 3:8-11, John Howard Yoder says that Paul's mission to the Gentiles, the uniting of Jew and Gentile in the peace of the cross, is the demonstration/announcement to the powers of God's manifold wisdom. This new way, this new creation, is a sign "to the powers that their unbroken dominion has come to an end."[20] The church engages in its mission to the powers by its very existence, by its liberation from the dominion of the powers. It "does not attack the powers; this Christ has done."[21] Christ's victory, says Yoder, is "a social, political, *structural* fact which constitutes a challenge to the Powers. . . . It is a declaration about the nature of the cosmos and the significance of history, within which both our conscientious participation and our conscientious objection find their authority and their promise."[22]

The most explicit description of Christ's triumph over the powers is this: he "disarmed the principalities and powers, and made a public example of them" (Col 2:15 RSV). The structure of this text shows a parallel pattern for 2:13-15. In each verse of the Greek, clauses a and c are participial; clause b is declarative, with the finite verb:[23]

v. 13 a. when *you* were dead in your transgressions
and the uncircumcision of your flesh,
b. HE MADE *YOU* ALIVE TOGETHER WITH HIM,
c. having forgiven *us* all our transgressions,

v. 14 a. having canceled out *the certificate of debt*
consisting of decrees against us and hostile to us,
b. HE HAS TAKEN IT OUT OF THE WAY,
c. having nailed *it* to the cross.

v. 15 a. When he had disarmed *the rulers and authorities,*
b. HE MADE A PUBLIC DISPLAY OF *THEM*,
c. having triumphed over *them* through him.
(cf. RSV)

The language of verse 15 evokes the scene of Emperor Vespasian and son Titus (army general responsible for Jerusalem's destruction in AD 70) leading Jewish captors and putting them on display, in the streets of Rome after the fall of Jerusalem (cf. the Arch of Titus in Rome). The text emphasizes that Christ's death on the cross has publicly displayed the defeated powers. From a gospel point of view, the imperial powers are no longer victor. Christ is victor over the powers!

Paul knew the Roman Empire's self-proclaimed Pax Romana from several sides. His many travels were possible because of its roads. The gospel spread through its commerce. He appealed to its law several times. At the same time, Paul endured much suffering for the gospel, which threatened imperial claims and the empire's local manifestations. Paul's hardships (listed in 2 Cor 4:7-12; 6:4-5, 8-10; 11:16-33) transpire within the governance of the Pax Romana. He willingly suffers *because* he gives his life to plant new kingdom communities, whose social composition and economic care for one another crosscut the imperial politics of the Roman world. To speak of believers as "one new humanity" (Eph 2:15b) deconstructs Roman imperial power and constitutes an alternative social, economic, and political order of life. From the gospel-*peace* perspective of Jesus Christ, the pseudo-nature of Rome's peace is glaring. Klaus Wengst in his study of the Pax Romana quotes several early sources depicting the violence of the Pax Romana. The Roman general Germanicus in the battle against the Germani calls on his soldiers "'to go with the carnage. Prisoners were needless; nothing but the extermination of the race would end the war.'"[24] The famed Roman historian Tacitus (AD 54-ca 120) puts on the lips of the Britain Calgacus a caustic description of the dangerous Romans: "'To plunder, butcher, steal, these things they misname empire; they make a desolation and call it peace.'"[25]

In the context of this Pax Romana, peace-through-oppression, Paul proclaims a counterpeace, a peace that repudiates domination over others and unites people of diverse backgrounds into the Christ-bond of peace. This is Paul's alternative peace-gospel, a subversive power in the Roman Empire, promising and inaugurating a new order of society; it is birthing a new socioeconomic, political creation based on Christ's atoning love and forgiveness and humans' learning the way of nonretaliation.

Paul stands in continuity with Jesus, as do the epistles of Heb, James, and 1 Pet, as well as the book of Revelation.[26]

Richard Hays rightly asserts that the entire NT advocates peace/peacemaking and reconciliation; it consistently repudiates use of violence to achieve peace:

1. "Those who are members of the one body in Christ ([Rom] 12:5) are never to take vengeance (12:19); they are to bless their persecutors and minister to their enemies, returning good for evil. There is not a syllable in the Pauline letters that can be cited in support of Christians employing violence."
2. "With regard to the issue of *violence*, the New Testament bears a powerful witness that is both univocal and pervasive, for it is integrally related to the heart of the kerygma and to God's fundamental elective purpose."
3. "One reason that the world finds the New Testament's message of peacemaking and love of enemies incredible is that the church is so massively faithless. . . . Only when the church renounces the way of violence, will people see what the Gospel means. . . . The meaning of the New Testament's teaching on violence will become evident only in communities of Jesus' followers who embody the costly way of peace."[27]

Hays represents well the growing number of Christian leaders in all denominations affirming a peacemaking, antiviolence stance. This signifies a "new reformation," occurring within the broader range of Christian churches today. It is significant that most renewal movements in recent

Christian history began with a strong emphasis on peace: the Puritans, the Friends (Quakers), Wesley (for the Methodists), Disciples, Adventists, Salvation Army, and Pentecostals. It is also significant that Jesus' peace teaching shaped, inspired, and empowered key moral leaders: Tolstoy, Gandhi, Martin Luther King, and voices such as Hannah Arendt.

The NT Scripture calls us to nonviolence (Hays in *The Moral Vision*) and its positive complement of peacemaking (as I seek to show in *Covenant of Peace*). I borrow the movement slogan of John K. Stoner: "What would it mean if every church were a *peace* church?" Active peacemaking, or "transforming initiatives,"[28] is what Jesus taught, as well as all the NT writers. In doing this, we seek to transform enmity into friendship, follow the way of Jesus, and perhaps have the courage to do as Dirk Willems did, save the enemy pursuing us even though it costs us our lives.

"Dirk Willems Saving His Captor's Life"*

* The etching, titled "Dirk Willems Saving His Captor's Life," appears in *Martyrs Mirror*, compiled by Thieleman J. van Braght, translated from the original Dutch 1660 ed. by Joseph F. Sohm, 2nd English ed. (Scottdale, PA: Mennonite Publishing House, 1950), 741. Used with permission.

Menno Simons describes the true brothers and sisters of Jesus Christ, "who are regenerated by Christ," and "partake of His Spirit and nature" as:

> People who are ever prepared according to the measure of their faith to do the will of the eternal Prince of Peace who has taught His disciples nothing but patience and eternal peace, saying, Peace I leave with you, my peace I give unto you. Again, Peace be with you. His kingdom is a kingdom of love, of unity, of peace, and of betterment of life; and not of hatred, turmoil, blood, unrest, and destruction. Again, in peace we are called of God. Let the peace of God rule in your hearts, to which also ye are called. Again, Blessed are the peacemakers. Paul says, The hope of God fill you with all joy and peace in believing.
>
> I am aware, my dear friends, that these Scriptures have reference for the most part to the inward peace which comes through Christ. Yet whoever has this inward, Christian peace in his heart will never more be found guilty before God and the world of turmoil, treason, mutiny, murder, theft, or of consenting to or taking part in them. For the Spirit of Christ which is in him seeks not evil, but good; not destruction, but healing; and not harm, but health. Such men seek to live everywhere in peace with all mankind as far as is possible. They follow peace with all . . . and holiness, without which no man can see the Lord. Heb 12:14[29]

In distinguishing true followers of Christ from the "abominable disturbances of the Münsterites," Menno writes:

> For we have, by the grace of God that has appeared to us, beaten our swords into plowshares, and our spears into pruning hooks, and we shall sit under the true vine, that is, Christ, under the Prince of Eternal Peace, and will never more study outward conflict and the war of blood. . . .

> We know and use no other sword than that which Christ Himself brought to earth from heaven, and which the apostles used and plied with the power of the spirit; namely, the one that proceeds from the mouth of the Lord. [Menno then quotes Heb 4:12.][30]

Menno, addressing beloved brothers and sisters in Christ in Prussia, October 7, 1549, writes:

> Do consider how you together with all Christians are received and called by the God of peace, under the Prince of Peace, by the messengers of peace, to the body of peace, with the Word of peace, into the kingdom of peace, out of mere love and grace. Therefore walk in that same peace, so that in that day you may in His grace be able to stand before your God with a confident and happy conscience when body and soul must part. . . .
>
> The Lord of peace grant you His peace in all places and in every manner. May that selfsame peace keep your hearts and minds in Christ Jesus. Amen.[31]

CHAPTER FOUR

Peacemakers: Salt of the Earth, Light of the World

Christ made peace with all our enemies too, on the cross. Let us bear witness to this peace to all.
—*Dietrich Bonhoeffer*, A Testament to Freedom

In the same chapter of the Sermon on the Mount where Jesus describes the peacemakers as children of God (Matt 5:9), he also calls his followers to be the salt of the earth and the light of the world (5:13-16). How do Christian peacemakers fulfill Jesus' call to be the salt of the earth and the light of the world? How does God's light shine forth into the world through peacemaking?

These questions provoke further questions. What is the peace message and mission? How do God's people perform that mission? Does this mission include witness to political institutions about peaceful solutions to existing conflicts? What is the peacemaker's style of life and action? By what methods, if any, do Christians speak to such institutions?

While these questions are difficult, numerous biblical teachings crucially guide us. Several biblical teachings form the bedrock and perspective of an answer. These teachings are the meaning of Jesus' incarnation and atonement, the nature and mission of the church, Christian response to evil and relation to temporal government, and the biblical view of morality, including war.

Incarnation

John's Gospel speaks of the Word becoming flesh (1:14), from which is derived the term "incarnation" (from Latin, *in carne*, in flesh). The crucial point of this affirmation is that Jesus took upon himself humanity and lived within time, space, and human relationships. Most significantly, he endured suffering, even suffering on the cross. This became a point of major disagreement in the early church, giving rise to the first major heresy called Gnosticism. Gnostics, though claiming Christian identity, did not accept a suffering Jesus, a Jesus of the cross. Nor would they acknowledge that Jesus truly came in the flesh. This heretical thinking apparently raised its head already in the NT church era, as the definition of "antichrist" in 1 John 4:1-3 indicates. Anyone who denies that Jesus Christ has come in the flesh is antichrist.

Perhaps for the same reason, Paul insists that his gospel message is the "message of the cross" (1 Cor 1:18), and he determines to preach nothing other than "Jesus Christ crucified" (1 Cor 1:23; 2:2). While Paul's theological contribution encompasses a broad range of topics and concerns, this central conviction shines in all his epistles. Though Paul does not use the precise word *incarnation*, his theology is indeed incarnational, as the classic text of Phil 2:5-11 declares:

> Let the same mind be in you that was in Christ Jesus,
> who, though he was in the form of God,
> did not regard equality with God
> as something to be exploited,
> but emptied himself,
> taking the form of a slave,
> being born in human likeness.

And being found in human form,
he humbled himself and became obedient
to the point of death—even death on a cross.

Therefore God also highly exalted him
and gave him the name that is above every name,
so that at the name of Jesus every knee should bend,
in heaven and on earth and under the earth,
and every tongue should confess that Jesus Christ is Lord,
to the glory of God the Father.

Further, when Paul reflected on the meaning of Christ for the church and the world, he affirmed that incarnation means reconciliation, both vertical and horizontal: "God was in Christ, reconciling the world to himself" (cf. 2 Cor 5:17 RSV). In Eph 2:14 Paul asserts that, having come in the flesh, *Christ is our peace*, breaking down all walls of hostility that separate peoples.

The shed blood of Christ on the cross is understood as the sin-offering atonement for all people, Jews and Gentiles, redeeming all from bondage and justifying all who believe (Rom 3:21-26; 7:14–8:6; indeed, all of Rom 1–8).[1] The crucified Messiah, therefore, draws all people to the loving heart of God, enabling the creation of a new humanity in which both Jew and Gentile are made one in and through Christ. Jesus' incarnation culminates in atonement, which is both vertically and horizontally an at-one-ment. God in Christ reconciles humans to Godself and to one another.

The incarnate Christ's life and teachings thus provide us a paradigm for our own discipleship. Through suffering the cross, Jesus has gained the crown (Phil 2:5-11; Heb 5:5-8; 12:2). Jesus' total life accords with his Gethsemane and Calvary suffering, thus making peace by the blood of the cross.

Jesus' victory does not come easily or automatically. Throughout his ministry he is tempted to compromise God's *peaceable* way to messiahship. Each of the three temptations (in Matt 4 and Luke 4) presents Jesus with a detour to the cross as essential to messiahship.[2] Jesus resists each temptation at the outset of his ministry in the wilderness; yet he also faces each of them later in his ministry. Each proposes a major compromise to his messianic mission and God's way to make peace.

In the first temptation Satan urges Jesus to satisfy his hunger by using his divine power to make bread out of stones (Matt 4:3-4; Luke 4:3-4). This suggestion appeals directly to Jesus' hunger. But the temptation, as many Bible scholars explain, also has deeper significance. In this temptation Jesus wrestles with the issue of what kind of Messiah he would be. Becoming a popular king by miraculously providing bread for the multitudes eventually becomes a live option in the life of Jesus (John 6:1-13). Jesus could become a *bread-making*, indeed a *welfare* Messiah (6:14-15). Jesus decisively refuses the temptation of seeking material security. For every age he has given us an example: "One does not live by bread alone, but by every word that comes from the mouth of God" (quoting Deut 8:3).

The second temptation confronts Jesus with the possibility of evading the cross by gaining popular Messianic support on a *religious* basis (Matt 4:5-7; Luke 4:9-12). The temptation is recorded in the form of an ancient prophetic expectation, that when the Messiah comes he will suddenly appear in the temple area (Mal 3:1). In light of this prophetic hope, Jesus indeed struggles with this possible route to messiahship. In Jesus' life-ministry, in his Palm Sunday entry into Jerusalem, Jesus sets the stage for a possible manifestation of this type of *religious, ecclesiastical* messiahship. Will Jesus evade the cross, the way of love and peace, by following an alternative route to messiahship?

No, Jesus refuses this temptation of becoming a popular, religious ecclesiastical leader by presuming upon his special power as Son of God and eliciting the applause of the crowd. Already in the wilderness his answer is, "Do not put the

Lord your God to the test" (quoting Deut 6:16). Jesus has clearly heard the call of obedience, the call to the cross, and he thus resists any ecclesiastical counterfeit. He is not about to become a temple chief priest as an alternative means to messiahship. Rather, he embraces the way of suffering love and atoning peace.

The third temptation confronts Jesus with a messiahship of political power as an alternative to the cross (Matt 4:8-10; Luke 4:5-8). This temptation is crucial because whenever we discuss the question of peace, it is precisely the question of political power that raises its head. The temptation that Jesus faces is to bow down to Satan himself and through worship of Satan gain the kingdoms of this world. This is the temptation to gain earthly power by earthly means. Jesus refuses. He commands Satan to leave him: "Away with you, Satan!" (RSV: "Begone, Satan!"). He then declares, "Worship the Lord your God and serve only him" (quoting Deut 6:13; 10:20).

All these temptations come into focus at some point in Jesus' life-ministry (cf. John 6:14-15, Jesus' Palm Sunday entrance into the temple area; and finally in Gethsemane). In Gethsemane, Jesus struggles with another possible evasion of the cross. He says he can call twelve legions of angels and confound and disempower those who have come to arrest him. Yes, he could fight against and defeat the Roman power; he would gain the world but lose the kingdom that he has proclaimed as he began his ministry in Galilee (Mark 1:14-15 and passim). Philip Yancey has put it thus: "As history has proven, especially in times when church and state closely mingle, it is possible for the church to gain a nation and in the process lose the kingdom."[3] Jesus as Son of God had the prerogative to manifest his Messiahship on a political platform, but Jesus did not yield to the temptation.

With this final temptation, Jesus resists the alluring alternatives that confront people of every age. He resists compromise on the basis of material power. He resists compromise for ecclesiastical power. He resists compromise for military power. These temptations clearly portray Jesus as one who categorically chooses the way of the cross, the way of suffering, peace, and reconciliation. From this evidence it becomes clear that the way of peace rests upon the bedrock of the gospel Jesus has lived and proclaimed.

These temptations connect to the life struggles that Christian believers face today.[4] Indeed, every temptation in Jesus' ministry is in effect a ploy to divert Jesus from God's commission to him to be the faithful Son, declared at Jesus' baptism. Though manifested in varied forms, including Peter's rebuking of Jesus when he speaks of his coming suffering, all the "testings" are Satan's efforts to enlist Jesus into his way of military power, even to liberate Israel from Roman occupation. Hence, Jesus' temptations are political to the core.

Every one of Jesus' testings (*peirasmoi*) in Mark and in Matthew and Luke prove Jesus' faithfulness to his baptismal designation as Son, Servant, Beloved One. Jesus is tested precisely on whether he will continue to be God's *peacemaker* (*eirēnopoios*), refusing vengeance against enemies or seeking to secure the future through violence.[5]

Indeed, Jesus' mission offers a qualitatively new way to establish God's reign, to fulfill the messianic hope. Jesus rejects both Zealot-type revolution and Essene withdrawal. He calls his followers to be "the salt of the earth" and "the light of the world." The image, "salt of the earth," likely refers to fertilizer (potash), rather than table salt that adds taste to food. The image thus calls for kingdom witness and growth, not a preservative within Christendom's society.[6]

This view of "the salt of the earth" fits well with "the light of the world" image. Echoing an important Isaiah text that calls Israel to be "a light to the nations" (49:6), Jesus calls his followers to carry forward this mission. All four Gospels have their own unique narrative voice beckoning readers to mission into the whole world (see chap. 10 below). Not confined to national boundaries, the great commission embraces the whole world. The Gospels' call to mission is fulfilled in Acts, where the gospel spreads through the power of the Holy Spirit from Jerusalem through Samaria and the Gentile world to Rome, and also in Paul in his lifework as apostle to the Gentiles (see chap. 8 below). In John the incarnate Jesus is "lifted up" on the cross so that he might draw all people to himself (John 12:32).

Atonement

A second area to consider in understanding Jesus lies in the cosmic significance of the atonement: Jesus' life, death, resurrection, and exaltation. The NT repeatedly speaks of Jesus' victory over evil. This emphasis is often called the Christus Victor view of the atonement.

The Gospels (Matt 12:27-29; Luke 10:18) teach us that Jesus in his incarnation and ministry has defeated and bound the powers of Satan. In Luke 10:18 Jesus says that as the disciples have extended the peace-gospel greeting, cured the sick, and proclaimed that the kingdom of God has come near, they have also discovered that the demons are subject to them (10:17). Jesus interprets this mission: "I saw Satan falling like lightning from heaven" (RSV). Satan loses his ultimate power because the Messiah has come. Paul declares that Jesus vanquishes the power of death, thus defeating the last enemy, and is therefore Lord of all (1 Cor 15:26, 54-56; cf. Acts 2:23-24, 36).

Jesus' victory over evil is manifest also in his rendering powerless the principalities and powers (1 Cor 15:24). Paul affirms in Col 2:10 that Jesus is head over all principalities and powers. These terms denote the temporal governments—but their meaning is thereby not exhausted. This triumphal affirmation is that Jesus is Lord over them all. This point is crucially relevant for understanding the Christian peace witness and responsibility. In the next chapter we look more closely at the crucial texts (Eph 1:19-23; Rom 8:35-39; Col 1:15-18; 2:10; 1 Cor 2:6-8; 15:20-28; 1 Pet 3:22). These texts emphasize that Jesus in his resurrection and exaltation has become Lord of all. He is head of everything. The picture in Ephesians is that Jesus is the head, the church is his body, and all powers outside those two realms are under the feet of Jesus. He is Lord over all. The church recognizes, knows, and confesses his lordship. The world denies it.

Because of Jesus' lordship over all, Jesus' atonement has both universal and cosmic significance, as claimed in numerous texts (Rom 8:18-25; Eph 1:10; Phil 2:11; Col 1:19-20; Rev 5:13). These verses declare that God's purpose in Jesus' life, death, resurrection, and exaltation is ultimately to unite all things in Christ. Thus, if the atonement has universal potential, God wills all people to be saved. Where and when war persists, people are killed who are either our Christian brothers or sisters or are candidates to hear the gospel, become saved, be baptized, and welcomed into the body of Christ. Consequently, the very exercise of war militates directly against both the unity of the church and fulfilling the great commission.

Here I summarize our examination of the meaning of the incarnation for peace witnessing. The peace witness is possible because Jesus has refused Satan's temptations to inaugurate the kingdom through material, religious, or military power. Peace comes rather through the gospel proclamation of Christ crucified and raised by God's power. Gospel, cross, and crown are inseparable. Only through the cross are we reconciled to both God and fellow humans. Only by the cross comes the crown, God's reward to the faithful.[7]

Based upon the fact of cosmic atonement accomplished in and through Christ, the peace witness should be announcement, not advice; petition in the name of Christ, not only political counsel. Christ's atonement opens the future; to it followers of Jesus bear witness through both deed and word.

As peacemakers, our mission of salt and light is to penetrate every realm of life and society with the fact and practical possibility of peace, reconciliation, and goodwill among people. We witness by life, deed, and word that hostility, conflict, and war are unnecessary and are outright denials of the mission of Christ.

Church

The church is first and foremost an international, transcultural community (Gal 3:28; Eph 2:11-22). As one body in Christ (Eph 4:1-16), the church renounces national*ism*, realizing that Christ's kingdom is ultimately not of this world (John 18:36). Committed and bound to an international family of Christian believers, the church regards this allegiance to be more primary than any national loyalty or responsibility. Hence the church decisively confesses: "We must obey God rather than any human authority" (Acts 5:29). Because the church is an international kinship, it considers participation in war a denial of its very universal, transnational nature. When one group of Christians takes up arms against another group of Christians, both groups deny their belief that Jesus and not Caesar is the supreme Lord. They sacrifice Christian faith for national security.

The early Anabaptist leader Michael Sattler specifically identifies this point in his discussion of the two orders of life to which the Christian is responsible. He refers to the one order as the order of sonship and the other as the order of service. Sattler distinguishes these two levels of obedience with the words "filial" and "servile." He uses the term "service" or "servant" to denote one who performs the duties and requirements of law—a use of "servant" quite different from that in Mark 10:45. In Sattler's usage, the servant lives on the level of legal mandate; the son, however, lives on the level of love and gospel ethic. Thus, the order of sonship transcends the order of legal service. The "son" is not to forfeit his calling for the lesser role of "servant."[8] The gospel transcends the law. Indeed, Sattler saw the law and temporal government as serving a legitimate function within God's total plan for history. But this is not God's primary venue to achieve God's salvation.

Gods' primary purpose is accomplished through the church, through God's redeemed community of sons and daughters (2 Cor 6:18, where Paul includes "daughters" in the royal promise given to David, in 2 Sam 7:13-14). Never should the community of sonship and daughtership jeopardize or sacrifice its calling, its commitment, in order to carry forward a lesser legitimate function in government.[9] The son gives filial obedience; the servant renders servile obedience, obedience to law, which is always only a temporary order of life to sustain society so that the gospel might be preached and God's primary saving-healing purpose for people accomplished (1 Tim 2:1-4).

Thus the Christian peace witness must be transnational whenever possible. In contemporary practical terms, this means that the church should send relief assistance, as needed, to both North and South Korea, both Shiite and Sunni Iraqis, and both Palestinians and Israelis. Our concern and commitment to the needs of all is universal, regardless of military zoning. As we issue statements of witness to temporal governments, we need to address both sides of the conflict insofar as this is possible.[10]

In our contemporary world, this often means witnessing first to the United States government. Because many of the U.S. leaders claim to be Christians, we have the responsibility of calling them to both the demands of the gospel and the demands of the law. They, of all world leaders, should seek wisdom to know and pursue the best possible temporal order wherein the way of "righteousness and justice and equity" is understood and flourishes (Prov 2:9). The Anabaptists, certainly Menno Simons, (see Appendix 1) frequently spoke forcefully to the magistrates on how they could do their jobs "better," to reflect biblical moral standards for godly civil leadership (Ps 72:1-7, 12-14; Isa 32:1, 16-17).

The church as church must act and speak on moral issues in contemporary society. Growing directly out of the church's loyalty to the gospel, the church must take a gospel stand regarding evils in the world: war, oppression of the poor, inequality, and injustice. The gospel does not annul the law. Instead, the gospel enables us to see the true intent and purpose of the law.[11] Christians, who through Christ know the "law written on their hearts" (Jer 31:33; Heb 8:10), should of all people leaven laws that turn people from evil to value the good and promote justice in the service of peacemaking.

Participation in Christ's body is therefore our primary calling. Consequently, when Christians take up arms in war, we sever the bond of Christ's peace, mocking his death and resurrection. As Myron Augsburger puts it, "To affirm that one is a member of the Kingdom of Christ means that loyalty to Christ and his Kingdom transcends every other loyalty. This stance transcends nationalism, and calls us to identify first of all with our fellow disciples, of whatever nation, as we serve Christ together."[12]

Christian participation in war cripples the mission of the church. "We cannot kill [one] for whom Christ died," Augsburger writes. "We cannot take the life of a person God purposes to redeem."[13] Killing the enemy deprives him of the opportunity to repent. "From an evangelical perspective," Augsburger argues, "it may be said that whenever a Christian participates in war he has abdicated his responsibility to the greater calling of missions and evangelism. . . . The way for Christians to change the world is to share the . . . good news of the Gospel rather than to think we can stop the anti-God movements by force."[14]

When Christians take up the sword, for whatever national cause, and thereby turn their backs on God's call to the church to demonstrate the peace of God's new humanity, the missionary cause around the world is set back by at least a generation; often it is rendered permanently incredible.[15] This reality is becoming apparent in Iraq, where Muslims, though perhaps gaining a shaky democracy, see the extension of the "Christian" West not through initiatives that make peace, but through war and bloodshed. They may even view democracy through the lens of a war resulting in the maiming or loss of many loved ones, producing many orphans and refugees.

When the church, by refusing war, treasures its unity in the body of Christ and demonstrates reconciliation as the service of "sons and daughters" (Mark 10:42-45; 2 Cor 5:17-21), it bears witness to the powers that a new order of life has come. Reconciliation of enemies, peacemaking, *has already happened,* through Jesus Christ!

Churches in the historic peace church tradition also have an important task, challenge, and opportunity to leaven the larger Christian body on peacemaking, nonviolence, and reconciliation. This opportunity presents itself in many venues: personal relationships, community events, ecumenical gatherings of various kinds, and also in the formal ecumenical structures. Fernando Enns (representing the German Mennonite Church) tells of several peace churches' involvements in the World Council of Churches, culminating in the Council accepting his proposal to make 2001-10 the international "Decade to Overcome Violence."

Spurred by the huge devastations of World War I, churches in various nations cooperatively developed conviction that the church must be the church and establish a new transnational identity. A decade later in 1948 in Amsterdam, the World Council of Churches was formally founded. From the beginning the Council's general secretary, Willem A. Visser 't Hooft, invited the historic peace churches "to share their convictions with the wider ecumenical family." Within the past several years, however, the historic peace church presence became especially significant, especially when the Balkan wars precipitated statements on human rights, conflict prevention, and outside intervention. Though the goals stated by World Council of Churches at Potsdam in 2001 were good, the addition of a sentence on the duty "to use armed force to help protect and assist people at risk in such situations" prompted historic peace church participants to object to such authorization of just-war assumptions (along with the Russian Orthodox Church, which saw this as a Western-dominated move, even if such intervention is through the United Nations). In response, the historic peace church representatives prepared a study document with alternative methods of protecting endangered populations. In 2001-4 the World Council of Churches received several statements from different groups requesting reconsideration of its 2001 statement. In 2003 historic peace church people met at Bienenberg, Switzerland, to develop a statement that built upon the five arguments in the study document. Here is the first of four significant paragraphs:

> The historic peace church position sets forth a vision of justice that is holistic and social, distinguishing it from a view that emphasizes individual autonomy and freedom, protection of private property, or a narrow perspective on human rights such as freedom of speech and association. The biblical tradition of covenant justice includes social solidarity, religious liberty, and a comprehensive vision of human rights.[16]

Underlying the statements contributed by the historic peace church caucus is the conviction that the church must not deny its essential identity in Jesus Christ by the means it uses to pursue peace, and that peaceable means must be employed to achieve the goal of peace. Only then will there be shalom for the communities of all parties involved, those in conflict and those seeking to intervene.

Shape and Method of Peacemaking

God called Israel to be a "kingdom of priests" (Exod 19:6 RSV) and a "light to the nations" (Isa 49:6). In this call of God for Israel, we learn the direction God was leading Israel to enable them to be a blessing—salt and light—to the nations (Gen 12:3).

In Exod 21:22-25 the eye-for-eye and tooth-for-tooth law of retaliation is operative. It may appear as though God is telling Israel to make sure that wronged persons get a square amount of vengeance. Actually, however, in their societal context this command was a limitation to vengeance. It restricted the amount of vengeance that could be meted out against the aggressor. The human impulse would be to retaliate by two eyes for one eye, but the divine command was a limitation of retaliation.

Later in the OT the prophets called for an ethic of social justice that paved the way for the radical love ethic of the NT. Key texts are Isa 58; Amos 5:21-26; Mic 6:1-8. In these passages the prophetic ethic challenges Israel to seek a way of justice, mercy, and love in all community relationships. Prophets Isaiah and Micah envision an end of war and the reign of peace fully manifest upon the earth (Isa 2:1-4; 30:15; 31:1-3; Mic 4:1-7).

The connections between Israel's calling enunciated by Isaiah and Jesus' calling of his followers is striking. Glen Stassen has identified seven themes that occur in nine key Isaiah passages and are integral to Jesus' proclamation of the kingdom.[17] With these themes I identify the Gospel that develops it most fully (see my *Covenant of Peace* Gospel-analysis):

Isaiah	**Jesus: Kingdom of God**
1. Salvation-deliverance	All four Gospels
2. Righteousness-justice	Matthew and especially Luke
3. Peace	Matthew, John, and esp. Luke
4. Joy	Luke
5. God's presence: Spirit and Light	Matthew, Luke, and John
6. Healing	All, but esp. Mark and Matthew
7. Return from exile	Mark and Matthew

These themes describe the shape and method of peacemaking to which God has called and continues to call the church. By living in the world, manifesting these divine actions and virtues, the Jesus community manifests an alternative identity and power in the world. These characteristics of the new Jesus community become the power of its mission in the world. The early church continued to proclaim these God-gifts in the world, in the name of Jesus Christ (see Acts 2–5) and through the power of the Holy Spirit. In this way the church became the salt and light of the society in which it lived.

The early Christians developed a radical sharing plan, selling possessions to assist needs so that no one among them was poor (Acts 2 and 4). This economic sharing continued in Paul's determination to collect funds from the Asian churches and bring them to Jerusalem, even at the cost of his life. In doing this Paul's commitment demonstrated and was a brilliant enactment of what he says: through the church the manifold wisdom of God is to be made known to the "principalities and powers" (Eph 3:10 RSV), the "rulers and authorities" (NRSV). In AD 251, the church in Rome had a massive program of caring for widows and the poor. The church, consisting of many house fellowships throughout the city, had 1,500 people on its roll for support. Bishop Cornelius was aided by six presbyters, seven deacons, seven more subdeacons, and ninety-four people in minor roles, all delivering a ministry of care for the needy.[18] These several models during the early centuries show how caring fellowship (*koinōnia*) empowered this material sharing; such models function as a powerful means to peacemaking, to be salt and light within the faith community and also beyond it. The church responded to the dire poverty and horrific suffering of the poor, those that the empire, in all its wealth and power, neglected, letting infants die and decay in Rome's street gutters.[19]

Interchanging with the theme of economic sharing is the

church's encounter with the political authorities. In Acts 3–5 the church chose fidelity to the gospel of Jesus Christ, resulting in both civil disobedience and punishment. The apostles declared, "We must obey God rather than any human authority" (5:29). The church's first martyr (Stephen) was killed because of religious and political conflict (6:8–8:1). Both Jesus and Paul were ultimately condemned and killed on charges of incipient political treason, creating riots, stirring up the people, refusing to support the status quo expectations of society.

The gospel is indeed revolutionary. It never is content to endorse the status quo structures of society. It calls its followers to a radical faithfulness that ever challenges the subethical standards of society. Indeed, the NT expresses critical attitudes toward social, economic, and political policy. In Luke 13:32 Jesus calls Herod a fox. In Mark 6:18 John the Baptist condemns Herod for marrying his brother's wife. In Acts 22:25 Paul questions the legality of the Roman tribunal's judgment. In Acts 24:25 Paul argues with Felix about "justice, self-control, and the coming judgment." The early church took seriously its mission to counter and transcend existing structures of social, economic, and political order. Not because of pragmatic reasons, not because it had some superior political theory, but precisely because it understood the gospel of Jesus Christ.

The objective of the peace witness is to "overcome evil with good" (Rom 12:21) through loving all people, even the "enemy," and praying "for those who persecute" us (Matt 5:43-48; Luke 6:27-36). Such a peace witness springs from our commitment to the gospel of our Lord Jesus Christ. The gospel itself becomes the criterion by which we decide what we should say and how we should say it. Concern to be faithful witnesses to the gospel takes priority over questions of pragmatic policy and effective results. The validity of the method through which we choose to speak depends upon the Christian integrity and the authenticity of the person and group who speak.

I began this book with the story of Tom Oliver, who through study of the Bible with his spouse came to believe that his participation in the U.S. Army was wrong. His arguments before the board of appeals were sound and persuasive. We owe gratitude to the board that heard them, acknowledged the persuasive strength of his position and presentation, and in light of Tom's integrity, granted his discharge without his serving prison time. Let us hear this and similar stories, such as Pentecostal pacifist Paul Alexander's in his speech to Mennonite Church USA 2007 assembly in San José, California,[20] to inspire us in our faith and convictions that Jesus, not Caesar, is Lord.

A Vision of Peace and Justice*

Leader We are a part of the body of Christ.

**People We are on a liberation journey to be
people of peace in our broken world.**

Leader We believe God's gift of peace is central
to the gospel of Jesus Christ.

**People The power of the gospel transforms us as we pray
and worship together;
it leads to practice peacemaking in our homes,
workplaces, schools, neighborhoods,
and here in our family of faith.**

Leader As individual members, and as a congregation
we disengage from the priorities of the world
that separate us from Christ.

**People Like Jesus we will risk our own lives and
privileges by standing with the people
at the margins of our community, society,
and world.
We will practice economic justice,
and stewardship of creation
as a sign of God's reign in our lives.**

*All God calls us to be followers of Jesus Christ and,
by the power of the Holy Spirit,
grow as communities
of grace, joy, and peace,
so that God's healing and hope
flow through us to the world*

Leader Let the peace of Christ rule in your hearts,
since as members of one body,
we are called to peace.

* Litany is from a Mennonite Church USA Church Bulletin for May 28, 2000: Easter Sunday. Written by Jennifer Davis Sensenig, Cedar Falls (Iowa) Mennonite Church. Used with permission.

Part 2

Critical Issues in Peace Witness and Mission

Send forth your light and your truth
let them lead me

CHAPTER FIVE

Christian Witness to Christ's Lordship over the Powers

That is our vocation: to convert . . . the enemy into a guest
and to create the free and fearless space
where brotherhood and sisterhood can be formed
and fully experienced.

—*Henri J. M. Nouwen,* Reaching Out: The Three Movements of the Spiritual Life

In chapter 4, I affirmed that Jesus Christ's victory over the powers is the theological basis for Christian witness to the powers. Here I take up the implications of that point for Christian witness and mission.

As Christians we are to witness to all peoples, regardless of nationality, status, gender, or even religion. The gospel is for everyone, as the NT makes abundantly clear. But does the church's mission include witnessing to Christ's lordship over the powers, whether to church or state institutions, or on specific policies in these institutions, including those of local, state, and national governments?

In addressing this issue, the starting point is the logic of the universality of Christ's lordship. Once we grasp this point, it becomes clear that we are not free to fence off certain arenas of life as immune to gospel witness. We are not to dodge our Christian witness by fighting, fleeing, or fencing. All of life's dimensions are spheres where the gospel witness is needed and relevant.

Further, the OT prophets regularly addressed their oracles, often of judgment, to their nation's leaders. Jeremiah is called to be a prophet to the nations (Jer 1:4-10). The prophetic literature constitutes about one-fifth of the canon! Further, some of the oracles are addressed to foreign nations (see Isa 13–24; Jer 46–51; Ezek 25–32). This prophetic tradition is an analogy for the church's role today in relation to the "powers" of the nations. As Revelation culminates its judgment of Babylon-Rome, it says, "The testimony of Jesus is the spirit of prophecy" (19:10d). This chapter and the next call us to give prophetic testimony to Jesus.

Christian Understanding of Government and Response to Evil

In Rom 12–13 two important themes interconnect. While the larger discussion focuses on Christian response to evil, an important and well-known admonition on how believers are to relate to government power is sandwiched into the larger thematic instruction on response to evil. The "stuff" inside the sandwich pertains to the "powers," while the "multigrain bread" is the Christian ethic of response to evil.

The "stuff" inside tells us that every authority or power that exists is ordained (KJV), instituted (RSV, NRSV), or ordered of God (the Greek verb from the root *tagma* provides strongest support for *ordered*). We can better understand this teaching if we look more closely at the word "power," which in Greek is *exousia*. *Exousiai* (pl.) is the term used in Rom 13:1, translated as "governing authorities" (NRSV). This word, together with *archai*, is used frequently and is translated as "principalities and powers," or "rulers and authorities" (NRSV). In Eph 1:21 two words are added to rule (*archē*) and authority (*exousia*): power (*dynamis*) and dominion or lordship (*kyriotētos*).

The OT phrase "Lord of hosts" helps us understand these "power" terms in the NT. "Lord of hosts" (Hebrew: *Yahweh Sabaoth*) occurs frequently in the OT (Ps 24:7-10; 46:7, 11; 84:1, 3, 8, 12; 89:5-9; 102:21; 148:2; Isa 5:16; 6:3).[1] In these texts *Sabaoth* is translated with the Greek *dynameis*, thus "Lord of the powers."[2] The Hebrew word *tsaba'* (sing.) means "military service" (e.g., Isa 40:2 RSV: "her warfare is ended"; NRSV: "served her term") or "army/troops," but also the "host" of heaven (e.g., Dan 8:10). This has led some to suggest that *Yahweh Sabaoth* may mean "Lord of the (heavenly) armies."[3]

Five dimensions of meaning are connected to this important term *Yahweh Sabaoth*: (1) The *Lord of hosts* dwells in the temple (above the ark of the covenant), where divine holiness lays humans low, with contrite heart (Ps 84:1, 3, 12; Isa 6:3). (2) "Lord of hosts" is associated with *Zion* as the temple mount, but even more closely with "Zion" as a theological symbol denoting Yahweh's holiness, kingship, and sovereignty, proffering security and defense for the covenant people who trust God for defense (Pss 20; 84). (3) *Yahweh Sabaoth* goes forth to battle, on behalf of Israel (Ps 24:8-10; 89:8-18, against primordial chaos and Egypt [Rahab], oppressor of God's people, Isa 14:22-27); (4) *Yahweh Sabaoth* also *restores* Israel from its devastating enemies (Ps 80:2-3, 7, 14, 19, where *God of hosts* is used in parallel to *Lord of hosts*). (5) The *Lord of hosts* also rises up against the nations that have devastated Israel, even "Assyria, the rod of my anger" (Isa 10:5), and crushes both Babylon and Assyria (Isa 14:22-27).

A related OT feature is the divine council or assembly. In this connection *hosts* is used also more broadly to denote other "powers": angels (Ps 148:2) or the gods of the nations (Ps 82), who are scorned to nothing (v. 5) because they do not do what the god-ruler of a nation should do: "Give justice to the weak and the orphan, and maintain the right of the lowly and the destitute" (v. 3). Instead, they "judge unjustly" (v. 2).

All powers in the heavenly court were intended to function as servants of God's purpose. But some became rebellious, resisting God's purposes and work. This is Satan's story, who sought autonomy to oppose God. Imagery later attached to Satan was earlier used to describe rebellious kings who arrogantly set themselves up against God ("King of Babylon" in Isa 14, esp. vv. 12-15 with the fallen-from-heaven "Day Star" = "Lucifer" [KJV]; "Prince/King of Tyre" in Ezek 28, esp. vv. 12-17 with imagery of the proud king cast to the ground). Thus, although government powers are ordained of God, they may refuse, deny, and rebel against God's sovereignty. Isaiah indicts Israel for their forsaking the Lord to go after diviners (magic), wealth (mammon), and chariots and horses (martial might): "Their land is filled with idols" (Isa 2:6-8). Thus, "the *Lord of hosts* has a day against all that is proud and lofty" (2:12). To illustrate in our day, we need think only of the Nazi Holocaust horrors during Germany's Third Reich and the Allies' firebombing of German cities. Still closer to home, the United States with its imperial tentacles is ever on the brink of the demonic, as disclosed by the atomic bombing of Hiroshima and Nagasaki, and the wars in Vietnam and Iraq.

Another related OT perception is the subservience of all powers to "the Son of Man" who will come on the clouds of heaven. A key text is Dan 7:13-14:

> As I watched in the night visions,
> I saw one like a human being [RSV: "Son of Man"]
> coming with the clouds of heaven.
> And he came to the Ancient One
> and was presented before him.
> To him was given dominion [LXX[4]: *archē*]
> and glory and kingship,
> that all peoples, nations, and languages should serve him.
> His dominion [*exousia*] is an everlasting dominion
> that shall not pass away,
> and his kingship
> is one that shall never be destroyed.

In Dan 7:27 the LXX uses both *exousia* and *archai* to designate temporal domains and governments: "The kingship and dominion (*exousia*) and the greatness of the kingdoms under the whole heaven shall be given to the people of the holy ones of the Most High; their kingdom shall be an everlasting kingdom, and all dominions (*archai*) shall serve and obey them." Here "the people of the holy ones of the Most High" share in the sovereignty of the Son of Man. This title is one that Jesus uses to denote his own role and mission. But in addition to its use with reference to future judgment and sovereignty (Mark 8:38; 14:62), Jesus also uses it to designate his earthly authority (to forgive sins; 2:10) and necessary suffering and resurrection (8:31; 9:31; 10:33-34).

All three of these streams of divine sovereignty in OT theological thought culminate in Jesus' lordship in the NT. The connection between *Yahweh* as Lord and *Jesus* as Lord is persuasive when the titles, roles, and actions of both are examined.[5] The NT regards Jesus as Lord with sovereign authority (*exousia*) over all temporal "principalities and powers," terms that the NRSV translates as "rulers and authorities" (*exousiai* and *archai*) in Eph 6:12. The NT proclaims the lordship of Jesus Christ over the powers. The church knows and affirms this (Acts 2:23-36; cf. 1 Cor 2:6; Phil 2:9-11). This confession of Jesus' lordship means that the church cannot remain silent as nations arrogate power to themselves that oppresses and destroys others, tramples the poor, and produces "bloodshed" (*mispah*) instead of God's expected "justice" (*mishpat*), or the "cry" of the poor (*tse'aqah*) instead of "righteousness" (*tsedaqah*)—Isaiah's puns against Israel's evils (Isa 5:7b).

The NT affirms that regardless of the response of these powers, Jesus is Lord (Col 2:10). Because of Jesus' resurrection and exaltation, all these powers have only limited authority and must one day bend their knee to Jesus Messiah's sovereignty (Phil 2:9-11). Because Christians derive ethics from God's kingdom reality and Jesus Christ's lordship, they seek to live in accord with that reality now.

Believers thus regard temporal government and even Satan with the awareness, the hope, and the assurance that they are overcome. They have been defeated! Jesus alone is Lord, and consequently this motivates Christian peace witness to political power. The authorities of the state do not have ultimate authority. They are temporal and ultimately will perish.

Within this theological context, Rom 13 is to be understood. At no place does the Bible state that the powers are either good or bad in and of themselves. Romans 13 and other texts call believers to be subordinate to the powers. But this is only one of three streams of emphases that I treat in chapter 6 (below) and also in *Covenant of Peace*.[6] Walter Pilgrim helpfully describes three different models of relationship: Subordinationist (Pauline), Critical Distancing (Jesus and the Gospels, Acts), and Endurance of Oppression and Persecution (Pet and Rev). While Rom 13:1-7 is Paul's most explicit statement of the subordinationist stance, yet Pilgrim rightly says that we need to observe six points of qualification:

> 1. Romans 13 does not intend to provide a developed Christian doctrine of the state, good for all occasions. Paul's aims were more limited. He speaks first of all to the historical situation in Rome. . . . Most important, his primary purpose is to offer ethical instruction on proper conduct toward rulers, not a political theory on the nature of the state.
> 2. Romans 13 and the other loyalty traditions [Pilgrim had discussed 1 Tim 2:1-4; Titus 3:1-2] cannot be used to give unqualified status to all earthly governments as somehow established by God nor as its corollary unconditional obedience. . . . Paul does not speak to the crucial issue regarding governments who oppose the good or do not resist evil. What if rulers betray their divine mandate for justice or fundamentally abuse or misuse their power? There is in Rom only a "deafening silence" on this question.

3. Paul elsewhere gives evidence that Rom 13 is not the whole of his attitude toward those who hold political office. For Paul and the early church, there is only one sovereign Lord: "Jesus Christ is Lord" (1 Cor 12:3; 8:5-6; Rom 10:9; etc.). On coins and inscriptions, the ruling Caesar claimed to be *divi Augustus* (divine Augustus). Paul preaches another as God and Lord. . . .

   Paul's own experience with Roman rule and the so-called *pax Romana* was decidedly mixed. Although a Roman citizen by birth, he often felt its harsh and cruel face. In 2 Cor 11:23-33, Paul enumerates at some length his sufferings, beatings, tortures, stonings, imprisonments, banishment, and nocturnal escape over a wall. Both Jewish and Roman officials were responsible for these actions. . . . Paul could scarcely have been naïve about Roman justice.
4. For Paul and the early church, the Christian's true citizenship belongs in the kingdom of God (Phil 3:20). . . . The government, as part of this present age, belongs to those structures that will one day pass away (1 Cor 2:6). [1 Cor 6:1-8 is one passage where Paul seems to oppose Christian involvement in the structures of the state.]
5. Central to Paul's message is "Christ crucified" (1 Cor 2:2; Gal 3:1; etc.). . . . The reference to a "crucified Lord" would constantly bring to mind the injustice of Roman power. . . . Neither Paul nor his hearers could be naïve or sentimental about the empire that nailed their Lord to the cross.
6. Finally, consider Paul's understanding of Christian suffering. He himself imitates Christ as one who bears in his body the "sufferings of Christ" (2 Cor 4:7-11; Gal 6:17; Rom 8:17; Phil 3:10). This suffering is a direct result of his faithfulness to the gospel and the cause of Jesus Christ.

Walter Pilgrim concludes this discussion:

> For the moment, Paul counsels acceptance of one's suffering for the sake of Christ. Here he is joined by the other New Testament writings advocating an ethic of obedience. But, as we will see, . . . this loyalty tradition constitutes only one stream of New Testament thinking regarding the state. Other voices, perhaps dealing with governments that have become increasingly the enemy of the church, will counsel forms of resistance quite different from this tradition.[7]

The more predominant and, I propose, normative NT view of the Christian attitude toward government bases itself upon Christ's victory and lordship over the principalities and powers (1 Cor 15:24-25; Eph 1:19-23; 3:10; Col 2:10, 15; 1 Pet 3:22). The powers have been stripped of ultimate power (Col 2:15). This truth reduces all governments to a temporal status with the precise function of restraining evil and promoting good until Christ's lordship is fully acknowledged. The believer who already confesses Jesus as Lord derives his basic direction for life and conduct not from the secular authorities, but from Christ, the commander-in-chief of God's army of overcoming love.

Romans 13 also describes the powers (the authorities, NRSV) as *servants of God* (v. 6). But this statement is immediately qualified by the phrase best translated from the Greek as "when they attend to this very thing." This qualification focuses criteria against which the performance of the authorities is to be measured and judged. These criteria are mentioned in the first part of both verses 3 and 4: "For rulers are not a terror to good conduct, but to bad; . . . for he is God's servant for your good." Precisely at this point the Christian peacemaker finds a responsibility: to help to define, in contemporary and specific political possibilities, the situational meaning of good and bad. We do this not because we lodge our hope in politics but because followers of Jesus Christ should know what the terms "good" and "bad' mean for human life and action.[8]

Although in Rom 13 the government is viewed as fulfilling a good function in the political realm, Revelation portrays the political powers in major rebellion and defiance of God's intended purpose. Some commentators suggest that in 2 Thess 2 the temporal power is regarded as the "restrainer of lawlessness" at one time, and at another time as the very demonic "lawless one." With or without this interpretation, the point emerges that governments are not to be described in static moral terms. They are merely better or worse, more or less faithful to the divine purpose. Ideally the government is to command the obedience, respect, and tax support of all its subjects and citizens (1 Pet 2:13-17). Whether or not the government realizes this ideal and intention is another question. If it is not realized, the Christian, though subject to the authorities (taking whatever consequences follow), may need to disobey the government (see my discussion of *hypotasso* in chap. 6 below). Indeed, the believer has the mandate and the responsibility to witness to the government in accord with the lordship of Christ, to enable government to know God's purposes for it.

Since governments often function as perpetrators of evil as well as restrainers of evil, *and since Christ has provided the final answer to evil,* we Christians are called *to bear witness* to Christ's answer, even to the government powers (Eph 3:8-10). The most important responsibility of the church toward government and to evil in society is to live as a new society demonstrating the reconciling reality of the gospel. We can then proclaim with integrity Jesus' victory: Christ has conquered, is conquering, and will conquer evil!

This thinking guides Paul in Rom 13:1-7. A *major* theme of Rom 12:9–13:10 is how to respond to *evil* (occurs eight times: 12:9, 17 [twice], 21 [twice]; 13:3, 4, 10). Christians should not repay evil for evil (12:17), but should seek to overcome evil with *good* (12:21; cf. 12:9; 13:3). Doing the good, making peace (12:18), and loving the neighbor (13:7-10) are the Christian responses to evil.[9] Avenging evil is forbidden to

Christians, for vengeance belongs to God (12:17, 19; 13:4), who delegates it only as a "trust" to authorities as servants of God's wrath (13:4-5).

Christians are called to a distinctive Christian ethic; they need not police society. They are not to resist evil by using evil means. Christ has shown a new and better means of resistance. Christian believers are not ministers of God's wrath (let the authorities be this), but the ministers of God's reconciling love (2 Cor 5:17-20).[10] Nor did Paul tell the Christians to withdraw from a difficult situation of societal evil; they are to stay in it, in Rome, to which Paul himself wants to go (Rom 15:22-29), and there demonstrate Christ's new response to evil. By so doing, they will also witness to the authorities (Eph 3:8-10) that it is *God* who really reigns. Not Caesar, but *Christ* is Lord. Christ's victory over evil guides the Christians' response.

From this point of view, in principle Christians are called to be in society, in the thick of the fray, resisting evil and working for good. To describe the methods we are called to use, we may point to a theoretical continuum of response ranging from inactivity (ignoring the evil) on one extreme, to lethal violence (killing people who do evil) on the other extreme.[11] Neither extreme is acceptable for disciples of Jesus, for neither is consistent with love. Abdication does not take evil seriously; lethal violence does not take the possibility of one's own evil seriously. Neither extreme genuinely considers the possibility of converting the enemy; the latter extreme actually makes the enemy's repentance and reconciliation definitively impossible. In other words, we cannot resist evil either by wishing it away or by using (from our point of view) a lesser evil. We cannot combat a big lie with a little lie. We must resist evil with good, and falsehood with truth.

New Testament Basis for Witness

Five streams of biblical teaching form the scriptural and theological basis for the position that Christians and the church as church are to witness to Christ's lordship over the powers. Jesus' lordship over all worldly and superworldly realms of authority is the grounding thesis here.

First, in his ministry Jesus proclaims that the kingdom of God (a political notion) has come near (or *is come*, Mark 1:14-15). Jesus' deeds of healing, exorcism, and forgiveness of sin witness to the coming of new kingdom power and reality. But Jesus never uses his power to destroy enemies; rather, he confronts demonic power, as the classic text puts it so clearly:

> If it is by the Spirit of God that I cast out demons, then the kingdom of God has come upon you. Or how can one enter a strong man's house and plunder his goods, unless he first binds the strong man? Then indeed he may plunder his house. (Matt 12:28-29 RSV; parallels: Mark 3:23-27; Luke 11:14-23)

When Jesus sends out his disciples, he gives them authority to heal, cast out demons, and proclaim, "The kingdom of God has come near" (declared twice, Luke 10:1-12). The apostles also extend the peace of the kingdom (*peace* occurs three times) as the test that opened or closed the door to their gospel message.[12] Jesus' and his disciples' mission challenged the powers of that day and finally led to his crucifixion. Jesus' power confronting the power of the political authorities lies at the very heart of the gospel. When the church faithfully follows Jesus, its Leader and Lord, it too will find itself confronting the powers of its day.

Second, Paul speaks specifically of Christ as head over the powers, and that Christ's victory on the cross is a defeat of the might of the powers. In the church's faith and proclamation, Christ is now both the de jure and the de facto head of all principalities and powers (the NT equivalent of governments, rulers, ologies, and isms): "You have come to fullness of life in him, who is the head of all rule and authority. . . . He disarmed the principalities and powers and made a public example of them, triumphing over them" (Col 2:10, 15). The same word for *head* in 2:10 to denote Christ's relationship to the powers is also used in Eph 5:23 to denote Jesus' relationship to the church. Further, God has made Christ "the head over all things for the church" (Eph 1:22). The *all things* subordinated to Christ certainly include the powers. Christ's cross and resurrection not only defeated the rulers and authorities (alternate translation: principalities and powers), but also made a public display of them, showing the futility of their power (Col 2:15; see chap. 4 above). Other texts, such as 1 Cor 2:6-8 and 1 Pet 3:22, make a similar point. Further, Paul speaks of Christ's present reign over all foes: "Then comes the end, when he hands over the kingdom to God the Father, after he has destroyed every ruler and every authority and power. For he must reign until he has put all his enemies under his feet" (1 Cor 15:20-28, quoting vv. 24-25).

Third, Paul speaks specifically of witness to the powers, "that through the church the wisdom of God might now be made known to the rulers and authorities [RSV: 'principalities and powers'] in the heavenly places" (Eph 3:10). The context here is Paul's apostolic call and mission, which led to the uniting of Jews and Gentiles in Christ. What the Roman government in all its power (even in its self-claimed Pax Romana) was not able to achieve, the gospel of Jesus Christ did achieve: the union of formerly hostile peoples into one faith body, living under the lordship of Christ. Paul sees this body as a manifestation to the powers of God's manifold wisdom.

The book of Revelation (see chap. 11 below) is a grand testimony to this point. It envisions the entire faithful church of its day, and in days to come, united in worship to God and the Lamb upon the throne ("throne" appears 46 times) as the Power against all worldly power. In the end, mighty Rome (Babylon) falls, and Jesus Christ's reign triumphs, manifest in the new heavens and new earth.

In both these texts the church is witness by its being, first of all. But it is also a witness through the words it speaks, both in Paul's life and in the words of Revelation. In Rev 18 particularly, the economic expansion and injustice of the empire is sharply condemned. The wealth of the empire stands under the judgment of God.[13] This is the church's witness, to speak just such words when empires seek to dominate the globe, as is happening now by U.S. efforts to economically (and indirectly politically) dominate the globe.

Fourth, Jesus and the apostles speak words about and directly to government rulers that demonstrate Christ's lordship over the powers. In John, Jesus declares to Pilate that his power is given him from above, inferring that the same heavenly Lord empowers Jesus in his life's ministry and death. Jesus pronounces restriction upon Pilate's power: "Pilate said to him, 'So you are a king?' Jesus answered, 'You say that I am a king. For this I was born, and for this I came into the world, to testify to the truth. Every one who belongs to the truth listens to my voice. . . . You would have no power over me unless it had been given you from above'" (John 18:37 RSV; 19:11a).

Further, in the early church preaching of Christ's resurrection, his lordship empowers the disciples to critique and even disobey the authorities, as shown in the following texts from Acts:

- 2:22-24, 36 holds the authorities accountable for crucifying Jesus, affirming also that it was in accord with God's plan.
- 4:7-29 again holds the leaders accountable for Jesus' crucifixion (v. 10), and the apostles refuse to obey the leaders' commands not to witness to Jesus, appealing to God's authority as greater than that of the leaders (vv. 18-20).
- 5:27-32: in another round before the authorities the apostles say, "We must obey God rather than any human authority."

- 22:25: Paul objects to the Roman centurion's flogging him: "Is it legal for you to flog a Roman citizen who is uncondemned?"
- 24:25: In discussion with the procurator Felix, Paul speaks to him about "justice, self-control, and the coming judgment," and Felix becomes "frightened."[14]

Fifth and finally, God's purpose for government stated in Rom 13 is set in the context of Rom 12, which consists of a clear and categorical call of submission and obedience to Jesus' lordship! In the next chapter I take up a textual study of Rom 13, in light of the text's call to pay all taxes. This topic is most difficult for those who consistently object to war, and specifically to Christian participation in war.

Understanding Rom 13 in light of Rom 12 does not allow Christian believers to fudge or renege on their calling to follow Jesus, even though it is also clear that the authorities may command, but believers cannot obey. Uncritical obedience to government, declaring "My country, right or wrong" or "My government deserves my ultimate loyalty," is not the teaching of the NT. Rather, as 1 Pet 2:11 puts it, we are "aliens and exiles" (KJV: "strangers and pilgrims"). This means our primary allegiance is to Christ's body universal, not to the nation-state. The criteria for obedience/disobedience come from the side of Christ's lordship, not from the authority of government.

Moral Norms for Government?

Another dimension of discussing the church's peace/salt-and-light witness in the social order is understanding God's moral expectation of humans. We focus the question: Does God have two ultimate moral codes, one for the church and one for the government? This is a problematic issue as the various solutions to resolving the ethical obligations of Christians in relation to government show.[15]

Viewing this matter from an Anabaptist perspective, the

only moral standard we know as Christians is rooted in the ethical norms of the gospel of Jesus Christ. In Rom 2:14-16 the apostle Paul indicates that the pagan who never heard of the Mosaic law or the Christian gospel may by chance do what the law requires and thus be in a better position for final judgment than the pagan who lives a more wicked life, or than the Jew or Christian who knows the moral norm of the gospel and fails to live in accord with it. But the final point of this passage is that ultimately all will be judged by the one gospel norm, the ethical norm revealed in the life of Jesus Christ. This means that all people falling short of obedience to the ethical norm of the gospel have no autonomous ethical norm by which God acquits or condemns. While this text speaks of the norm of the law, the gospel fulfills the "just requirement of the law" (Rom 8:3-4) and is the *telos*-end (fulfillment) of the law's ethic (10:4).

This issue has implications for the expected morality that characterizes government policy. Christians cannot expect government to exemplify moral norms that the gospel has given for the church's obedience. At the same time, however, Christians may expect a better-than-now-is performance from government. There is always the possibility for those outside the gospel to do better than they are doing. Consequently, when the church addresses the government, it speaks in terms of specific alternatives. It articulates specific possibilities for the government that are not being followed but that could be followed and that more closely approximate the norms that we know they will never fully attain.

The chief reason why Christians must speak to specific alternatives is because the Bible does not teach any political theory that Christians should seek to sell to government. While Christians may advise certain political actions that they believe to more closely approximate the Christian ethic, yet they can never propose a form or theory of government in the name of Christ. All the Christian has to propose is the kingdom of God. And that proposal is for a radically new order of society that allocates government order to secondary significance.

The church's mission with regard to the morality of government is thus to pray and witness in order that the highest morality possible might be achieved. With Paul we believe that some levels of morality, or immorality, are preferable to others and more amenable to God's moral standards. It is meaningful and important to acknowledge that governments may carry on their work more or less in accord with the purpose and plan of God. This purpose and plan are not to realize the kingdom of God through government structure, but to seek for the more amenable political policies possible so that the Christian gospel can be advanced and God's mercy and justice be more closely approximated in the temporal order.

War

To sharpen the issue, we pose the question: Is war wrong, or is war wrong only for the church and not for the government? This is implicitly answered by the foregoing discussion on the biblical view of morality. For outside the moral norm of the gospel, all other action, though we may call it more or less moral, is actually more or less immoral. And within this realm of immorality, there has been war, there is war, and there will continue to be war. This does not make war right. It only underscores the fact that war is and sin is. The reason why war continues is because of human sin, rebellion against the lordship of Christ. War continues because people ignore, deny, and refuse God's norm of morality as revealed in the gospel of Jesus Christ. From a theological viewpoint, then, based upon the NT teaching, all war is sin and wrong.[16]

In the history of the Christian church, however, there have been ways in which war has been supposedly justified. Chief among these is the just-war theory. This theory seeks to make war in certain cases legitimate. Many theologians and ethicists, however, question whether there ever was a just war, whether this theory ever was tenable, and whether any war was fought for a truly just cause. From a theological viewpoint, a wide consensus emerges that war has always been wrong, continues to be wrong, and always will be wrong.

However, from a political viewpoint, the major opinion of theologians and ethicists yields a different emphasis. Many theologians and ethicists contend that war is politically necessary as a way of balancing human evil egoisms. Reinhold Niebuhr has argued and advanced this viewpoint, known as Christian realism.[17] This view contends that war is a fact of political necessity, but though necessary, it is never right. These ethicists say that when we engage in war, we do compromise the gospel norm. But we can do no other. We trust for God's forgiveness.

From this perspective of analysis, some wars may be unnecessary and *therefore* wrong, not only in a theological sense but also in a political sense. Many Christian ethicists on the basis of political, not theological, judgment regard the war in Vietnam to have been unnecessary and wrong—likewise, the Iraq war that began in 2003. These wars therefore are immoral even by the Niebuhrian "realism." This is why we heard and now hear statements such as "The war in Vietnam/Iraq was/is immoral and unjust." That statement can be made as a consequence of the theological assertion above, that all wars are wrong and sinful, and therefore this war is immoral and unjust. But it can also be made as a consequence of a political judgment. Such a statement then does not derive from the previous premise that all wars are wrong and sinful, but from the premise that some wars are necessary, others are unnecessary, and the Vietnam and Iraqi wars are of the latter kind. Therefore they are immoral and wrong.

What then does this discussion mean for our presence in the political order as nonresistant, pacifist Christians? It means, first, that the witness and affirmation that all war is wrong and sinful should be continuously proclaimed to government leaders by Christian peacemakers. It is an indiscriminate gospel call to repentance and full obedience to the way of Christ and to a primary allegiance to the kingdom community.

It means also, in fidelity to our salt-and-light mission, that we should discover how to witness against a war that is popularly judged politically unnecessary and therefore morally wrong on political analysis. The crucial question confronting the church today is how to speak on this second level without distorting the quality of our trans-situational witness? The recent work evolving out of a Mennonite Central Committee study on peace theology speaks of using a "middle language," developed from John Howard Yoder's model of "middle axioms" described below. Lydia Harder draws on the biblical wisdom tradition as a scriptural model that connects the prophetic-covenantal ethic with life in the world.[18] The model is useful and merits further explication.

In reading Proverbs recently, I noticed in 8:13-21 numerous moral attributes of wisdom applicable to moral address to government leaders, civic or national:

1. Fear of the Lord, recognizing that we are only human and mortal (cf. also Pss 9–15, which are strong in wisdom tradition).
2. Hatred of evil and love of the truth (8:13; how badly needed these days!).
3. Hating perverted, deceitful speech (8:13c).
4. Looking to wisdom, not folly, for courage and strength (8:14).
5. Wisdom enabling rulers to rule justly and with righteousness (8:15, 20).
6. Wisdom as source of riches, honor, and prosperity (shalom; 8:18-19), but recognizing also that wisdom is valued above jewels (v. 11) and "gold, even fine gold" (v. 19).
7. Wisdom as source of "creative ordering" of the world with God (8:22-31).

Chapter 14 has several relevant proverbs: "Those who oppress the poor insult their Maker, but those who are kind to the needy honor him" (14:31). "Righteousness exalts a nation, but sin is a reproach to any people" (14:34). Psalm 94 also contributes to this wisdom tradition, especially verses 4-6 castigating the speech and actions of the "arrogant," and posing the piercing question in verse 20: "Can wicked rulers be allied with you, those who contrive mischief by statue?" We might construct a profile of virtues in this "middle language," by which people in the biblical faith tradition address rulers to call them accountable to a standard that even apart from covenantal faith they would recognize as wise, prudent, and productive of security and shalom.

The wisdom model also needs case studies to demonstrate how it works. Harder's example of her father involved in cooperatives, a form of community-governed institutions, is helpful. A story from my own genealogical history illustrates this wisdom approach during the American Revolutionary War, as told by John Ruth in *'Twas Seeding Time*. A Rosenberger family brought two Swartley brothers to the New World as indentured servants, settling in the Franconia, Pennsylvania, area. In the course of time both Swartley young men married a Rosenberger daughter.[19] John's wedding to Magdalena took place during the peak of the war, imperiling the shalom of the wedding reception. Hungry soldiers seeking food for the army often would rampage a festival and take the food. The women who prepared the reception meal at Deacon Henry Rosenberger's Skippack home feared just such a catastrophe, and not in vain. Sighting soldiers advancing over the rise from Towamencin, the women consulted in consternation and decided on a plan, a fine Christian response. Several met the soldiers as they approached and invited them as welcomed guests to the wedding meal. It worked. The banquet symbol in the Gospels' appropriation of the wisdom tradition, to which Lydia Harder refers, disarmed the potentially hostile situation, extending kingdom hospitality to hungry soldiers.[20]

Wisdom can perhaps help us with the "middle language," but it will need stories of people, from the past and present, who embody this ferrying of the gospel into the everyday challenges of life where a myriad of current cultural forces threaten security. How to "ferry across" to imperial military actions and the economic exploitation of our time, let alone the rising violence within civil society, presents a daunting challenge. The model developed by the Mennonite Central Committee Peace Theology study is provocative;[21] it needs life-stories to illustrate its working in both civil government and national plans and exploits of domination.

Our Calling

As Christians we may participate in all aspects of our society consistent with our calling. Conversely, we may not accept positions of responsibility that exclude love as the answer to evil. The extent of participation in societal structures will and should raise difficult questions for Christian believers. In our attempts to answer them, we must maintain a genuine flexibility in decision making. The individual Christian's conscience and the discernment of our communities of faith are essential guiding resources. In no case, however, may we Christians take positions that lead us, either personally or by the logical extension of our actions, to take the life of the enemy or evil one. This is incompatible with the way of Christ. To serve therefore in regular or revolutionary armed forces, in the military branches of the civil service, or in industries manufacturing armaments violates the Christian ethic of peacemaking, doing good and loving the neighbor; indeed, God may be calling those who have jobs in these areas to take the risky step of resigning and seeking other employment.[22]

There are indeed many avenues of service and witness that are open to Christians.[23] Clearly, we will engage in the ministry and struggle of prayer for governments, our enemies, and our persecutors.[24] Nonviolent Christians have discovered that through prayer for impossibly fraught situations, God has worked miracles of deliverance.[25] Christians may also, as a rule, teach in schools, hold public health positions, and serve as traffic wardens (though psychological force and on occasion physical force for restraint will be used in these occupations, we Christians should refrain from using any type of force that is not an expression of care for the well-being of the persons to whom the force is applied).[26] We may engage in trade union activities, in nonviolent demonstrations, and even in civil disobedience for prophetic witness.

In many societies we will not be able to serve as judges or police, because these occupations have been ruled out by the obligations they have either to take life or to sanction the taking of life. However, in societies (such as the United Kingdom) that have rejected the death penalty and have a largely unarmed police force, these may be appropriate avenues of Christian involvement. Significantly, the early church allowed believers to carry out police duties; but if they took life, it excommunicated them.[27]

Christians in positions of public responsibility must recognize, however, that the laws and institutions of most societies often function to protect the self-interest of certain privileged groups of citizens. For this reason, when we Christians seek to advocate policies that express the biblical mandates for justice, peace, and respect for life, we may well lose our jobs.[28] Even so, we support the efforts of fellow believers deliberately to take such positions in order to witness to the gospel; we advocate such effort not because we think that we can thereby Christianize the system, but because we seek to demonstrate Jesus' kingdom way in the structures of society.

The primary challenge to the Christian, then, is not to avoid sinful involvement; it is rather to select involvement that gives positive expression to Jesus' teachings. The challenge before us as Christians is not to be agents of *state-government* law and justice, but to be ambassadors of *God's* way of setting things right (justification) through Jesus Christ. Our vocational employment, therefore, should seek to express our Christian vocation of bearing witness to *God's* justice and peace.

More than four decades ago John Howard Yoder wrote *The Christian Witness to the State*,[29] which presents a theological basis for just such a witness. Although the title of the book makes the state the (indirect) object of the witness, I prefer to make *the lordship of Christ* that object. The state is one arena, then, where that witness to Christ's lordship is directed. But over the years this issue has been controversial. One former colleague of mine, who shared an office with me, contended that this is wrong, that the state lies outside the lordship of Christ. It is under God (he would cite Rom 13:1-7), and our witness to Christ is that of salvation for all people, period. Jesus Christ is head over the church but not over the government. Therefore, Christian witness does not bear on institutions as such, certainly not governmental policies and practices.

I disagreed and pointed out that Paul declares Jesus head over the principalities and powers (Col 2:10). To this my colleague had no answer, but he continued to believe that witness to government was theologically misplaced. As happens in the face of such divergent positions, I gathered the NT texts that bear on this issue. I also read *The Complete Writings of Menno Simons* in order to ascertain what the Anabaptist tradition was on this topic. Appendix 1 prints relevant texts from Menno Simons as well as one from Michael Sattler. The clarity of their precedent in setting forth such witness persuades me that Anabaptists assumed this to be part of their responsibility as faithful witnesses to Jesus Christ. The Anabaptists did not hesitate to speak to government leaders about their infidelity to biblical morality. Government leaders then claimed to be Christian, but this is also true of many political leaders today, especially in the United States.

John Howard Yoder's Views on the Powers and Witness to the State

An important part of John Howard Yoder's contribution in his 1964 book *The Christian Witness to the State* is his distinction between church and state entities. The church does not speak to the state as though it should operate on the same moral standards that guide the life of the church. Rather, he suggests that the church's witness to the state be envisioned via a "spring-tension" relationship, which respects the fact of one ultimate morality expressing God's will for human life, and the fact that "the state" does not function on those standards. Nevertheless, the state has no independent God-given moral code. Influenced by the post-1948 World Council of Churches language of J. H. Oldham, and later John C. Bennett, Yoder used the concept of "middle axioms" as a means of witness to advocate moral values that stand in continuity with what the church holds for its own practice, but yet does not ask government to function up to the moral standards of the church. The goal of the witness is to assist the state to be more moral than it is, to choose the better of several alternatives, none of which expresses fully God's kingdom vision.

To illustrate, Christians who seek to obey Jesus' command to love enemies—many, however, don't accept the command as meant for them, but explain that it applies only in some limited sense[30]—witness to government on the course of action that will least alienate the enemy and possibly open doors for cooperation and mutual assistance in the future. When the United States began voicing its consideration of invading Iraq (the second time), it was clear to me that this would alienate more than strengthen either country in the long run. Accordingly, I wrote a letter to *The Peoples Forum* of my local newspaper and sent copies to my representative and senators. With the passing of several years after the U.S. invasion, it is clear that warmongering in Afghanistan and Iraq has not only galvanized terrorism; it also has made terrorists more determined and more hateful of Western imperialism. John Paul

Lederach said about this bad political decision: If only the leaders of the two nations would have gathered around the table to discuss their fears and differences, they could have avoided the horrible consequences of thousands of casualties (American, coalition, and Iraqi) and the mounting numbers of widows, orphans, and refugees. They did not consider other alternative actions, more congruent with "love of the enemy."

Government leaders often marginalize the witness of faith-voices because they assume that they do not have adequate information. But in this case it has become clear that government leaders not only had inadequate information, they also had false information, manufactured from who knows where. Further, faith communities often have information about various countries around the world arising from nongovernmental organizations or mission personnel in those countries. But the driving force of such witness to government is not that of superior intelligence or better information, but of dogged commitment to speak the truth of the gospel, often through middle-axiom language. For witness on the matter of paying taxes used for an ever-spiraling military budget, see the next chapter. As Christians, we are called to be vigilant in our witness to Christ in all spheres of life, and in humility and honesty indeed to speak truth to power. We are to seek the welfare of not only "our" country's people, but also shalom for all peoples.

Conclusion

Christ's lordship over the powers is the bedrock confession for Christian believers (see Phil 2:5-11): it provides the theological basis for Christian witness to the state (meaning government policies and practices at all levels). We should see this Pauline and Petrine declaration in continuity with Jesus' ministry of exorcism, which is indeed a key sign that the kingdom of God has come near. As Luke 10:18 (RSV) says, the apostles' extending the *peace-gospel* and announcing the coming of the *kingdom* occurs simultaneously. This mission-action is the basis for Jesus' exclamation: "I saw [Greek: was seeing] Satan fall like lightning from heaven." The dawning of God's kingdom through the receiving of the gospel marks Satan's loss of control over humans. The same biblical theology that supports Christian witness to the state also supports Christian deliverance ministry. Both appeal to the sovereign lordship of Christ.

Two stories illustrate how these ministries are intertwined. George McClain, in *Claiming All Things for God*, relates how ritual use of exorcism was used to free social and political systemic power from demonic control. The setting was Louisville, where the board of the United Methodist Church was to meet. The time was 1987, before the formal ending of apartheid in South Africa. For several years strong protests were lodged against the United Methodist General Board of Pensions for not divesting funds from South Africa corporations, but the board did not heed the pleading. In the summer before this event, McClain had shared his frustration at a spiritual retreat that he led, "Journey Inward, Journey Outward." A member of the retreat suggested a service of social exorcism that she prepared on behalf of this blockage. Spirits of Fear and Intimidation, Lust for Power, Mammon, and Patriarchy were named, for these seemed to be the blockers preventing open consideration of the issues.

Several weeks after that session, the chair of the board, who was firmly against divestment, announced his resignation. With this background to the Louisville meeting three months after the retreat, McClain called together a small prayer group the night before a larger group was to hold a public service of social exorcism outside the Seelbach Hotel, where the board was to meet the following day. The pronouncements of disempowerment were not against board members, but against the "Powers" that blocked change. For the first time the board was open to the pleas of the Methodist Federation for Social Action, which McClain represented. Dialogue in smaller groups continued into the night, and the way opened for change in the board's policies.[31] Though McClain defers on drawing a cause-effect relationship, what appears to have been divine intervention is striking.

The other story comes from East Germany, occurring several years later, in 1989. Yearning for an end to the Communist suppression of freedom, a growing number of people in East Germany gathered for weekly prayer in the churches, to cry out to God for help, to change the tyranny of the political system. Believers and unbelievers came together to pray and to search for God's help and way. As one East-German-born Christian from Grand Rapids put it, with tears in her eyes, the people who had never come to church just came, and they began to call upon God for help, voicing simple but powerful earnest prayers. In the Nicholas church (*Nikolaikirche*) in Leipzig, many began to meet regularly on Monday nights.

Then the political situation became very tense, and the people feared the troops of the Communist Party would come and crush their hopes by force. But the church called on both the government and the people to refrain from violence. This petition not to resort to violence was read from every pulpit in the city and over the municipal public address system. They called all those who wanted to do anything for their country to come tonight to the church. Some seventy thousand people showed up. After the secret police felt the power of this faith movement, they left the mass of people. The people, weeping with joy, praised God for a new Red Sea miracle.[32]

In my articles in *Even the Demons Submit*, I narrate stories that show Christ's delivering power in encounter with demonic oppression, manifest in the human person.[33] The theological affirmation of Christ's lordship over the powers is the basis for both types of witness. Both testify to the resurrection power that has defeated the power of Satan, in varied evil manifestations. Indeed, Jesus is Lord of all. Not all the redemptive payoff comes in this life, for evil continues to abound in structures and personal experience. Nonetheless, the church is called to faithful witness in all spheres of life.

Addendum

While Yoder's contribution to "witness to the state" has had significant effect upon a generation within the historic peace churches, his work on "the powers" (especially chap. 8 in *The Politics of Jesus*) has been even more influential, but not without major critique. I describe different interpretations of the principalities and powers in chapter 8 of *Covenant of Peace*. Aside from these different exegetical views, one's understanding of the church's mission in relation to the powers is perhaps even more important. Thomas McAlpine identifies four main approaches:[34] Reformed, which seeks to transform the powers to be more accountable to Christian moral standards; Anabaptist, which emphasizes the importance of the church as a contrast community to the powers; and the Third Wave approach (Peter Wagner), which seeks in its missionary strategy to confront evil spirit-powers exerting control of specific territorial domains.[35] McAlpine's fourth approach is sociological-anthropological, which is comparatively descriptive of evil as understood by various societies in relation to their differing worldviews.

These differences center on whether the Christian mission witnesses to the gospel by confronting evil in the spiritual realm through binding and casting out demons, or whether one confronts evil in the structural systems that dominate and oppress people. The distinction sharply put is whether one thinks and speaks of personal (and territorial) spiritual oppression, or of political, socioeconomic, and systemic structural oppression. My own position is that this matter is not an either-or but both-and.

In a speech that originated in a Walter Wink Symposium at Eastern Mennonite University in March 2000, I developed this point at some length.[36] Likewise, I have shown that Jesus' ministry of exorcism has continuing significance for the ministry of the church.[37]

Rather than repeat these contributions, I take up, as representative voices, the issues as they are focused in letter exchanges between John R. Stott and John Howard Yoder.[38] Stott's concern, arising from Yoder's teachings and writings on the powers, focuses on two points: (1) Does Yoder adequately respect the evangelical belief in the spirit realm (here, *evil* spirit powers)? (2) Does Yoder too easily demythologize the NT testimony to these realities by narrowing "evil" to political and economic structures and systems?[39]

The influence of Yoder's work on the powers is enormous. Ron Sider, Walter Wink, Ched Myers, and numerous other writers assume a Yoderian theology of the powers. These writings are not limited to North America but show up in "revolutionary theologies" throughout the world. Wink treats the theme in such a way that two new perspectives appear: an explicit articulation of a postmodern worldview, and a Jungian psychological theory: taken together, they replace the transcendent and immanent with an *inner* and *outer* face.[40] Yoder's responses to Stott indicate a firm embracing of both the transcendent and immanent dimensions of evil, and on this a crucial difference emerges between Yoder and Wink, since Wink's worldview collapses the transcendent-immanent distinction.[41]

Yoder's contribution on the powers has also shaped the working theology of peace and justice activist groups, in such publications as *Sojourners* and *The Other Side,* and activist groups such as Christian Witness for Peace and Christian Peacemaker Teams. The influence of his work on the powers within the Mennonite world predates his 1971 *Politics*. It began in the midfifties with his 1955 paper on "The Lordship of Christ over Church and State" and became more influential through his 1964 publication by the Institute of Mennonite Studies, *The Christian Witness to the State*. The midsixties' initiatives among Mennonites to witness to the U.S. government were based on Yoder's contributions, with some modification, as noted above.[42]

Thousands of students who studied at Eastern Mennonite University and Seminary, Associated Mennonite

Biblical Seminary, and other Mennonite colleges and universities have been shaped in their theology and preaching by these Yoderian emphases. Yoder's thought became the dominant ethos of Mennonite discussion about peacemaking for over two decades, as shown by the study of Kraybill and Driedger on Mennonite peacemaking. Three periods of shifting dominant emphases outline an effective history of this theological emphasis:

Witness to the State	1960-1968
Nonviolent Resistance	1968-1976
Peace and Justice	1976-1983
Peacemaking	1983-1990[43]

In my perception, peacemaking, mediation, and conflict transformation have been prominent emphases for the decade 1990-2000, which together with restorative justice continues into the present decade. In these areas Yoder's theology has been less significant,[44] and earlier Mennonite emphases on the way of love in human relations together with emphases from the social sciences have become more dominant. This is clear also in the 1995 *Confession of Faith in a Mennonite Perspective*, in which emphases on nonresistance and the way of love are more prominent than is Jesus' lordship over the powers, even in article 23, "The Church's Relation to Government and Society."[45]

Recognizing Yoder's widespread influence on the church and scholarship (not only Mennonite, but also among others and internationally), two issues remain problematic.[46] First is the relationship between Jesus Christ's victory over the powers and Jesus' exorcisms in the Synoptic Gospels. While Yoder separates these two[47] and never writes on the latter to my knowledge, several scholars have developed continuity between the two, from two angles of consideration: (1) "Power" language occurs also in the Gospels (especially Wink and Tambasco).[48] (2) The victory of Christ over the powers, which as Yoder holds did not destroy the powers, requires ongoing Christian resistance to the powers, often designated as "spiritual warfare." In Christian reality these two dimensions of emphases are integrally related to Christ's victory over the powers, as is OT warfare also.[49]

Samples of this larger viewing of the "powers" agenda are Thomas Yoder Neufeld's dissertation on Eph 6 and his 2002 commentary on Ephesians. Yoder Neufeld works in detail with the trajectory from the OT to NT in order to understand Eph 6. God's work as Divine Warrior is "democratized" so that the saints, the church, participate with God in the battle against evil.[50] Clinton Arnold puts spiritual warfare into the context of the Ephesian believers' past religious allegiances in the Artemis cult, in various forms of magic and astrology, and in other mystery cults, in all of which great fear of demonic powers played a major role. Hence Christ's victory is a conquest of the powers, and the believers are called to stand against them with the divine armor: "Victory over the 'powers' is not assured apart from the appropriation of the power of God. Failure to resist allows the devil to reassert his dominion."[51] Leivestad treats Eph 6 together with numerous other "victory" texts (like Eph 4:8-10) and the NT as a whole. His work shows a strong stratum of unity in NT thought, and especially between the seven letters of Paul and Ephesians and Colossians.[52]

Just as Yoder's work on Jubilee is brilliant in the scope of concern it addresses, so also is his work on the "powers."[53] But in each there is a reductionism in view of Yoder's specific goal to demonstrate that the NT is not irrelevant to social ethics. Since he never took up the task of a more comprehensive constructive theology, the Jubilee connection to evangelism and deliverance from Satan in conversion and exorcism does not appear. On the "powers," the Christian fight against them in every sphere of temptation is not addressed at length. Likely Yoder would respond by explicating further his statement that the Gospel writers do not comment on how Jesus struggled against "pride, envy, anger, sloth, avarice, gluttony, and lust." They focus on how Jesus "faced again and again . . . the temptation to exercise social responsibility, in the interest of justified revolution, through the use of available violent methods."[54]

The reductionism of temptation to this one central theme by Yoder triggered Jeffrey Gibson's doctoral dissertation's analysis of eight temptations of Jesus in Mark and Q sources.[55] As noted earlier in chapter 4, Gibson substantiates Yoder's thesis, though not all will agree with his exegetical decisions.[56]

While Yoder brilliantly recovered the NT for social ethics, the associative dimensions of these themes in personal and communal practices have been shortchanged, both in Yoder's writings and in the ecclesial communities that Yoder's contribution so much influenced. One might rightly counter this critique by pointing out that Yoder began a good work to which other contributions have added wider dimensions, as in Thomas Yoder Neufeld's, Thomas Finger's, and my own writings.[57] I recognize truth in this but also observe that these associative dimensions of Jubilee and the "powers" have received minimal emphasis in the very communities of faith where Yoder's contribution has been so influential.

This shortfall may explain in part what Stephen Dintaman has lamented as "spiritual impoverishment" in Mennonite efforts to transmit and live out the Anabaptist vision. Our social ethics and peacemaking efforts need to be rooted in the empowerment of the Holy Spirit (a major theme of Luke's Jubilee story) and in the vitality of "joyous, healing, and empowering fellowship [that] always precedes fruitful discipleship."[58]

A Peacemaker's Confessions

Those conflicts and disputes among you are, where do they come from? Do they come from your cravings that are at war within you? (James 4:1).

*All rests ultimately in the disarmament of the human heart and the conversion of the human spirit to God, who alone can give authentic peace (*The Challenge of Peace, *p. 286, Pax Christi, June 1985).*

Keep your heart with all vigilance, for from it flow the springs of life (Prov 4:23).

I am a peacemaker. Disarm my heart from the evil that binds it.

I confess that little and big wars go on inside my heart—wars between good and evil, hope and despair, love and hate, courage and fear, selfishness and unselfishness.

I confess to holding on to unresolved bitterness that infects and cripples my peacemaking.

I confess to talking and preaching peace but sometimes being too busy to make peace, too afraid to face the violence in me and around me.

I confess my tendency to violate others—to manipulate, dominate, and put others down.

I confess to attacking others verbally, to making harsh and self-righteous judgments of others, sometimes making such judgments against myself.

ALL: Lord, have mercy on me.

I confess turning deaf ears, becoming hardened and unresponsive to the cries of the poor and the oppressed in my community, in Chicago, Northern Ireland, Middle East, Central America, Africa, Philadelphia . . .

I confess keeping silent when I should have spoken and acted for justice because I was afraid or selfish.

I confess to creating divisions, quarrels, conflicts, of using destructive words, and to actions against those close to me and then being slow to seek forgiveness.

I confess my complicity in supporting structures that bind and oppress, and to permitting them to go unchallenged in my community, nation, and world.

I confess to having racial and sexual prejudices, to practicing discrimination, using exclusive language, and being exclusive.

I confess to taking more than my share of the resources of your world, of confusing my needs with my wants.

ALL: Lord, have mercy on me.

I confess to using pious words and flimsy excuses for not getting involved in the ministry of reconciliation, to which you have called us all.

I confess my difficulty in loving the oppressors, sometimes the heads of state and those who separate evangelism from peacemaking and justice.

I confess that sometimes my peacemaking reflects defensiveness, arrogance, and rigidity rather than the spirit of Christ.

ALL: Lord, have mercy on me.

ALL: Wash me thoroughly from my iniquity, and cleanse me from my sin! Create in me a clean heart, O God, and put a new and right spirit within me. Cast me not away from thy presence, and take not thy Holy Spirit from me. restore to me the joy of thy salvation, and uphold me with a willing spirit. Amen (Ps 51:2, 10-12).

By Atlee Beechy, presented on 7/26/99 as part of his devotional for MC USA Peace Executive Meeting [expanded form of his "Confessions of a Peacemaker," in *Seeking Peace, My Journey* (Goshen, Ind.: Seniors for Peace, distrib. Pinchpenny Press, 2001), 202]. Used with permission from Susan Mark Landis, MC USA Peace Advocate (SusanML@MennoniteUSA.org).

CHAPTER SIX

Christians and the Payment of Taxes Used for War

All wars are civil wars, because all men [people] are brothers [and sisters]. . . .
Each one owes indefinitely more to the human race than to the particular country in which he [or she] was born.
—*François Fénelon*, via A.Word.A.Day (www.wordsmith.org/awad)

The basic sources of authority through which Christians learn the will of God are Scripture, church, and Spirit. This study seeks to understand how one of these sources, Scripture, directs Christians on the morally agonizing question: Should Christians who seek to follow the Prince of Peace support a war-oriented federal budget? Can we be good Samaritans and support a systemic spiraling of weaponry that maintains "the balance of terror" and portends cosmocide?

To ascertain the directive of Scripture, I will first briefly summarize (1) the nature of biblical ethics; (2) the political character of Jesus' life, death, and resurrection-exaltation; and (3) the early church's view of political government. In the fourth and major part, I will discuss at length the NT texts that speak to payment of taxes. Fifth and finally, I will suggest a hermeneutical path from the text to our present situation.

Biblical Ethics

In the OT, God's people learned how to think and behave from their relationship to God in the covenant. Clinton Gardner points out that the demands of the covenant required all of Israel's life, even its political and economic structure, to be conformed to the will of God.[1] Biblical ethics and Christian ethics are covenant ethics. The values of God's people are rooted in their jealous allegiance to their covenantal God.[2]

Israel's primary ethical values were righteousness and justice, related directly to God's holiness (Ps 89:14; Isa 5:16; 6:1-5; see chap. 1 above). The burden of the prophets was hence twofold: (1) to call the people into covenant obedience to God, and (2) to thunder forth the ethic of social righteousness. Amos declares: "Let justice roll down like waters, and righteousness like an everflowing stream" (5:24). Or hear Isaiah: "Seek justice, correct oppression; defend the fatherless, plead for the widow" (1:17 RSV). And in Micah's summary: "What does the Lord require of you, but to do justice, and to love kindness, and to walk humbly with your God?" (6:8).

The NT extends the ethical logic of the OT. The imperative grows out of the indicative. Because we belong to God, we then do what is *fitting* for God's children (Eph 5:4). We seek to walk worthy of the calling to which we have been called. Throughout the Gospels and epistles, believers are called to follow the ethic of love (Matt 22:37-39; Rom 12:19-21; 13:8-10; James 2:8), since God, to whom we belong, is love (1 John 4:16).

Scripture thus roots the moral imperative in God's own being, God's claim upon the covenant people, and the people's response to be and do what God requires.

The Political Character of Jesus' Life, Death, and Resurrection

While Jesus was not a revolutionary in the Zealot mold of violence, the political dimensions of Jesus' life, death, and resurrection are prominent. In chapter 2 I presented two lenses through which to view Jesus, both with political import: Jesus as political king, and Jesus as Prince of Peace. Certainly Brandon is quite wrong in his almost complete identification of Jesus with Zealotism;[3] yet it would be just as wrong to imagine a Jesus who is politically innocuous. What we should learn from the biblical portrait of Jesus is that commitment to God's kingdom and God's love for all people will mean costly discipleship. It is not abnormal if the way of faithfulness to God's kingdom brings us into political conflict with the kingdoms of this world.

The Early Church's View of Political Government

The NT gives us three different views of the church's attitude to political government. In the first, Rom 13:1-7; 1 Tim 2:1-4; Titus 3:1; and 1 Pet 2:13-17 present a positive view of government, calling for Christian subjection since the authorities are God-ordained. In the second, Matt 4:8-10; Mark 10:42-43; Luke 4:5-8; 1 Cor 2:6-8; 6:1-6; Eph 6:12; and Rev 13 present a negative view, in which government is either ignorant of God's will, resists God's purpose, or deifies itself.[4] Because of these opposite emphases, both views reflect circumstances of the times as well as a theological dual dimension of government.[5] The early church fathers continue these two differing views. The "apologies" convey generally positive attitudes toward government; the "martyr accounts" often give negative portraits of the authorities, notably the emperors.

I propose that the third and more-predominant normative NT view of the Christian attitude toward government bases itself upon Christ's victory and lordship over the principalities and powers (1 Cor 15:24-25; Eph 1:19-23; 3:10; Col 2:10, 15; 1 Pet 3:22). This truth reduces all governments to a temporal status, with the precise function of restraining evil and promoting good until Christ's lordship is fully acknowledged. The believer who already confesses Jesus as Lord derives his direction for life and conduct not from secular authorities, but from Christ, the commander-in-chief of God's army of overcoming love.

The key points emerging from this brief survey of biblical ethics, the Gospels' portrait of Jesus, and the early church's view of government are these:

1. Ethical values are rooted ultimately in God. The behavior of God's people is determined by their relationship to God.
2. Jesus' own life, death, and resurrection both challenge and transcend worldly political claims.
3. Believers derive their political ethical direction not from the varied situations of political governments but from Christ's lordship.

New Testament Texts That Speak to Payment of Taxes

Matthew 17:24-27, the Temple Tax

> When they reached Capernaum, the collectors of the temple tax came to Peter and said, "Does your teacher not pay the tax?" He said, "Yes, he does." And when he came home, Jesus spoke of it first, asking, "What do you think, Simon? From whom do kings of the earth take toll or tribute? From their children or from others?" When Peter said, "From others," Jesus said to him, "Then the children are free. However, so that we do not give offense to them, go to the sea and cast a hook; take the first fish that comes up; and when you open its mouth, you will find a coin; take that and give it to them for you and me."

Though many might cite this text to support payment of taxes, it has little relevance to this discussion. The tax under question is not a tax that directly benefits Rome, but Judaism itself. It is the half-shekel temple tax, instituted in Exod 30:13. Jewish law requires every Jewish male at least twenty years old to pay this tax annually. It is more accurate to call this tax the annual temple tithe. Even the Zealots who oppose Rome's rule with dagger and sword have no problem in paying this tax.

The punch line of the text comes not with the decision to pay or not to pay the tax (and certainly not in the method of securing the tax money), but in the subtle declaration that Jesus is the son of the Lord of the temple.

His words "Then the children are free" mean that Jesus is the son of the temple's ruler and thus exempt from payment. Then in order to avoid offense, Jesus orders the payment. But, clearly, the emphasis falls on Jesus' sonship, not on the payment of tax.

Mark 12:13-17, Taxes to Caesar

> They sent to him some Pharisees and some Herodians, to trap him in what he said. And they came and said to him, "Teacher, we know that you are sincere and show deference to no one; for you do not regard people with partiality, but teach the way of God in accordance with truth. Is it lawful to pay taxes to the emperor, or not? Should we pay them, or should we not?" But knowing their hypocrisy, he said to them, "Why are you putting me to the test? Bring me a denarius and let me see it." And they brought one. Then he said to them, "Whose head is this, and whose title?" They answered, "The emperor's." Jesus said to them, "Give to the emperor the things that are the emperor's, and to God the things that are God's." And they were utterly amazed at him.

Before focusing on the meaning of Jesus' oft-quoted "Render to Caesar" statement (RSV/KJV), I make four observations on the *historical context* of this Scripture:

1. The goal of this encounter is to entrap Jesus. The crafty opponents are specified: "some Pharisees and some Herodians." The Pharisees resist the tax in principle but compromised in practice, to make life possible under Roman occupation. The Herodians, a party we know little about except that they favor King Herod and the Herodian rule of Palestine, cultivate good favor with Rome and hence support payment of this tax. Both parties must suspect Jesus' position to be otherwise, or else the question would not be a trap from their point of view.
2. The tax denoted in the text is a specific tax (not taxes in general). It is a poll tax instituted in AD 6. A census taken close to that time (cf. Luke 2:2) to assess Jewish resources provoked the wrath of the country. Judas of Galilee led a revolt (Acts 5:37) at that time, which was suppressed only with some difficulty.[6] Many scholars date the origin of the Zealot party and movement to this incident.[7] Blood has already flowed because of this tax, and Jesus' answer to the question is calculated to be grounds for his arrest (see Mark 12:12; Luke 23:2).
3. The Sicarii or Zealots categorically refuse payment of this tax. They regard this tax as "an introduction to slavery and an affront to the sovereignty of God."[8] The land of Palestine belongs to God. God has given it to Israel. No other nation has a right to it. A head tax levied by Rome is utterly abhorrent. Such is the Zealot view. In this incident particularly, one wonders whether the Pharisees and Herodians suspect Jesus of Zealotism and are seeking therefore to publicly expose him as a tax resister, a position that would inevitably lead him to the Roman death penalty for Zealots, crucifixion.
4. Rome required that the poll tax be paid with the *denarius*, a silver coin worth about twenty cents. During Augustus' reign (27 BC-AD 14), several hundred different *denarii* were issued. But during Tiberius' reign

> (AD 14-37), only three types of *denarii* were struck, with only one circulating widely, from Lyon to India.[9] The Zealots would not have been caught alive with this coin in their possession. On its obverse side the coin showed "a bust of Tiberius . . . adorned with the laurel wreath, the sign of his divinity."[10] The legend read: TI(BERIUS) CAESAR DIVI AUG(USTI) F(ILIUS) AUGUSTUS, meaning "Emperor Tiberius august Son of the august God." On the other side was the title PONTIF(EX) MAXIM(US), meaning high priest, with Tiberius' mother, Julia Augusta, sitting on the throne of the gods.[11] The coin was "the most official and universal sign of the apotheosis of power and worship of the *homo imperiosus* (the emperor) in the time of Christ."[12]

Within the context of these considerations, Jesus' first word of response, "Why are you putting me to the test? Bring me a denarius," touches the moral anguish of the Pharisees and Herodians. But the agony of the moment intensifies when Jesus asks, "Whose head is this, and whose title?" I expect that the Herodians, sooner than the ambivalent Pharisees, reply: "The emperor's." In that word lay the despair of the nation.

Then comes Jesus' stunning response: "Give to the emperor, . . . and [give] to God. . . ." What does belong to the emperor? What does belong to God? The difficulty of arriving at an assuredly correct interpretation is illustrated by the following typical textbook commentary:

> (1) Some see it as a clever evasion. The answer "was primarily intended to be non-committal." Jesus was really anti-Roman, but he refused to get caught on either side of the question before him. . . . (2) Jesus clearly asserted that the tax should be paid. Coins with Caesar's image on them belonged to the emperor. He had a perfect right to demand them. (3) Others see the answer as advice

> which caught the testers. They had Caesar's idolatrous coin in hand. Of course they were obligated to return it to him. It was his property. (4) Still others view the answer as an endorsement of the Roman head tax comparable to the advice Jesus gave Peter to pay the Temple tax (Matt 17:24-27). Some think Jesus simply reaffirmed the Jewish position of loyalty to God and the government except when the latter demanded apostasy. . . . (5) Others argue that Jesus approved the double obligation to God and government, but he left to the individual the determination of the proper claims of each.[13]

While one might advance arguments supporting each of these various interpretations, three considerations illumine interpretation of the text:

1. The historical and literary contexts favor the interpretation that Jesus' answer condemns the position of the testers. The preceding parable, spoken against the wicked tenants of the vineyard (Mark 12:1-12), condemns the position of the religious leaders, those who question Jesus' authority (11:27-28). The test question about the resurrection posed by the Sadducees (12:18-27), which follows the tax question, receives an answer that also condemns the position of the questioners. The same point applies to the scribe's question regarding the greatest commandment (12:28-34), though in a milder manner. Hence, if this interpretation of the passage is correct, Jesus' reply would sound as follows: "[Then] [*with irritation*] *render* to *the emperor* the things that are the emperor's, and [*with strong affirmation*] to God the things that are God's."[14] Jesus thus forbids the payment of the tax by those who are faithful, implying that once one has compromised so much as to possess the idolatrous coin, the tax matter has already been settled in principle.

2. Mark 2:1–3:6 records five additional encounters between Jesus and the religious authorities. Like the three in Mark 12, all five have the same questioning, accusing intent from the adversary (vv. 2:7, 16, 18, 24; 3:2), and each ends with a succinct, incisive reply from Jesus (2:10, 17, 19-22, 27-28; 3:4).[15] Significantly, this series of episodes ends with the Pharisees seeking counsel *from the Herodians* in order to determine "how to destroy him." These two groups do not appear together again in the Gospel until 12:13; then comes the tax question—implementing the plot to destroy him.[16]

   Jesus' answer, "Render to the emperor," is also quite similar in type to the answers given in 2:1–3:6. In these cases we observe that (1) Jesus' position opposes that of the Pharisees, and (2) his answer transcends the mentality of his questioners. By applying these principles to Jesus' answer to the tax question, we must conclude that Jesus' answer opposes the Pharisee's position. But this does not necessarily classify Jesus with the Zealot's position of tax refusal, although it appears that the Pharisees do in fact so accuse Jesus (see exposition of Luke 23:2 below).
3. A further consideration enters the case. In 3:4 Jesus responds with the typical rabbinical formula: "Is it lawful to do good or to do harm on the sabbath, to save life or to kill?" The Pharisees *cannot* answer. Then in 12:14, having now collaborated with the Herodians, the Pharisees phrase their question also with the rabbinic formula: "Is it lawful to pay taxes to the emperor, or not?"

The question "Is it lawful?" merits more attention. In Mark 12 Jesus answers not on the level of legality, but points beyond the letter of the law to the basic morality and religious authority upon which the law rests. Clearly, the Pharisees regard Jesus as a lawbreaker. Hence, when Jesus in 3:4 responds, no doubt with tongue in cheek, "Is it lawful?" it appears to indicate that (1) the Pharisees are still committed to *their law* above everything else, (2) they plan to use the power of their law against Jesus on a very sensitive issue (they have come "to entrap him"), and (3) they know that the tax question is so politically volatile that if Jesus hedges in any way in his response, they would have a case for the cross.

In light of these considerations, in our effort to derive contemporary moral guidance from this text, we must be careful that we do not simply adopt the position of the Pharisees, that law is the final word on moral issues. Significantly, Jesus' reply points beyond the rights of the emperor to the rights of God. God's claim and the emperor's claims must never be put on the same level. The text may not be interpreted in such a way as to *equalize* God's and Caesar's rights. As Donald Kaufman rightly says, "Jesus' view of life implies a reservation in regard to the state but none in regard to God. For [Jesus] there was never any doubt that God was supreme even in the realm which Caesar claimed for himself."[17]

What guidance, therefore, does this text give to the question of paying taxes used for war? (1) In view of the hypocritical and accusing intent of the questioners as well as the cryptic nature of Jesus' response, we acknowledge that Jesus and the opponents of Jesus hold differing views on this sensitive issue. (2) We do not allow ourselves to take the Pharisees' side in making law the sole judge of moral obligation. (3) We see clearly that Jesus' answer does not tell us to give Caesar *whatever* he asks for.

Luke 23:2, Charges Against Jesus

> They began to accuse him, saying, "We found this man perverting our nation, and forbidding us to pay taxes to the emperor, and saying that he himself is the Messiah, a king."

The Jews accuse Jesus of forbidding the payment of taxes to the emperor. How do we assess this accusation? Two observations are relevant:

1. In view of the historical and literary contexts of the question in Mark 12, this charge appears to have some foundation. The Pharisees and Herodians have identified Jesus with the Zealot cause and proceed accordingly. Like other Zealots, his doom is the cross.
2. Yet Luke carefully shows that Pilate finds Jesus innocent of the charges (23:4, 14, 22). How do we resolve this apparent contradiction?

One might resolve the problem by holding that Mark and Luke simply present different perspectives. Such a response, however, fails to go to the heart of the matter, since a careful reading of Luke 23 shows that Pilate's declarations of innocence are not based on any evidence that clears Jesus of the charges. In the face of Jesus' equivocal answer to Pilate's query whether he is the king of the Jews (23:3) or silence before Herod (v. 9), Pilate pronounces that he finds nothing worthy of death in Jesus. The charges are never factually cleared or confirmed. In fact, the Jewish leaders' rephrasing of the charge in their persistence to nail him—"He stirs up the people by teaching throughout all Judea, from Galilee where he began even to this place" (v. 5)—is precisely what Luke accentuates as a main feature and effect of Jesus' ministry (4:14-15, 28, 31; 5:1-3, 15; 6:11, 16; 7:17; 11:29; 12:1; 13:22, 14:25; 16:14). The effect of Pilate's pronouncement, rather than denying the charges, ironically vindicates Jesus by allowing Luke to thus portray Jesus as a righteous sufferer, fulfilling the work of the servant in Isa 53 (Luke 22:37; 23:47) and a prophet rejected by the people. Like Moses and Elijah, who were also accused of perverting the people (with identical terms used in the LXX: Exod 5:4; 1 Kings 18:17), Jesus upsets the tenuous and unjust peace of the existing social order.[18]

The reliability of these three charges against Jesus is thus never established, nor are they proved false. Instead, three different perceptions emerge: the Jewish religious leaders', Pilate's, and Luke's. As believing readers of the Gospel, we are expected to identify with Luke's view of Jesus, which shows Jesus as a righteous prophet whose radical loyalties to the kingdom of God cannot be grasped by the political mentalities of either the Jewish leaders or the Roman procurator. His crucifixion reflects the verdict: *Zealot*—political insurgent. But the Gospels tell us more. Jesus is a *righteous* prophet (Luke 23:47, KJV), rejected by God's people, dying a martyr's death. In my judgment, Oscar Cullmann's analysis of Jesus' political standing is helpful:

1. Throughout his entire ministry Jesus had to come to terms with Zealotism.
2. He renounced Zealotism, although he also assumed a critical attitude toward the Roman State.
3. He was condemned to death as a Zealot by the Romans.[19]

In this is a crucial and hard learning for us: We must recognize that our prophetic witness to kingdom priorities may and likely will be misunderstood as a challenge of political power or even an attack against it. Whether in conscientious objection to war or war-tax resistance, we must accept the liability that political forces will brand both our resistance and nonresistance as dangerously revolutionary. Religious people may consider it as perverting the people or stirring them up. But it might well be that such discrepancy between their perception and our self-understanding is the critical test of our faithfulness to the ethic of Jesus.

Romans 13:6-7, Pay Taxes Due

> For the same reason you also pay taxes, for the authorities are God's servants, busy with [RSV: "attending

> to"] this very thing. Pay to all what is due them, taxes to whom taxes are due, revenue to whom revenue is due, respect to whom respect is due, honor to whom honor is due.

Of all the NT texts that speak about paying taxes, this is the clearest and most relevant to the contemporary discussion. Five aspects of exegetical inquiry enable us to understand the text and to ask the appropriate questions for the use of the text in our contemporary situation.

Structure of the text. The text's structure shows that Paul's counsel, "Pay all of them their dues" (Rom 13:7 RSV), is the main point of 13:1-7. As Victor Paul Furnish notes, the main "topic in 13:1-7 is not 'the state' and the main appeal of these verses is not to 'be subject' to it."[20] While the admonition to 'be subject' does occur in verse 1 and again in verse 5, this is preliminary to the main appeal of the text in vv. 6-7.

Perry Yoder's analysis of the structure of these verses substantiates this point.[21] "Let every person be subject to the governing authorities" is the thesis of the text, followed by supporting theological and practical arguments in verses 1b-2 and 3-4 respectively. Verse 5 restates the thesis and is again followed by theological and practical considerations ("to avoid God's wrath" and "for the sake of conscience"). But this entire argument stands in support of verses 6-7, which appear to be addressed to a specific problem facing Christians in Rome.[22]

Literary context. Two observations are crucial. First, in its description of the new life in Christ and the call not to be conformed to this world, chapter 12 provides Christian ethical norms. Christians are not to be conformed to the values and practices of the world (v. 2). Verse 9 calls for love that is genuine; vv. 14 and 20 apply that love to relationships with persecutors and enemies. Verse 21 challenges the believers not to be overcome with evil, but to overcome evil with good. Immediately after 13:1-7, verse 8 calls for a life that is debt free, except to love. Finally, verses 10-13 focus upon the impending ultimate eschatological event.

By observing this literary context of moral concern, we learn that the new life in Christ with its moral imperative of love provides the perspective for answering specific questions about proper Christian response to specific political demands and laws. The government itself, while it has authority and passes laws of all kinds, does not provide moral guidance. Some laws may be compatible with the Christian morality of *agape*-love, and some may not be: Christians must decide their responses in accord with the call not to be conformed to worldly evil and to pursue the way of love (12:2).

Second, the larger literary context of Romans indicates that Paul plans to visit Rome, and possibly make Rome his base for missionary work in Spain (15:22-29). As elsewhere (1 Tim 2:1-4), Paul's counsel on the Christian's response to government is influenced by missionary considerations. To resist payment of taxes would jeopardize the presence of Christianity in Rome, possibly triggering another edict of expulsion as happened eight years earlier. At this point the literary observations call for comment about the historical context.

Historical context. From Acts 18:1-2 we learn that Priscilla and Aquila had left Rome because the emperor, Claudius, had expelled the Jews (including Christians) from Rome. The Roman historian, Suetonius, reports concerning Claudius: "Since the Jews constantly made disturbances at the instigation of Chrestus, he expelled them from Rome."[23]

Between AD 49, the year of Claudius' edict, and 57, the approximate time when Paul wrote Romans from Corinth, Christians returned to Rome. Further, in 54 a new emperor, Nero, began his reign. The pattern of imperial response to Christians (and Jews), while it depended upon the patchwork pieces of the past, was in a new state of formation. By 64, Nero fiercely persecuted Christians, but in 57-58, when Romans was written, the political atmosphere was more open.

Another Roman historian, Tacitus, tells us that Nero faced a growing tax revolt in his early years of emperorship. The government had levied two types of tax: the direct or fixed "poll" tax (Latin: *tributa*; Greek: *phoros*; RSV: "taxes") and the indirect or commission tax (Latin: *portoria*; Greek: *telos*; RSV: "revenue"). Government officials collected the direct tax; the indirect was hired out to agents for the highest bid, a system that led to extortion and exploitation of the people. This generated a tax revolt. In his desire to please the people at the beginning of his reign, Nero was about to rescind the commission tax:

> His impulse, however, after much preliminary praise of his magnanimity, was checked by his older advisers, who pointed out that the dissolution of the empire was certain if the revenues on which the state subsisted were to be curtailed: "For, the moment the duties on imports were removed, the logical sequel would be a demand for the abrogation of the direct taxes."[24]

When Paul writes, "Pay all of them their dues" (Rom 13:7 RSV), he is likely telling the Roman Christians that they should pay the direct tax (*phoros*) to the government officials and the commission-tax (*telos*) to the contracted tax agents.[25]

Paul's theological and cultural heritage. In both Judaism and Hellenism, it was commonly held that rulers receive their authority from God (or the gods). Because, especially in Judaism, they do not possess it as an inherent right; they are accountable to God. This order (*tagma*) is the basis for Paul's thesis with its arguments of support in verses 1-5.

Particularly within several OT traditions, prophets severely criticize governing leaders for their failure to govern justly or trust Yahweh, as in Elijah's confrontation with Ahab (1 Kings 21), Isaiah's oracle to Ahaz (Isa 7), Jeremiah's judgment upon Zedekiah (Jer 21). In the NT as well, Christian believers sometimes are critical of the laws of government and even disobey them when they conflict with God's purpose (Acts 4–5; 22:25; 24:25; Revelation, cf. also Luke 13:32; Mark 6:18; 13:9-27).

While Paul says in verse 1 that the "authorities" (*exousiai*) are under the authority of God, he elsewhere emphasizes that all such authorities have been stripped of ultimate power because of Christ's victory and lordship (Rom 8:38-39; 1 Cor 2:6-8; 15:24-25; Eph 1:20-23; 3:10; 6:12; Col 2:10, 15).

To keep within Paul's and the Scriptures' larger emphases, we must not use Rom 13 to support unconditional obedience to government and its derivative, an unqualified mandate for payment of all taxes. What Paul says in this specific situation cannot be hardened into a "Christian law." The enduring law, rather, is in verse 8: "Owe no one anything, except to love one another."

Analysis of key words. The command "to be subject" in 13:1 is based upon the Greek word *hypotassō*. The noun form is *tagma*, which connotes "order." Paul uses *hypotassō* also for mutual subordination (Eph 5:21) and wifely subjection to the husband. But for children to parents and slaves to masters "obey" (*hypakouō*) is used (6:1, 5; cf. Col 3:20; 1 Pet 1:14). Though *hypotassō* appears to be interchangeable with *hypakouō*, "to obey," in a few instances (cf. "submit" in Titus 2:9; 1 Pet 2:18; 1 Tim 3:4 with "obey" in Eph 6:1, 5; Col 3:22), they are not fully interchangeable. Submission is not the same as obedience. The instances of interchange occur only in the slave-master and child-parent relationships. The different words are used by different writers, and we need to take care not to conflate meaning from one writer to another, or even from one context to another. The most that can be said is that while the writer of Ephesians and Colossians used the word "obey" (*hypakouō*) to describe the slave-master and child-parent relationships, the same writer does not use that word to describe the response of other subordinates (political and domestic), nor do the writers of Titus and 1 Pet use the term "obey" for the slave's response. The conduct expected of

Christians in response to an "order" (*tagma*) in the social structure is not absolute obedience. Absolute obedience is reserved for God alone (as in Dan 1:1-17, refusal to drink and eat the king's rations; Acts 5:29;[26] Rev 20:4). The verb "to be subordinate" (*hypotassō*) means submission, not revolt, but allows the possibility of "not obeying," suffering the penalty for disobedience.[27]

The phrase "attending to this very thing" (Rom 13:6 RSV) should likely be translated as a temporal participle, reading "when they attend."[28] This means that Paul tempers his admonition with the principle of discrimination. Certainly Paul would not regard every ruler in whatever act done as a *servant* of God; sometimes rulers act against God's purpose. In such cases, only in the same sense that Satan or evil may be designated as "serving" God in some ultimate sense, could it be said that evil rulers are servants of God. Paul, likely, was not thinking of such theodicy in this text; his counsel is framed by the situation at hand, where he discerns good intent on the part of the rulers. But with a temporal participle, he acknowledges that it may not always be so.

In accord with this interpretation, verse 7 also contains language of discrimination. John Howard Yoder comments on this verse:

> We are not called to submit to every demand of every state. When Paul instructs the Roman Christians (Romans 13:7) to give "tax to whom tax is due, toll to whom toll, respect to whom respect, and honor to whom honor," this is the opposite from saying that tax, toll, respect, and honor are due the state. He is saying, as the similarities to Matthew 22:21 and 1 Peter 2:17 confirm, that we are to discriminate and give to each only his due, refusing to give to Caesar what belongs to God.[29]

On first thought, Yoder's interpretation contradicts the findings from the reconstruction of the historical background.

Those findings indicate that Paul takes a rather categorical position, telling the Roman Christians to pay both kinds of taxes. But on closer analysis, the little phrase "their due" calls for moral discernment on the part of those paying the tax.

Here, precisely, is where the moral imperatives from the literary context of Rom 13:1-7 must be considered. The moral instruction in 12:1-21; 13:8-13 is clear:

1. "Do not be conformed to this world [= its evils]," but "present your bodies as a living sacrifice . . . to God [not to the nation]" (12:1-2).
2. "Do not repay anyone evil for evil" (12:17).
3. "If it is possible, so far as it depends on you, live peaceably with all" (12:18).
4. "Never avenge yourselves, but leave room for the wrath of God, for . . . 'Vengeance is mine, . . . says the Lord'" (12:19).
5. "If your enemies are hungry, feed them; if they are thirsty, give them something to drink" (12:20).
6. "Do not be overcome by evil, but overcome evil with good" (12:21).
7. "Owe no one anything, except to love one another" (13:8).

If the flow of the entire narrative is consistent, then Paul assumes that the payment of the taxes specified does not conflict with these clear moral imperatives. Similarly, only when we fulfill these moral imperatives through responding to the present dilemma of paying taxes used for military weapons—even for mass destruction—will we truly hear Paul's and Jesus' intentions for our morality. Further, let us remember the missionary consideration: which course of action will better further the gospel and witness to God's kingdom worldwide?

From Text to Present

Though we might wish it otherwise—to obtain direct biblical counsel on payment of taxes for war—the text gives no indication that the moral issue concerning the use of the tax, whether for the Roman military and political oppression of the *Pax Romana*, entered into Paul's consideration. Nor do the secular contemporary sources connect the tax revolt to protest of Rome's military policies. In other words, Paul is not asked nor does he answer: What is the Christian moral obligation on tax payment when the tax is used mostly for military defense and war? One might argue that Paul does answer the question by his categorical statement (13:6-7), because he knows what taxes are used for, having seen Rome's military presence all over the empire as he traveled. But to deduce this from Paul's counsel parallels the argument used in the 1800s that Paul endorses slavery as an institution because he prescribes Christian conduct for slaves and masters. This reading makes Paul say something more than he has explicitly said. To use biblical texts this way is misuse of the Bible.

Wider Biblical Considerations

In finding biblical directive on any moral issue, it is imperative to consider the entire biblical witness on a given issue. The following ten strands of biblical teaching bear on this particular moral issue of paying taxes that are used for war purposes:

1. The Decalogue's sixth commandment, "You shall not kill" (Exod 20:13 RSV), means that it is God's prerogative to take life, not ours. As a disciple of Jesus Christ, I cannot kill or approve killing one for whom Christ died. Wilma Bailey in her 2005 book[30] has persuasively shown that the Hebrew word here (*tirtsakh*, from root *ratsakh*) more likely means "kill," not "murder." Her conclusion is based on a contextual

study of the thirteen uses of the word in the OT. The change to "murder" in the NRSV is unwarranted. If we object to killing in war, should we not be consistent and refuse tax that supports preparation to execute war?

2. The OT prophets, beginning with Moses, called for trust in the Lord as the true and adequate defense. They criticized the buildup and use of military power. Isaiah 2 and Mic 4 speak of "beating swords into plowshares." Further, Isa 2:6–3:17 condemns Israel for its idolatries: running after other gods and relying on military might. For these, judgment comes. Paying taxes to finance war aids and abets this idolatry.
3. The OT gives examples of those who refused to obey the orders of kings:
   - The Hebrew midwives: Shiphrah and Puah (Exod 1:5-22)
   - Moses' mother and Pharaoh's daughter (Exod 1:22; 2:10)
   - Daniel and Esther (see books of that name)
   - Jeremiah, in speaking against the king's policies, and counseling subjection to God's imminent judgment through enemy invasion.
4. Jesus commanded, "Love your enemies and pray for those who persecute you." Also, he said, "Blessed are the peacemakers." Both are linked to being "children of God." Peacemaking is thus the identity mark of God's children (Matt 5:9, 43-48).
5. Jesus taught, "Give to the emperor what is his, and give to God what is God's." The two are not equal. What we owe to God stands above and prior to what we owe to the state (cf. Matt 22:21).
6. Jesus, even as king, repudiated domination over others, refused use of the sword for self-protection, and chose the way of the cross. In the NT we are called to imitate Jesus in this regard.

7. Both Daniel's and the apostles' testimonies concur with this model: "We must obey God rather than any human authority" (Acts 5:29).
8. The NT epistles speak of God as "God of peace" eight times. Nowhere in the NT is God designated "God of war." This bold innovation from Paul's writings is most significant.[31]
9. The church, composed of former enemy peoples, is now at peace in one Christ-body. This peace-union, God's new creation in Christ Jesus, manifests to the principalities and powers the manifold wisdom of God (Eph 3:9-10). Is not this "mystery" of God's wisdom jeopardized when we support war that results in "Christians" in one nation killing "Christians" in another nation?
10. Jesus' lordship extends over both the church and the powers (Col 2:10, 15).[32]

Conclusion

How then should peacemaking Christians in the United States respond to the war-tax dilemma? On one hand, specific scriptural references, most notably Rom 13:6-7, are readily at hand to support payment of all taxes. On the other hand, the moral imperative of love for all, nonconformity to the world's values, and concern for the worldwide missionary cause raise major reservations, and for some, a decisive directive not to pay taxes used for war.[33]

To be sure, for those Christians who see Paul's command to be subject to the authorities as requiring participation in military service, this topic is not an issue. They would accommodate it with just-war rationale. But this study supports those who have understood the Bible to forbid the Christian's participation in war. What is at stake in the holding of these different positions, with both appealing to Scripture, are several crucial principles of biblical interpretation. We give priority to the NT over the OT, thus relegating

Israel's practices of warfare to a level of non-normative morality. But as recognized above, the OT also bears witness to resisting the authority of governmental powers when it conflicts with God's will. On moral issues, the life and teachings of Jesus are central for moral guidance. Further, Paul's specific counsel to "be subject" to the authorities does not mean indiscriminate obedience. When given only these two alternatives, Christians committed to Jesus' peacemaking commands are thus called to disobey government rather than participate in the military. On the issue of tax payment specifically, we answer yes in principle—but no if that response violates the moral principles that frame Paul's specific counsel in 13:1-7.[34]

Similarly, we repudiate basic biblical principles of morality when we use Rom 13:7 to indiscriminately support payment of taxes used for war. When we do that, we use Paul's specific counsel to legitimate a practice that repudiates the basic moral principles out of which the original specific counsel arose. The difference in the historical cultural situations and the questions addressed account for this problem. Changed circumstances and questions call for different specific counsels even though the basic moral principles remain the same.[35] For example, the basic principle behind holy war in the OT is trust in Yahweh, a principle that carries through into the NT. But God's commands to fight against enemies cease with Jesus' command to love the enemy, and with the early church's redefining the boundaries of God's peoplehood (Eph 2:11-22; Col 3:11). Changed historical realities along with unfolding revelation from the OT to the NT necessitate new moral considerations. If that were not so, Jesus Christ's coming would be superfluous. The salvation encounter with Christ would not mean any moral change.

Personal response to the issue. In an effort to follow the basic moral principles of the NT, submission to governmental authority, nonconformity to the world, owing nothing but love, overcoming evil with good, and promoting the missionary cause of the gospel—I have resisted payment of a percent (30-60 percent) of my annual tax. Mary (my spouse) and I do this as a form of witness. This resistance to tax payment is not against payment of taxes in principle, since we want the government to tax in order to provide health, education, and social services to the poor, disabled, retired, and even universal healthcare coverage. We believe this witness accords with the gospel of peace, trust in God, and the way of love.

We've written letters to Internal Revenue Service, our representative and senators, the House Ways and Means Committee.[36] Our resistance has taken the form of writing a second check, payable to Public Health Service (formerly Health, Education, and Welfare). We ask the IRS to forward the PHS check in an envelope we enclose, addressed and stamped. Two times the amount has actually gone to a specific public health organization via IRS forwarding the check to PHS, and PHS allocating it to a specific need. One Monday morning we received a surprise phone call from St. Elizabeth Hospital in Bethesda, Maryland. The woman calling thanked us for our generous contribution to the hospital (of which we knew nothing), and informed us that they were using it to improve services for their senior longer-term residents in the hospital. However, several years later IRS levied our bank account and collected the amount sent to PHS for at least one of the two times the check was sent to PHS. Thus, in principle, the IRS did not accept the earlier PHS check as a bona fide tax payment. In most years the IRS has simply endorsed and cashed both checks.

Our hope and prayer is that the *witness* given through the letters and phone conversations accompanying such action speak a word faithful to the gospel and also sensitize others to kingdom values and the gospel's critique of national priorities.

We welcome Christian discernment and counsel to test this way of Christian faithful response to God's peace for humans.

God of War*

God of war, sometimes visible and invisible,
Showed up after his work of Terrorism,
Stood on the platform with his baton,

And started conducting.
Then the U.S. high-tech vultures rushed to Afghan
And started unsparing bombardment.

His seeds bore splendid fruit again!
Joy danced on his face.
This god, who has been worshipped

In the mosques
Under the mask of Allah
And in the church

Under the mask of Christ,
Has been ceaselessly whispering to them,
"Make wars."

Now so showily waved he his baton,
Both camps responded in ecstatic unison,
"Kill them! Kill them!"

As he conducted more, their hatred
Increased more. His kingdom had been
The battlefield, but now it is the whole globe.

* Reprinted from *The Poetry of Yorifumi Yaguchi: A Japanese Voice in English*, ed. Wilbur J. Birky, by Good Books, Intercourse, PA (2006), 145-46. © by Good Books (www.GoodBooks.com). All rights reserved. Used with permission. Yorifumi Yaguchi is a 1965 Goshen Biblical Seminary graduate. He is a professor of poetry and American literature at Hokusei Gakuen University in Sapporo, Japan, and a leader in the Japanese Mennonite church.

Even when he stopped conducting and disappeared,
He never failed to sow his seeds again.
It is this God who entices us,
"Go to war! Kill them!
I will install you
in my Yasukuni shrine[37] as gods,
As I did before." And our prime minister,
Half-rising, is almost ready
To follow him, like a patient infected with high fever.

—Yorifumi Yaguchi

CHAPTER SEVEN

The Bible and Israel: Two Interpretations and More

Holy Land has to do with welcoming
refugees and immigrants
and trying to remove the causes
and alleviate the problems of . . .
population dislocations. . . .
Where land is sanctified,
it engenders contentment and stability and
fosters love of home. . . .
Unholy land produces refugees,
sanctified land performs a redemptive function.
—*Marlin Jeschke,* Rethinking Holy Land (2005), 144.

This study began at the end of an Eastern Mennonite University alumni and friends tour to the Middle East in June 1975. I had served as Bible teacher for the group. It became clear that tour members held opposing views regarding Israel's right to the land. Some held that Israel is God's chosen people and has always had an undisputed right to the land, including the areas where Palestinians lived. Others were unsure, and still others were certain that that view was wrong but were unable to articulate an alternative. Hence, at the end of the tour, in our hotel in Rome, I presented a sketchy version of "Two Interpretations" for our Sunday morning sermon and discussion. And discussion there was. My notes for this presentation were scant, but one tour member taped the presentation and later typed up a transcript.

My second visit to this topic came late in 1990 at the Associated Mennonite Biblical Seminary in a public debate one month before the United States went to war in Iraq. A local Elkhart pastor, Stephen Swihart from the Church of the Living Word, presented a pro-Israel interpretation, justifying U.S. entry into the war because of concern for Israel's security. I presented a version of what appears below, seeking to show that there is more than one way to understand Israel's right to the land and God's promise of the land to Israel.

Aspects of this issue arose again in local newspaper letters (including my own) as President George W. Bush prepared for the invasion of Iraq in 2003. In this context one of my AMBS colleagues asked permission to use this text in her theology-ethics class, at which point I returned to the topic, revising my earlier work further. She expressed her view that this piece and more work on this topic needs to be available for the larger church.

Since that time I have had the privilege of reading Roy Kreider's *Land of Revelation: A Reconciling Presence in Israel* (Herald Press, 2004), as well as editing the fine commentary on Romans by John E. Toews (Herald Press, 2004). Kreider presents a sympathetic view toward Israel based not on political right to the land but upon God's call to be a Christian presence in Israel, with compassion for the spiritual needs of the people. The subtitle, *Reconciling Presence*, sums up well the Mennonite witness in Israel since its beginning in 1953. These contributions, together with a recently published book by John H. Yoder (see below), prompted me to extend my earlier contribution of "Two Interpretations." In the latter part of this chapter, I reflect upon the difficult theological and Christian mission issues that arise for the church, in its relation to Israel, and to the Jewish people worldwide. The current number of Jews in Israel is close to the number in United States, each with five million plus.

Interpretation I

This view holds that the Bible speaks about the present state of Israel, and that the creation of the state of Israel in 1948 is a direct fulfillment of biblical prophecies. This view appeals to the following biblical data:

1. The *covenant promises* that God made to Abraham and David

   The Abrahamic covenant

   Gen 12:1-3. God promises a land, a great nation, and to be a blessing to the nations.

   Gen 17:4-8 (see also vv. 9, 10, 19). God promises descendants innumerable.

   The Davidic covenant

   2 Sam 7:12-16, 24-26. God promises an heir on the throne forever (Father/Son).

   1 Chron 17:11-14. God promises an enduring throne and kingdom to David's offspring.

2. Jeremiah's prophecy of the new covenant with Israel and Judah

   Jer 31:31-34, 38-40. New covenant is unlike old one; the law is within and all will know God.

   Jer 33:7-26. God will restore the fortunes of Israel and Judah; a "righteous branch" will spring forth to establish "justice and righteousness" in the land.

3. The Songs of ascent extol Jerusalem and Zion

   Pss 120-136, especially Pss 122 and 132:11-14; also Ps 147. These Psalms praise God for blessings and renew hope for restoration of losses (e.g., Ps 126; cf. Ps 80).

Commentary. In these texts emphasis falls on "forever and ever," "an *everlasting* throne," and "establishing Zion for ever."

4. Prophecies of *Israel's return* to the *land*

   Jer 23:3; 33:7-13. God will restore the fortunes of Israel; gather home a remnant.

   Ezek 11:16-17; 28:25-26; 34:11-31; chapters 36-37 and 40-48, with Ezekiel's vision of the new temple.

   Joel 3. Verses 9-13 may refer to the great battle of Armageddon.

   Amos 9:11-15. God promises to repair the fallen booth (temple).

   Zech 2:6-12. God will plunder the captor nations to which God sent them; God's people will come home singing, and God will dwell in their midst. Verse 8c, "One who touches you touches the apple of my eye."

   Zech 8:2-8, 22-23. Jerusalem will again be a city of peace, with aged and children in the streets.

   Zech 10:8-12. God will redeem Israel bringing them home; will make them a glory.

   Zech 14. Verse 4, the Lord's "feet shall stand on the Mount of Olives, . . . [which] shall be split in two." Verse 20 speaks of "the bells of the horses" with inscriptions on them, "Holy to the Lord."

   Commentary. Throughout these texts and others we hear the promise that the Lord will gather home his dispersed people in all the earth. This is understood to refer to the large-scale return of Jews to Palestine, which has taken place since 1948.

5. *Millennial view* of end times correlated with *mass salvation of Israel*

   The rapture: Jesus will come on the clouds of heaven

and "catch up" (rapture) all believers. See Rev 4:1; 1 Thess 4:16-17; and 2 Thess 2:3, where some say the word "rebellion" (RSV) should be translated "rapture."

The tribulation period of seven years, based upon visions in Daniel and Revelation (the seven seals, seven angels, and seven bowls of wrath). See also Mark 13; Matt 24; and Luke 21. During this period certain things occur:

- The salvation of Israel, Rom 9-11, especially 9:4 and 11:26: "And so all Israel will be saved."
- Fulfillment of Jesus' parable of the fig tree in Mark 13:28-31 (par. Matt 24:32-35; Luke 21:29-33), in which the fig tree symbolizes Israel (cf. Jer 24). The fig tree putting forth its bud is taken to refer to Israel's coming to nationhood in 1948. Within one generation of this event, *all these things will take place.*

The 1,000 Year Reign on Earth, the Millennium (Rev 20).

This is followed by a new heavens and earth (Rev 21–22).

Commentary. Those who hold this view do not agree among themselves on the order of the first three items above. Some put the tribulation before the rapture. Some also put the salvation of Israel, at least in its beginning stages, before the rapture. This view also speaks of first and second resurrections, which happen before and after the millennium. The great white throne judgment comes immediately after the second resurrection.

Critical Evaluation of Interpretation I

Strengths

1. The position appeals to many texts located in various parts of the Bible and hence appears to be what the whole Bible really says on the subject.

2. Interpretation is *readily* understood, taught, and preached. Hal Lindsay's book *The Late Great Planet Earth* was widely read by laypersons in the 1970s. More recently, the *Left Behind* novels by Tim LaHaye and Jerry B. Jenkins popularized this view. It follows a *literal* interpretation of Scripture, pasting bits and pieces together, and thus, once accepted, needs little explanation. It originated in the nineteenth century under the influence of John Nelson Darby (1800-1882), founder of the Plymouth Brethren. It gave rise to Dispensationalism, which was popularized by the Scofield Bible (Oxford Univ. Pr., 1909).
3. Creation of Israel as a state in 1948 is a visible linchpin that makes the view appealing and convincing.

Weaknesses

1. The verses cited to support the covenant promises are all one-sided. Proponents do *not* cite the texts that stress the *conditional* nature of the covenant:

   Exod 19:5-6. "*If* you obey my voice . . . "

   1 Kings 9:4-9 and 2 Chron 7:19-22. If Israel disobeys, they will be cut off, scattered among the nations, and become a proverb and byword among the nations.

   Deut 28:15-46 makes it clear that the promise of the land is conditional on their obedience; it foretells what did happen years later: Israel's exile. In 2 Chron 36:21 the exile is viewed as punishment for not obeying the sabbatical laws. Strikingly, the land did have rest for *seventy* years during Babylonian exile!
2. Prophecies of return ignore the historical and NT context of their cited Scriptures.

   Almost all the OT texts were written before and/or in reference to Israel's exile into Babylon (586-539 BC) and therefore refer to the homecoming in 538

BC. For example, Ezek 37 likely refers to Israel's return home in 538 BC. Ezek 39:23-25 explicitly mentions return from captivity. See also Jer 27:22; 29:10-11; 30:3. It is clear that the exile left deep marks on all the OT canonical literature. Read the laments in Pss 74; 79; 80; and Lamentations.

Some of these texts are regarded by NT writers as fulfilled in Jesus and early church developments, such as these:

- Amos 9:11-15 is fulfilled by Jesus' coming and the Gentile mission, according to Acts 15:16-18.
- Jer 31:31-34 is fulfilled by the covenant Jesus made with believers, according to Heb 8:8-13.

In some texts, like Isa 49:14-16a, one must distinguish between Zion and Jerusalem, as well as between Zion as symbol and Israel (Judah) as nation.[1]

3. The millennial view of end times is weakly supported by Scripture.

One cannot find the whole scheme in any one biblical author. The scheme is possible only by pasting together bits of information from various sources scattered over hundreds of years of writing. Again, the meaning of these texts in their contexts is often ignored (e.g., Daniel's and the Gospel's use of the phrase "abomination of desolation," referring to 168-165 BC and AD 40 respectively; or when you see Jerusalem surrounded by armies in Luke 21, referring to the fall of Jerusalem in AD 70).

As far as we know, neither Jesus nor Paul held this view since the entire scheme is not in either the Gospels or Paul's writings alone.

Texts purportedly referring to the rapture are all open to serious question when studied in context.

Should "*all* Israel" being saved (Rom 11:26) be taken literally? If so, then Rom 11:32 would indicate that "*all* people " will "receive mercy." Does this mean that everyone will be saved? The literal interpretation thus becomes difficult.

4. The interpretation of Israel's mass return to God through Christ is a relatively late emphasis in Christianity. One does not find it in the writings of the early church fathers and the Reformers. It appears to have arisen in nineteenth-century Darbyism somewhat parallel to the rise of Zionism as a political philosophy.[2]

   Nowhere in the NT is there a statement that Israel shall return to the land, but God's judgment upon Israel occurs often with implied loss of special covenant role (notably Matt 21:33-43). The lack of NT texts on the "return" theme verifies the point that the OT texts speaking of the return do refer to the return from the exile in 538 BC.

   View is hard pressed for a *Christian* answer to the role of the Christian Arab in the end-time drama as well as a *Christian* response to the plight of the Palestinians, since the return of the Israelis is "an act of God."

5. This interpretation exploits the "conquest ideology" of the Old Testament, used to justify and legitimate Euro-population taking over land in the "new world" after 1492, planting both Dutch and British settlements in South Africa, and most recently Israel's expansionist policies in Palestine, based on Zionist ideology. This use of Scripture, to justify violations of human rights and war to secure land, discredits Christianity. The colonialist land-conquest ideology results in either "conquer and destroy" or "conquer and corral" the indigenes, and this is certainly not the way of Jesus who gave himself for humanity's sins, rather than inflicting violence and death on others.[3]

6. This view also fuels gross misinterpretation of Revelation, and other biblical apocalyptic literature. Rather, than understanding Revelation as a call to continue faithful amid suffering and persecution, it uses apocalyptic code imagery to prognosticate on schedules and dates of end-time disasters. It misses the heart of Revelation's vision in which the slain Lamb (Jesus) provides the pattern for Christian response to imperial persecution. Numerous scholars have exposed the error of this use of Revelation and help us truly understand Revelation (esp. Barbara Rossing, Loren Johns, and Richard Bauckham).[4]

Interpretation II

This view does not identify present-day events in Israel as fulfillment of biblical prophecy, but rather stresses that God's promises to Abraham and David are fulfilled through Jesus Christ and the Christian church. The only plan God has for Jews is the same as for all people, to receive Jesus as Messiah, Savior, and Lord. The Bible is not clear on the matter of Israel's mass conversion. However, both these points do not necessarily mean that God's special covenant relationship to Israel as a people has ceased or no longer has significance.

This view appeals to two basic considerations: that the *covenant promises are both conditional and unconditional*, and that within *Scripture we encounter unfolding revelation.* These considerations are developed in four key theses:

1. The Mosaic covenant (Exod 19:5-6) and the Solomonic covenant (1 Kings 9:4-9; 2 Chron 7:19-22) are God's covenant to Israel *as a nation* (Mosaic) *and in relation to the temple* (Solomonic). Both *are conditional.*

   The condition is Israel's obedience.

   The history of Israel shows that they disobeyed and broke the covenant (Kings and Chron).

   The prophets clearly say that Israel *broke the*

covenant (Jer 7:1-15; 26:1-6; 31:32; Hos 1; 8:1) and that Israel will therefore go into exile (721 and 586 BC).

The promise of nationhood and temple are renewed for a second chance beyond exile (Hos 1:10-11; 3:1-5; Ezek 36–37, 40–48), but the promise of *nation* and *temple* remains conditional.

In the NT the people's rejection of the Messiah appears to mark the end of the conditional promise to Israel. Nationhood and temple imagery are applied to the Christian church (1 Cor 3:9; Eph 2:19-22; 1 Pet 2:4-10), including the "great nation" promise made to Abraham (Rom 4:16-17). Some early church fathers regarded the fall of Jerusalem in AD 70 as God's judgment.

2. The Abrahamic covenant (Gen 12:1-3; 17:4-8) and the Davidic covenant (2 Sam 7:12-16) are God's covenants with Israel *as a people*. Both are unconditional.

   The NT sees both covenants fulfilled in Jesus and his messianic community, beginning with the first disciples.

   Christian believers are the true descendants of Abraham and heirs of the promise to Abraham (Rom 4:13-16; Gal 3:6-9, 14; 4:21-31). Thus the church is called the "Israel of God" (Gal 6:16).

   The reign of Jesus as King, begun at his resurrection, fulfills the Davidic promise (Rom 1:3; Acts 2:22-36; 15:15-18; 1 Cor 15:24-26; Rev 4–5; 11:17-18; 17:14; 19:11-16). Matthew's Gospel also shows Jesus as the Davidic king.

   The promised new covenant (Jer 31:31-34) is fulfilled in Jesus' covenant in his blood (Matt 26:26-30; Heb 8:8-13).

Commentary. This view holds that God's covenant promises to Abraham and David are fulfilled and universalized in Jesus Christ and his followers, both Jews and Gentiles. Even the promise of the land is universalized. The *meek/faithful* will inherit the earth/world (Rom 4:13; Matt 5:5; 1 Cor 3:22-23; Rev 21:1-4).

3. The OT promises and prophecies must be correlated with God's unfolding salvation drama in history.

   Israel's recitals of God's salvation history should be correlated with the Abrahamic promises as follows (based upon recitals in Deut 26:5-9; Josh 24; Pss 135–136; Neh 9; Acts 7; 13:13-17):

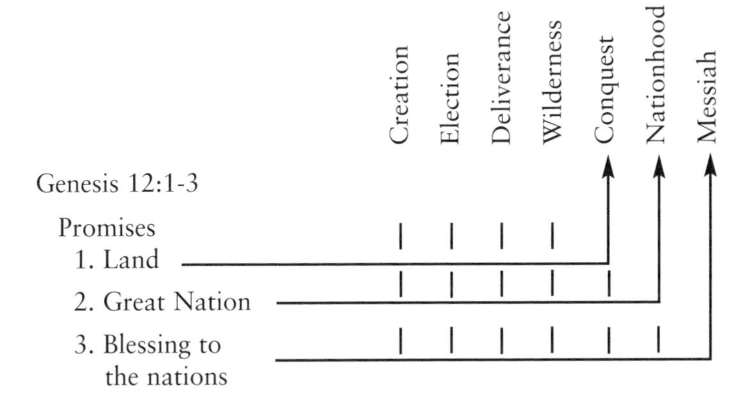

- The promise of land had its fulfillment in the conquest; the promise of nationhood had its fulfillment from David to the exile; and the ultimate promise of worldwide blessing had and continues to have its fulfillment in Jesus Christ.
- God's purpose in calling Israel was to bring blessing to the whole world, not to bless it for its own sake alone (Gen 12:3; Amos 3:2; Isa 42:6; 49:6; Jonah, and entire NT).

4. Almost every NT book stresses the failure of the Jews to accept Jesus as Messiah, with the gospel going to the Gentiles, and affirms that both Jews and Gentiles have election status before God.
   - The Jews' rejection of Jesus as Messiah means (or may mean) that the kingdom and its promises are taken from Israel (or the religious leaders, allowing for a faithful remnant of Jews) and given to others (Matt 21:33-43; Mark 12:1-12; John 12; Acts 13:44-48; 18:6; 28:23-28; Rom 9–10; 15:7-13). We can understand most of these texts as "warnings" to Israelites hearing Jesus' pleading and thus not a settled doctrine. See the latter sections of this chapter.
   - Both Jews and Gentiles receive God's blessings on the same terms: "by grace through faith in Jesus Christ" (Rom 1–4; 11; Eph 2; Gal 2–5; etc.).
   - Rom 9–11 is first and foremost an affirmation of the *righteousness of God* in that Israel is not rejected for salvation through inclusion of the Gentiles (cf. 3:21-26). The *righteousness of God* means that *all Israel* and that *all Gentiles* are potential recipients of God's salvation.
   - The book of Acts shows that the Jewish question, "Will you at this time restore the kingdom to Israel?" (Acts 1:6 RSV), had to be replaced with a vision of sharing the kingdom with the whole world through the power of the Spirit (1:6-8; 8:12; 14:22; 19:8; 20:25; 28:23, 31).

Critical Evaluation of Interpretation II

Strengths

1. Draws on Scripture from all parts of the Bible and takes into account the historical contexts of the Scriptures.
2. Uses the Gospels and epistles most heavily and stresses the NT's fulfillment of the OT.

3. Emphasizes the centrality of Jesus Christ (not time schemes) as the common basis of salvation for Jew and Gentile alike. Hence, this position gives a clear mission mandate to all people in any period of time. But see below for the special relationship between Judaism and Christianity.
4. Affirms the same message for the Jew and Arab in the present Middle East conflict, promotes love for both, and need not push one down because of "God's plan."
5. Since the Jews missed the Messiah the first time because of their political interpretation of this Messiah, this view learns from the mistake and does not look for a literal political fulfillment of the OT prophecies, many of which were already fulfilled in OT times, according to this view.

Weaknesses

1. This view is more difficult to grasp and appreciate since it requires a careful study of the total unfolding drama of the Bible with *close attention to the historical context of Scripture.*
2. If certain prophecies in the OT are pressed for *literal* fulfillment, this view does not have a clear explanation (e.g., Ezekiel's vision of the temple in chaps. 40-48, since the postexilic temple did not literally fulfill the description).
3. This view has no special theological value to attach to the present state of Israel, which for many evangelical Christian and Jewish Zionists becomes a liability since they want a theological justification for Israel's claim on the land.[5]
4. Since this view does not try to locate a specific literal fulfillment of certain prophecies, those who are committed to Interpretation I tend to regard adherents of Interpretation II as not wanting to believe the Bible. This has the effect of associating this interpretation with a low view of biblical authority.

5. This view may be judged as anti-Semitic since it tends to hold that Christ and the church displace Israel as the recipient and arena of God's continuing work in history.

While Interpretation II is stronger in its biblical theological notions, especially in its manner of treating both OT and NT texts in their historical contexts, it also is not adequate since it borders on a "replacement" view, that the church displaces Israel as God's covenant people. This cannot stand, in light of the NT's and especially Paul's view that Gentiles are incorporated into God's covenant with Israel.

Paul's Apostleship

Paul designates himself as "an apostle to the Gentiles" (Rom 11:13). Galatians 1:1–2:14 and Eph 3:1-13 give the overwhelming impression that Paul understands his conversion as an apostolic calling, bestowing upon him the God-given commission to take the gospel of Jesus Messiah to the Gentiles. It appears that Paul was uncertain about his status before the judgment seat of God if the Gentile converts did not stand faithful to the gospel. In his earliest letter, Paul says with a tone of both joy and desperation: "For what is our hope or joy or crown of boasting before our Lord Jesus at his coming? Is it not you? Yes, you are our glory and joy!" (1 Thess 2:19-20). Then in 3:8 Paul says: "Now we live, if you continue to stand firm in the Lord."

The letter of 1 Thessalonians, likely written in AD 50, was penned likely less than a year before the Jerusalem conference described in Acts 15. What is the real issue at this conference? Many say that the issue is whether or not believing Gentiles must be circumcised. But this answer is only superficial. The nitty-gritty of the Jerusalem conference is *the* theological issue of first-century Jewish Christianity: *Is the coming of Jesus as Messiah the time when the Gentiles are to come into God's kingdom and peoplehood as Gentiles?* If so, then in principle circumcision is not required. If not, then God's economy requires Gentiles to enter under the Jewish knife. In Mark's Gospel, Paul's letters, and the entire NT witness, the answer to this italicized question is a resounding "Yes."

The Jewish question of the apostles in Acts 1:6 about the kingdom being restored to Israel is answered by the universal vision of Acts. Through the power of the Spirit, the kingdom of God will extend to Samaria, the Gentile world, and even Rome (Acts 1:8; 8:12; 14:22; 20:25; 28:23, 31). The decisive moment at the Jerusalem conference is when James, yes, *James*, puts his finger on the prophecy of Amos (9:11-12) and identifies the present events in the life of the church as the promised rebuilding of the fallen booth of David *for the sake of the Gentiles!* The text says:

> "After this I will return, and I will rebuild the dwelling of David, which has fallen; from its ruins I will rebuild it, and I will set it up, so that all other peoples may seek the Lord—even all the Gentiles over whom my name has been called. Thus says the Lord, who has been making these things known from long ago." Therefore I have reached the decision that we should not trouble those Gentiles who are turning to God. (Acts 15:16-19)

That settles it! The messianic age has arrived, and Gentiles as Gentiles, not as Gentiles-made-Jews, are to participate in the salvific, redemptive blessings of God's economy.

Lest it be missed, the triple narration of Paul's conversion in Acts underscores Paul's apostolic call to the Gentiles. In chapter 9, the Lord's revelation to Ananias declares that Paul "is an instrument whom I have chosen to bring my name before Gentiles and kings and before the people of Israel" (v. 15). In Acts 22 we learn that on Paul's first visit to Jerusalem after his conversion, the Lord tells Paul, "Go, for I will send you far away to the Gentiles" (v. 21). In the third narration, Jesus commissions Paul even while he is lying stricken on the road:

> Get up and stand on your feet; for I have appeared to you for this purpose, to appoint you to serve and testify to the things in which you have seen me and to those in which I will appear to you. I will rescue you from your people and from the Gentiles—to whom I am sending you to open their eyes so that they may turn from darkness to light and from the power of Satan to God, so that they may receive forgiveness of sins and a place among those who are sanctified by faith in me. (26:16-18)

This text, together with Gal 1:16; 2:7-8 and Eph 3:1-2, 6-8, indicates that Paul, given a crucial calling and ministry, receives momentous, far-reaching insight into God's economy of salvation: to know Jesus as Messiah is to welcome believing Gentiles as Gentiles into God's peoplehood. Paul lives and dies for this precious truth that God's salvation is *for all people*. That includes *us*, whoever *we* are! Each of the Gospels too has its own way of affirming Gentile inclusion as recipients of Messiah Jesus' mission.[6]

A Closer Look at Romans 9–11

Paul regards the issue of the relation between Gentiles and Jews so important that it forms the hinge section of Romans, chapters 9–11. This section is the climax of Paul's most exhaustive treatment of a wide cluster of salvation themes (chaps. 1–8); it also serves as the context for discussing the moral life of the ethnically diverse community (chaps. 12–16). John E. Toews, in his Romans commentary, is correct in pointing out that God has been and will be faithful in keeping covenant with Israel as a people, even though that people narrows to a faithful remnant. Toews puts it well:

The central theme of chaps. 9–11 is the faithfulness of God. That theme is stated clearly in a thesis statement in 9:6: the word of God has not failed, and the rhetorical question in 11:1: has God rejected his people? The answer is developed in two ways. First, Paul resumes the diatribe style of question and answer. He knows that his opening defense of the reliability of God in 9:6-13 will raise objections. Therefore, he uses the diatribe style to pose questions that will determine his overall argument. The major questions are clearly indicated by the use of introductory formulas. The first two in 9:14 and 9:30—*Is there injustice with God*? and *Why* are the Gentiles attaining a righteousness they did not pursue while the Jews are not fulfilling the law they are pursuing?—are introduced by *what, therefore, shall we say*? The other questions in chaps. 9 and 10: 9:19, 20-21, 22-23, 32; 10:14-15, 18-19 are clearly second-order questions. The third and fourth major questions in 11:1 and 11:11: *Has God rejected his people*? and Have the Jews *stumbled so as to fall?* are introduced by *I, therefore, say. . . .* Three of the four major questions are denied by the *Absolutely not*! answer, while none of the other questions are negated. Secondly, Paul shapes his answer by the exposition of Scripture: 35 of the 90 verses in chaps. 9–11 contain direct quotations of biblical texts (the 39% citation is higher than any place else in Paul; the next is 28% in Rom 4, and 25% in Gal 3). Chapters 9–11 offer an interpretation of Israel's Scripture. If the question is *Has the word of God failed*? then the answer must come from an explanation of the word of God. That is what Paul offers throughout Rom 9–11.

At a structural level, this reinterpretation of Israel's Scriptures retells Israel's story from Abraham (9:6f.) through the Messiah's fulfillment of that story (10:4) to Paul's own mission to Israel and the world (10:14-21). It is at the same time a retelling of the story narrated by Paul already in 7:7–8:11. God's gift of the Torah became an occasion for stumbling (7:7-25 and 9:30–10:3). God again brings the Torah to fulfillment through Messiah Jesus (8:3-4 and 10:4).

> The argument of chaps. 9–11 is introduced with Paul's personal lament about Israel's state, 9:1-5. It is the first of four times Paul interjects himself into the discussion in these chapters, each at an important turning point in the argument. In 10:1-2 he prays for Israel's salvation and bears witness that she has a zeal for God, albeit an ignorant zeal. There is evidence in 11:1 that God has not rejected Israel because he has called a remnant. In 11:13-14 he defines his own ministry to the Gentiles as a means *to make my fellow Jews jealous, and thus save some of them.* Paul's story is an integral part of Israel's story.
>
> The thesis of chaps. 9–11 is stated in 9:6, the word of God has not failed. Everything that follows in chaps. 9–11 is designed to support the opening assertion that God is faithful and can be trusted. The argument proceeds in three main sections:
>
> 9:6-29 God's word has not failed.
> 9:30–10:21 Christ is the fulfillment of the Word of God.
> 11:1-32 God has not rejected Israel.
> A doxology concludes the argument, 11:33-36.[7]

In his "Text in the Life of the Church" section for this portion of Scripture, Toews describes the early church trend to lose the emphasis of God's faithfulness to Israel and stress instead a "displacement theology" that began in the second century church already with Justin Martyr,[8] followed by a "theology of predestination" that Origen began and Augustine developed. This "theology" emphasized God's *foreknowledge* of those who would believe and those who would not believe, leading to saving grace and damnation respectively. Jewish unbelief in Jesus as Messiah fell into the latter category. Toews, rejecting both these positions, then affirms "God's election of Jewish and Gentile peoples."[9] Toews concludes:

> As Paul argued earlier in Romans, God in Christ elects all humanity to be the people of God (5:12-21) and desires

> them to become children of God in Jesus. That does not mean that all humans are saved, just as God's election of Israel did not mean that all Jews were saved. Paul is clear that only those human beings who exercise faith in Christ and have the Spirit enjoy the saving blessings of God's election (see 3:22-26; 4:1-25; 9:30-32; 10:9, 16, 20-21).
>
> Election in Romans 9 is an affirmation of God's faithfulness. God remains faithful to election, to the choices made in history. But Romans 9 also indicates that the boundaries of election have been opened up beyond the Jewish people to include Gentiles. That is a word of divine grace and mercy for both Jews and Gentiles; it is not a word of judgment on the Jewish people.[10]

The view Toews sets forth here concurs with that of Jewish scholar Alan Segal, in his treatment of the same topic. Segal's commentary on Rom 11:26 interprets Paul's view correctly and succinctly:

> Although Paul polemicizes against his enemies [Segal has already dealt with Paul's vituperative language in Galatians], he does not exclude either Christians or Jews from the saved. All Israel is saved, he says, in typical Pharisaic manner (*pas Israel sothēsetai* [Rom 11:26]). It is clear, however, that they will not be saved until they are transformed spiritually.[11]

Though Paul expected transformation for both Gentiles and Jews as they became members of the new Christ body, Segal also contends that Jews could accept the Messiah without "converting." They would continue their religious practices and regard Jesus Messiah as the fulfillment of these practices. Paul, however, was "converted" (title of Segal's book) to the priority of Gentile admission into the messianic faith. Segal holds that Acts 15 affirms a compromise, affirming both models of Jewish Christianity. But Paul expected that continuing transformation into the image of

Christ holds for both types of in-Christ/Messiah believers, Jewish as well as Gentile.[12]

This important perspective of two ways for Jews to be incorporated into the new body of believers of Jesus Messiah, however, does not yet address the key issue of the Jews' continuing covenant status outside Jesus Messiah. "Supersessionism," which need not deny God's covenant relation to Israel,[13] may too easily become another form of "displacement theology," or lead to a "two-covenant theology,"[14] popular today in ecumenical circles. Both fall short of expressing Paul's nuanced treatment of this delicate topic.[15] Most certainly, any form of "anti-Judaism" or worse, "anti-Semitism," is beyond the pale of right understanding, though several texts in Matthew and John taken out of their first-century context readily support this view.[16] Here careful exegesis, placing the texts in particular historical settings, is most important.[17] Toews' conclusion is helpful:

> The church's story is part of the larger story of Israel as the people of God. Christians worship the God of Israel, the God of Abraham, Isaac, Jacob, Ruth, Mary, Jesus, and Paul. Jesus is the Messiah of this God who brings to fulfillment the promises of this God. Any claim to obscure or reject the church's worship of the God of Israel, YHWH, casts doubt on the trustworthiness of the God the church proclaims. If God does not keep faith with Israel, how and why can this God be trusted to keep faith with any other peoples? The church's place within God's covenant is secure only if the Jewish people remain part of the covenant. The Jews are the trunk, the Gentiles the branches. Without the God of Israel and the Jewish people, there is no Messiah and no Christian church.
>
> The Jewish faith is not simply one more religion among the other religious traditions, e.g., Hinduism or Buddhism. The Jewish people are half-brothers/sisters of Christian people—they come from the same parents chosen to be the people of God in the world. They continue

> to be God's people despite their refusal to believe that Jesus is the Messiah. God's grace toward Israel persists despite the fact that she rejects this grace for the present time. The Christian mission to the Jewish people, which continues the mission of Peter and Paul, is to call this people to the fulfillment of its faith in Messiah Jesus, not to the conversion to a different God and a different faith.[18]

Toews imagery of "trunk" and "branches," derived from the olive tree image in Rom 11:17-21, fits well with Will Herberg's genial perception of the relationship between Judaism and Christianity. In a chapter on the relationship between the two religions, he speaks of a "double covenant" (subtitle of the chapter: note the singular "covenant" modified by "double") and enumerates ten points of structure and faith common to both religions.[19] He describes the relationship as one of mutually related vocations: "The Jew's vocation is 'to stand,' the Christian's to 'go out'—both in the same cause, the cause of the kingdom.[20] In another essay he expands on this point:

> Yes, each needs the other: Judaism needs Christianity, and Christianity needs Judaism. The vocation of both can be defined in common terms: to bear witness to the living God amidst the idolatries of the world. But, since the emergence of the church, and through the emergence of the church, this vocation has, as it were, been split into two parts. The Jew fulfills his vocation by "staying with God," "giving the world no rest so long as the world has not God. . . ."[21] The Christian can fulfill his vocation only by "going out" to conquer the world for God. . . . This is the unity of Judaism and Christianity, and this is why a Jew is able to see and acknowledge Jesus in his uniqueness as the way to the Father.[22]

In my reading over the years on this thorny and challenging issue of the relationship between Judaism and Christianity, I have not found a better description than Herberg's. He maintains the clear biblical teaching of one covenant, and he rightfully stresses the absolute necessity that Christianity not cut its biological tie to Judaism. Historically, this severing of relationship, starting with the church in the second century and culminating in the Holocaust, has been most unfortunate. John Howard Yoder gave considerable attention to this topic, contending in his book, published posthumously, that "It Did Not Have to Be." Yoder argues that during the first century, Christians (the "Nazarenes" or followers of the Jesus Way) were part of the pluriform nature of emerging Judaism. Many continued to worship with Jews in synagogues and to varying degrees continued practices of ritual and moral purity laws.

Yoder contends that Christianity in the first three centuries and Judaism for most of the last 2500 years bear witness to a Jeremiah-type existence: make your home and witness in the circumstance of diaspora. Only when Christianity became an established state-church and "empire" in nature did it seal its cleavage with Judaism and then persecute Jews. Heirs of the Radical Reformation must repudiate this, and the church as a whole must repent of its grievous sin.[23] In his insightful article "The Power of Diaspora," Alain Epp Weaver points also to the model of diaspora as "a political form [that] counters nationalism, since diaspora involves the "dissociation of ethnicities and hegemonies."[24] Epp Weaver also cites a book by noted Jewish scholar Daniel Boyarin and his brother Jonathan, *Powers of Diaspora*. The Boyarins celebrate "the diasporic genius of Jewishness, that genius that consists in the exercise and preservation of cultural power separate from the coercive power of the state."[25] Daniel Boyarin has since expanded his treatment of the issue, holding that the "border" between Jews and Christians developed more gradually than previous scholars assumed. It was the result of a long give-

and-take between the communities, stretching into the first four centuries or more. One illustrative detail: while the *Logos* conception (God as Word) was accepted widely in rabbinic Judaism, only in the second century AD was it viewed as heresy, due to the Christian claim (John 1:1-18).[26] Daniel Boyarin's work generally concurs with Yoder's theses, though there are some significant differences.[27]

Boyarin's article, "Judaism as a Free Church: Footnotes to John Howard Yoder's *The Jewish-Christian Schism Revisited*," published in *CrossCurrents* 56 (2007) along with five panelist's responses, promises a way forward in mutual understanding between Judaism and Christianity that extends earlier emphases promulgated by Herberg, Rosenzweig, Roy Eckhart, and Gregory Baum of one covenant, two vocations. As Boyarin puts it, quoting his earlier writing: "'The genius of Christianity is its concern for all the Peoples of the world; the genius of rabbinic Judaism is its ability to leave other people alone.'"[28]

But the new dimension in the Yoder/Boyarin perspective is privileging the Jeremiah-type *diaspora* existence for Jews and for Christians: an antizionist Jewish existence (Boyarin) and Christian anti-(Constantinian)establishment existence. While Boyarin will not "excommunicate" Jews who believe otherwise, and must cling to land for home, Yoder's position is more nonnegotiable, appealing to foundational NT texts and the early church: "strangers and pilgrims" and "Every land is fatherland . . ."

Another key difference in Boyarin's and Yoder's notions of "free peoplehood" is that Yoder links "free church" to its *missionary* nature and calling; Boyarin disagrees, contending that *diaspora* existence for the Jew does not and should not entail *missionary* aims and actions. Put in lay language, Judaism's mission is to keep the home-fires burning. But further, Boyarin challenges Yoder's reading of history on two points: that first-century Judaism was missionary and that only "free churches" are missionary—other Protestant, even

Catholic, are also missionary. Laura Brenneman's response speaks to this issue, and proposes a median link: the (free) church must be missionary, but it must be a "not-in-charge" mission,[29] echoing the Roy Kreider approach described above.

Connecting to the critical issue of *land* in the larger discussion of this chapter, Alain Epp Weaver's response article is most helpful, taking up the current struggles for a viable future for Israelis and Palestinians living on land claimed by the other. Epp Weaver, weighing in on Cartwright's and Och's (editors of the Yoder volume) criticisms of Yoder, as well as Boyarin's, embraces Boyarin's proposal of a third way between *diaspora* and Zionism for Israel: the "notion of a diasporized state—what we might call a diaspora or exilic consciousness within the land, one in which sharing the land with others is a normal state of affairs." This contrasts to the prevailing separatist ideology in which the dominant power player (Israel) calls the shots—even in a two-state model. This also means recovering the pre-1948 Zionism and the pre-separatist ideology; rather, we need a bi-national vision of peaceably shared land at the core of thought and action.[30]

While Boyarin and Yoder forge new thinking about the relation of Judaism and Christianity—indeed historically, theologically, and perhaps politically as well—it is important also to understand Zionism in those dimensions as well. The thirty-three essays, including the Introduction, in *Challenging Christian Zionism: Theology, Politics, and the Israel-Palestine Conflict* are insightful and comprehensive in scope. The word *history* also belongs in the title, for the first two essays and a part of the third trace the historical roots, first in the United Kingdom (Irving to Balfour: 1820—1918) and second in the United States (Blackstone to Bush: 1890—2004). On the British side of Zionism's origins the biblical-theological influence of Irving and Darby coalesced with the political-theological endorsement of Lord Shaftesbury (1801—1885) and Lord Balfour (1848—1930) leading to the Balfour Declaration.[31] In the United States Darby's dispensational scheme exerted strong influence on Dwight Moody and William Blackstone (1841—1935), the latter a student of the former. Blackstone's *Jesus Is Coming* (1878, trans. into 42 languages) and Cyrus Scofield's Bible (1909) lit fires fueled by both Zionism and Dispensationalism that continue to burn wildly in influential media: e.g., Jerry Falwell and the *Left Behind* series.[32] The wide-ranging scope of the essays in *Challenging Christian Zionism* enables us to grasp how use of Scripture, intertwined with politics, has strategically shaped the current world conflict in the Middle East, extending to two Iraqi wars, not to speak of Israel's 1967 War, U.S. funding of Israel, and the importance attached to maintaining Israel's political sovereignty over the region.

Returning to the major, and more irenic, issue of this chapter, how two peoples dwell together in *one* covenant that the same God formed through Abraham-Moses-David and again through Jesus Messiah, I point to the ten provocative essays in *Jews and Christians: People of God*, ed. by Carl Braaten and Robert Jenson (Eerdmans, 2003). These are theologically rich, with Jenson in chapter 1 attempting a "*Christian Theology of Judaism.*" Such will distinguish Judaism from "canonical Israel," avoid Christian supersessionist claims, and yet not fudge on Christianity's messianic beliefs and commitments. Such a theology will seek to understand both Judaism's and Christianity's claim to identity as *people of God*.[33] In the quest to understand, respect for each other is assumed, dialogue may be helpful, but relationship is essential, a motif echoed in later essays, especially by Neuhaus: "When we Christians do not walk together with Jews, we are in danger of regressing to the paganism from which we emerged"[34] (and I add, the paganism of our environment in today's increasingly pluralist and pagan world). In valuing relationship Christians and Jews complement each other, keep the other honest in their distinctive vocations, and remind the other of the one God they worship. Jews keep Christians from idolatry; and Christians keep Jews from election-*hybris*. Both are messianic: one says Jesus messiah; the other, messiah coming.

The Olive Tree, for the Healing of the Nations

Paul's choice of the *olive tree* as the metaphor to describe the relationship between Jews and Christian believers is most fitting. As it is today, olive oil was valued for its healing properties and was used in healing. It is striking that Paul employs this imagery just before speaking about the incoming of the *full number* of Gentiles, and thus *all Israel will be saved* (Rom 11:25-26). This does not mean every single Gentile or Israelite; these terms are corporate. Paul speaks about a "fullness" of both, determined by belief of both. First is the Gentile inclusion, and this in turns provokes Jewish belief. *All Israel* seems to be used here not ethnically, of Jews, but of the fullness of both groups, incorporated into God's covenant made first with Abraham. In this conception of the relationship and unity of the two peoples—actually *Gentiles* are not a people until thus incorporated, and then they cease to be Gentiles in the proper sense of the word[35]—Paul declares, lest it be forgotten, that "the gifts and the calling of God are irrevocable" (11:29). At the same time, Paul makes it absolutely clear that entry into or continued standing in God's election is by grace and mercy, for both Jew and Gentile. Only by remembering this point will people of both origins relate to each other and live together in unity and peace. Paul's letters as a whole function specifically to keep this calling before the nascent churches composed of Jewish and Gentile Christians.

What then of Christian mission in relation to Jewish people? Herberg says, "No proselytizing,"[36] and I agree. But that does not fence Christian believers from *mission*. The moving account of Christian presence in Israel, as narrated by Roy Kreider, demonstrates this point. Any notion of mission must begin with God, with *missio Dei*. If indeed mutuality between Jews and Christians is to flourish as part of God's mission for both, then Christians and Jews need to be in life-relationship, which too often does not happen, at least not in mutually strengthening ways. By this I do not mean simply "dialogue," but life relationships. If in that relationship one sibling embraces the faith-eyes of the other, a Christian embracing Judaism as sometimes happens, or a Jew embracing Jesus as Messiah, as happened dramatically at times in the Kreider story, then again we can speak only of God's grace and God's mission.

Finally, we must with Paul bow humbly before the inscrutable ways of God:

> O the depth of the riches and wisdom and knowledge
> of God! How unsearchable are his judgments
> and how inscrutable his ways!
> "For who has known the mind of the Lord?
> Or who has been his counselor?"
> "Or who has given a gift to him,
> to receive a gift in return?"
> For from him and through him and to him are all things.
> To him be the glory forever. Amen. (Rom 11:33-36)

Hear This Story of Hope for Israelis and Palestinians

The newspaper *Ha'aretz* reported on November 2005 an extraordinary act of kindness of a Palestinian father whose twelve-year-old son, Ahmed al-Khatib, was accidentally shot and killed by the Israel Defense Forces. The family of Ahmed agreed to donate the son's organs "for the sake of peace between peoples." From this act of kindness, "three Israeli girls, two Jewish and one Druze, underwent surgery Sunday to receive Al-Khatib's lung, heart, and liver. Twelve-year-old Samah Gadban had been waiting for a heart for five years when doctors called her family late Saturday and told them of the Al-Khatib donation. By Sunday afternoon, the Druze girl had a new heart and was recovering at Schneider Children's Medical Center in Petah Tikvan.

Samah's father, Riad, said: "I don't know what to say. It

is such a gesture of love. . . . I would like for [the family] to think that my daughter is their daughter."

In total six Israelis received organs. "The boy's liver was divided in two and given to a six-month-old baby and a fifty-six-year-old woman; his kidneys were given to a five-year-old boy; and his lungs were given to a five-year-old boy and four-year-old girl."

What an act of kindness transcending ethnic and national rivalry and hostility, so often the dominant experience between these peoples.

Part 3

Peace, Mission, and Worship

Send forth your light and your truth,
let them lead me,
let them bring me to your holy hill
and to your dwelling

CHAPTER EIGHT

Biblical Perspectives on Mission

The church exists by mission as fire exists by burning.
—Emil Brunner

During visits in 1975 to numerous cities of first-century Christianity, I frequently asked myself, By what power and vision did the apostle Paul dare to preach to the famed Athenian philosophers, to confront Ephesian and Corinthian civil religion, and to challenge imperial Rome's political sovereignty?* Who was this Paul who headed for the cultural, commercial, and political urban centers and dared to defy the sacred cows of the Roman Empire, whose emperor himself claimed to be "the august son of the august god"? Did the sending churches back home at Jerusalem and Antioch know what a powerful gospel and cultural change agent their missionary Paul really was?

Reflection upon these questions prompted insights into several areas of thought crucial to the Christian's missionary task, the apostle Paul's and ours.

The Pattern for Growth: Jerusalem to Rome

The book of Acts tells the phenomenal story of how Christianity, beginning in Jerusalem as a localized religion,

* Adapted from *Mission Focus: Current Issues,* ed. Wilbert R. Shenk; foreword by Arthur F. Glasser (Scottdale, PA/Kitchener, Ontario: Herald Press, 1980), 1-25; used with permission.

grew into a worldwide movement of Christian disciples throughout Palestine, Asia Minor, Greece, and Rome. The structure of Luke's story accentuates the remarkable growth of this messianic movement. As Bruce Metzger suggests, Acts consists of six periods of church expansion, each period concluding with a summary-statement of church growth:

> *Period I.* Acts 1:1–6:7. The gospel spreads throughout Jerusalem. Summary: "And the word of God increased; and the number of disciples multiplied greatly in Jerusalem, and a great many of the priests were obedient to the faith" (6:7 RSV).
>
> *Period II.* Acts 6:8–9:31. The church is extended throughout Palestine, including Samaria. Summary: "So the church throughout all Judea and Galilee and Samaria had peace and was built up; and walking in the fear of the Lord and in the comfort of the Holy Spirit it was multiplied" (9:31 RSV).
>
> *Period III.* Acts 9:32–12:24. The gospel moves beyond Jewish boundaries. Cornelius becomes a believer, and the church begins in Antioch. Summary: "But [despite persecution] the word of God grew and multiplied" (12:24 RSV).
>
> *Period IV.* Acts 12:25–16:5. Cyprus and Asia Minor receive the gospel, and new churches are founded. Summary: "So the churches were strengthened in the faith and increased in numbers daily" (16:5).
>
> *Period V.* Acts 16:6–19:20. Through Paul's second and third journeys, the gospel is carried into Europe, with churches established in Philippi, Athens, Corinth, and Ephesus. Summary: "So the word of the Lord grew mightily and prevailed" (19:20).
>
> *Period VI.* Acts 19:21–28:31. Paul's missionary labors culminate in Rome through his arrest and appeal to Caesar. Summary: "He lived there two whole years at his own expense and welcomed all who came to him,

proclaiming the kingdom of God and teaching about the Lord Christ with all boldness and without hindrance" (28:30–31).[1]

Who Enters the Kingdom?

Underlying this pattern of phenomenal church expansion is the important theological issue of first-century Christianity: Who receives the kingdom of God? The "kingdom of God" functions as a key term in Acts. During the forty days between the resurrection and the ascension, Jesus, when he appears to the disciples, speaks concerning the kingdom of God (1:3). Hence comes the disciples' question in 1:6: "Will you at this time restore the kingdom to Israel?" Tucking away the question of time into the Father's sovereign purpose, Jesus answers: After receiving Holy Spirit power, you will be my witnesses (1) in Jerusalem (1:1–8:3), (2) in all Judea and Samaria (8:4–12:25), and (3) unto the ends of the earth (13:1–28:31).

Not until the gospel arrives in Samaria does the key term "kingdom of God" occur again. Then *in Samaria*, Philip is preaching "the good news about the kingdom of God" (8:12). The term does not occur again until Paul takes the gospel to *the Gentile world* (13:1ff.). Then the phrase occurs three times! At the end of his first missionary journey, blessed by Gentile believers, Paul warns, "It is through many persecutions that we must enter the kingdom of God" (14:22). In his Ephesian ministry, Paul spends three months arguing "persuasively about the kingdom of God" (19:8). And in his farewell speech to the Ephesian elders gathered at Miletus, Paul describes his missionary labors thus: "I have gone about proclaiming the kingdom" (20:25).

When the book reaches its climax, so also does the author's use of the term "kingdom of God." After arriving at Rome, the capital of the empire, we are told that Paul is "testifying to the kingdom of God" (28:23). Four citations of OT Scripture then follow, all stressing that God's sovereign purpose is being accomplished in the Gentiles' acceptance of the gospel. The concluding verse reports that Paul spends two years in Rome, "proclaiming the kingdom of God" (28:31).

Quite clearly and precisely, the missionary vision of Acts is that the kingdom of God must no longer be considered Israel's private possession. It is a liberating power, calling all people—Jews, Samaritans, and Gentiles—into a common fellowship under Christ's lordship. The Christian church, originating in Jerusalem, must grow until it is found throughout the empire and especially in Rome. Paul himself must contribute to the gospel's growth in the capital city. For Paul, Rome symbolizes the center of world power and culture. Not until the gospel reaches the capital is his mission complete, his task fulfilled.

The Role of the Sending Church

In reflecting upon this rapid spread of first-century Christianity, one does well to ask: What was the role of the sending church in this missionary enterprise? Which was the sending congregation: Jerusalem, Antioch, or Ephesus? Each center plays a significant role in the missionary task.

Five considerations show how Jerusalem takes initiative in the missionary enterprise. (1) On the occasion when the gospel first moves beyond Jewish geography into Samaria, Peter and John go down from Jerusalem to Samaria, to extend the Pentecost-community of faith to the new believers (8:14-15). (2) Upon hearing of the birth of the church in Antioch, the Jerusalem church sends Barnabas to Antioch to affirm the Lord's salvific work and thus firmly link Antioch to Jerusalem as common centers of God's peoplehood (11:12-24). Barnabas also goes to Tarsus and brings Paul to assist the continuing missionary work in Antioch (11:25-26). (3) In the description of the first Pauline missionary journey, two textual notes indicate the importance of Jerusalem in the team's missionary origin: (a) Barnabas, Jerusalem's missionary to Antioch, is mentioned first in the selected pair, Barnabas and Saul (13:2).

(b) John [Mark], also from Jerusalem, goes with them as their *hypēretēs* (the Greek word in 13:5), which means an officially appointed "minister of the word" (cf. Luke 1:2). John Mark's presence on the missionary team is Jerusalem's guarantee that the gospel will be faithfully transmitted and proclaimed. (4) The Pauline mission among the Gentiles is accountable for its ecclesiastical authority to the church in Jerusalem (Acts 15). (5) Paul's determination to take the relief gift to Jerusalem (Rom 15:16, 24-33; Acts 21:7-15) symbolized both his commitment to the unity of the church and his awareness that Gentile Christianity stands indebted to Jewish Christianity. For these convictions he is willing to live and die.

From beginning to end in Acts, Jerusalem plays a key role in the missionary enterprise. This mutual responsibility, both in financial resources and discernment of the practical meaning of the gospel for church life, should be instructive to us today.

Antioch also plays a crucial role in the Pauline missionary enterprise, developing into a leading center for Gentile Christianity (11:20ff.). The church at Antioch, equipped with prophets and teachers (13:1), becomes the commissioning body of the first missionaries. The text indicates that the Holy Spirit initiates the missionary movement (13:2). The perception that Barnabas and Saul should be set apart for the missionary task apparently comes not to the whole church but to the prophets and teachers as they are worshipping and fasting. It may well be that these leaders sense an oversupply of prophets and teachers and discern which ones among them are best gifted for a new task. Further, it appears that this group of leaders functions as the representative body in commissioning this team for missionary work.

At the end of the first journey (14:26), the missionary team returns to Antioch. They call the church together to hear their report on God's work among the Gentiles (14:27). Again, the sending church is vitally involved in the missionary enterprise even though this sending church may think of itself as a new congregation formed by missionary assistance from Jerusalem. The missionaries recognize the role of both Antioch and Jerusalem.

Later in Paul's ministry, Ephesus becomes the headquarters of his labors. For three months Paul teaches in the synagogue, arguing persuasively about the kingdom of God. When opposition arises, he finds a new center, the hall of Tyrannus, in which he continues teaching for two years. From this ministry, the gospel spreads throughout all Asia (19:10). In his farewell speech to the Ephesian elders, Paul indicates that his ministry in Ephesus lasted for three years (20:31). He writes his letters to Corinth (and possibly the Galatian epistle) during his stay at Ephesus.

While Ephesus is nowhere designated as the sending church for Paul's missionary team, it is clear that it becomes an on-the-field center for the missionary movement in Asia Minor and Europe. Seven Asia Minor churches are mentioned in Rev 2–3, with Ephesus listed first. This may suggest that Ephesus functions as a recognized originating center for the gospel's spread.

In all of these cases—Jerusalem, Antioch, and Ephesus—the role of any given Christian center is not static. Although the specific role of each congregation is determined by the dynamic of the missionary movement itself, each congregation is involved in the missionary cause in a continuing role. So it must be for congregations today if they are Spirit-led, gift-discerning, mission-oriented congregations.

The Power for Growth

The book of Acts says that Christianity's growth from Jerusalem to Rome comes through the power of the Holy Spirit. Acts 1:8 tells us that the spread of the Christian witness will happen after Jesus' followers receive the power of the Holy Spirit. Pentecost heads the story of the Christian mission (Acts 2).

The missionary significance of Pentecost is threefold: the

release of new power, the perception that Jesus is both Lord and Christ, and the formation of a new community, which through the miracle of tongues overcomes historical linguistic boundaries. Throughout Acts we are reminded of fresh outbursts of the Spirit's power, usually by the term, "filled with the Holy Spirit" (Acts 2:4; 4:8, 31; 6:5; 7:55; 9:17; 13:9, 52).

In Acts this spiritual power is not a nebulous good feeling. It is integral to the messianic scandal, the bold conviction that a specific man, Jesus of Nazareth, is both Jewish Messiah and universal Lord (Acts 2:36). The goal of the missionary, therefore, is to call for belief in this messianic scandal, an offense to both Jews and Greeks (1 Cor 1:22-24) and then expect the formation of a believing community.

Standing in the ruins of ancient Corinth or sitting on the rocks of the Areopagus (Mars Hill) under the shadow of the Acropolis, one of humanity's great cultural achievements, one feels overwhelmed by the boldness and courage of the apostle Paul. Paul proclaims a gospel not of noble ideas or social betterment but a gospel of a new political reality. Jesus is Messiah and Lord of all; he calls all people into full allegiance to his lordship. Jesus is Lord because God raised him from the dead. The resurrection of Jesus, therefore, is the foundation for all missionary motivation and vision. Paul's speech to the Athenian philosophers makes this point unmistakably clear: Paul is preaching "Jesus and the resurrection" (17:18), and according to the final words of the sermon, God "has given assurance to all by raising [Jesus] from the dead" (17:31b). Verse 32 then says that some mocked when they heard about the resurrection of the dead.

This reality of the risen Christ, infused by the dynamic of the Holy Spirit and the vision of a new universal peoplehood, supplies the power of the missionary movement. Neither mocking nor persecution can halt it. Beyond Paul and his colleagues is the Lord himself—the Lord of a new people, the Lord over the emperor, and the Lord of the gospel the missionaries preach.

Courage to Confront and Conquer

Only by coming to terms with the unique power behind Paul's work can one begin to comprehend how Paul confronts the three major pagan bulwarks of Roman society (and ours).

Confronting human achievements. In Athens, Paul confronts the proud achievements of human intellect. Close to where Paul stands to address some Stoic and Epicurean philosophers towers the famed Parthenon, a showcase of architectural excellence. To its left are the well-proportioned Propylaea, the small graceful temple of Wingless Victory, and the Erechtheum with its exquisite beauty. In the midst of these monuments to Athens' cultural grandeur stands the large statue of Athena, the goddess of beauty and perfection. Further, these philosophers can boast of Plato, Socrates, and Aristotle. To entertain themselves, they listen to what this new babbler, Paul, has to say.

Hats off to Paul! He takes the opportunity. While recognizing the validity of some philosophical insights, Paul nonetheless stands firm, both in denouncing Athenian idolatry and in affirming that history—past, present, and future—hinges upon an appointed person whom God has raised from the dead.

It is customary to say that Paul's effort failed, implying that we should now know better than to confront philosophers with the gospel. Yet the text reminds us that "some" believed: Dionysius the Areopagite and a woman named Damaris, among others. The fourth-century Christian historian, Eusebius, tells us that this Dionysius became the first bishop of the church at Athens. This indicates that Paul's effort meets with greater success than is usually acknowledged. And likewise, it indicates that Paul's encounter with philosophy should urge us to speak the gospel courageously to today's esteemed philosophers, artists, and scientists. If this point is taken seriously, it will mean that our church's educational enterprise will also be part of our church's missionary commitment.

Confronting civil religion. In Ephesus and Corinth Paul sabotages first-century civil religion. Early in the first century, a trend began that developed into an open clash between the Roman government and Christianity. After his death in AD 14, Augustus Caesar was acclaimed as son of the deity. Within several decades emperors were regarded as gods to be worshipped throughout the empire.

To facilitate this new emperor cult, many temples were built in major cities from Rome to Baalbek. Both Ephesus and Corinth were among these centers selected to promote the new imperial cult. But this emperor worship did not replace the earlier cults oriented to the fertility cycles of life, both human and agricultural. The older worship of Ashtarte, Aphrodite, and Venus continued. Cultic prostitution was commonplace.

With this joining of emperor and fertility worship, a powerful civil religion emerged, functioning as the economic infrastructure of the economy of the Roman cities. This combination of sex, politics, and religion was a winner for human desire.

Into the midst of this political playboy paganism, Paul comes with the gospel of the risen Lord Jesus Christ. So effective is the gospel against this civil religion that a riot breaks out in Ephesus (Acts 19:23-41). Demetrius' protest indicates that Paul's Ephesian ministry, two to three years long, has created economic paralysis. Fewer and fewer people are buying the pagan cultic products. In Demetrius' words,

> This Paul has persuaded and drawn away a considerable number of people by saying that gods made with hands are not gods. And there is danger not only that this trade of ours may come into disrepute but also that the temple of the great goddess Artemis will be scorned, and she will be deprived of her majesty that brought all Asia and the world to worship her. (19:26b-27)

In Corinth also, Christianity apparently has effect on the local economy, at least upon the city treasurer, Erastus. Acts 19:22 reports that Paul sends Erastus into Macedonia to visit young churches. In Rom 16:23 Erastus is mentioned as the city treasurer, presumably of Corinth, since Paul writes Romans while at Corinth. At the site of ancient Corinth is an inscription on the pavement in front of the first-century theater that reads: "Erastus, the treasurer of the city, personally paid for laying this pavement." It appears that the Erastus of Rom 16:23 is the same Erastus mentioned in this inscription.[2] Since the event of Acts 19:22 is several years later than the inscription, it is possible that this Erastus quits his job as city treasurer, involving complicity with Corinth's civil religion, and takes up the new task of assisting Paul in his missionary work.

From these two incidents we can observe two models of Christianity's confrontation of civil religion: (1) in Corinth, by calling a given person out of the system; and (2) in Ephesus, by changing the religious allegiance of a sufficient number of persons so that economic crisis and paralysis results.

Challenging Rome's political supremacy. In Thessalonica and Rome, Paul challenges the political supremacy of Rome. According to Acts, Paul goes to Rome as a prisoner to appeal his case to Caesar, but we are not told what happens to that appeal. Eusebius, quoting Tertullian, tells us, however, that both Paul and Peter were beheaded and crucified under Nero.

Paul's earlier troubles in Thessalonica forecast this imminent clash between Christianity and Rome. In Thessalonica the Jews accuse Christians of inciting the people against the empire, "acting contrary to the decrees of the emperor, saying that there is another king named Jesus" (Acts 17:7; cf. Luke 23:2). To preach as Paul does—that Jesus is Lord—is a political put-down for Rome, for if Jesus is Lord, then Caesar is not Lord. No one can serve two masters.

Within the next several decades many Christians were

killed because they refused loyalty to Caesar. Christianity became a subversive irritant to Rome's political arrogance. Polycarp's martyrdom, dating from AD 155, clearly indicates that the issue was political: whether Jesus is Lord or whether Caesar is Lord. This missionary movement from Paul to Polycarp shows that the gospel threatens any nation that demands unconditional allegiance from its subjects or citizens.

Conclusions

The pattern for missionary work and church growth is to begin at home and push outward and onward until all people have opportunity to become members of the kingdom of God.

1. There must be sending congregations who identify gifts and missionary candidates and who maintain relationships with missionaries sent out. This supporting role in the missionary enterprise must be adapted to the changing needs of the missionary movement.
2. The power for church growth comes from the Holy Spirit, who enables faithful missionary witness. The gospel centers on the risen Lord and inspires the vision of a believing community composed of persons from all nations and walks of life.
3. The NT missionary gospel will challenge and dethrone idolatrous claims upon human lives, whether these claims come from intellectual philosophy, appealing civil religion, or arrogant political powers.

Reflection

How might the patterns of mission in this chapter
be appropriated by your church
as it envisions its mission?
What challenges to the present-day culture does that mission entail?

The Way to San José

How did they get there
    to MCUSA at San José?

I heard Jennifer preach, powerfully,
    enlisting us to God's warfare
By truth, justice, gospel of peace, faith, salvation, Word of God—with
echoes from Joseph—to overcome evil with good through Jesus Christ.

How did she get there, growing up Baptist,
    singing her way through Carleton College?
An MVS** brochure in counselor's office
    hooked her, then seminary, pastor, and to San José.

I heard Pentecostal Paul preach,
    Thank you, thank you for living peace, he said,
You show a way I did not know,
    Please, please, don't keep quiet—your peace.

How did he get there, growing up with "tongues of fire"?
    in PhD studies learned of Pentecostal peace at the start.
Then he found Yoder and with theological depth,
    affirmed his Pentecostal forbears' peace.

I heard Evangelical Shane preach,
    calling us to be "geysers in the desert"
Communities of faith, pointing others
    dying in the desert to waters of shalom.

How did he get there? Through wife's mother's living-room décor,
    Amish and Mennonite, including history book on same,
He now knew peace in his head; studied at Fuller Seminary, then
    through wife's adversity, with PMC*** meals and love, in heart.

"The way" to San José?
    mission, peace, and worship:
A cord of three strands, when
    twined cannot be broken.
        —Willard Swartley

*The Mennonite Church USA biennial convention was held at San José, July 2007
**Mennonite Voluntary Service   ***Pasadena Mennonite Church

CHAPTER NINE

The Evangel as Gospel of Peace

How beautiful upon the mountains
Are the feet of the messenger
Who announces peace,
Who brings good news,
who announces salvation,
who says to Zion, "Your God Reigns."
—Isaiah 52:7

This text from Isaiah is the starting point to present the evangel as *persona* and voice of the gospel of peace.[1*] This text, though not identified in C. H. Dodd's influential contribution to the OT substratum of NT theology, is as crucial as any other OT text in shaping the NT's portrait of Jesus. Jesus is the *evangel-messenger* (the *mebasser*) of Isa 52:7. Further, this evangel *gospelizes peace.* Numerous key words in this text, *gospel, peace, salvation, the Lord reigns*, recur in the NT writings, indicating how foundational this text is. A look at the text with key words in Hebrew and Greek transliteration illumines some fundamental connections, even to our English language:

* This chapter has been slightly modified from its publication in *Evangelical, Ecumenical, and Anabaptist Missiologies in Conversation: In Honor of Wilbert R. Shenk*, ed. James R. Krabill, Walter Sawatsky, and Charles E. Van Engen (Maryknoll, NY: Orbis Press, 2006), 69-77; used with permission.

How beautiful upon the mountains
are the feet of him who announces gospel (*mebasser*),
who proclaims (*mashemia*) peace (*shalom*),
who announces the good gospel (*mebasser tov*),
who proclaims (*mashemia*) salvation (*yeshuah*),
saying to Zion, "Your God reigns (*malak Elohayikh*)."

The Hebrew *mebasser* and *mashemia* become in the Greek Septuagint one word, the participle, *euangelizomenos*. This one word includes both the subject, *the one announcing* and *gospel*, which in English translation unfortunately regularly becomes the object of the verb proclaim. But from the Greek grammar perspective, *gospel* is already in the participle. The *objects* of the verbal *gospel-proclaiming* are *peace, good*, *salvation*, and "*Your God reigns*," in both the Hebrew and Greek. This is important for three reasons. First, when this text is quoted in the NT (see below), this is the perception of the authors (Luke and Paul). Second, if the Christian church through the centuries had perceived the centrality of *peace* to the gospel, its method of witness and expansion would have avoided both coercive tactics in its mission and its too-frequent persecution of Jews and Muslims. Third, to hold this perception means that the church would not and could not have aligned itself with the empire strategies of "conquer and baptize." Nor could the church have participated in empire warfare. The church would have had to remain a true peace church. The self-understanding of the *evangel* would have been *messenger of the gospel of peace* as one with *messenger of the gospel of salvation*.

Thus, the *gospel* declares *peace*, and it is *good*, perhaps echoing the refrain in Gen 1. This verse (Isa 52:7) forms the backdrop to the famous Isa 53 text (the unit actually begins with 52:13), which influenced Jesus' own perception of his ministry. But it is less well known that 52:7 also played a crucial role in shaping Jesus' ministry, as well as the early church's understanding of Jesus and his mission.[2] A crucial text of Isa 61:1-2a, "The Spirit of the Lord is upon me," complements Isa 52:7 for Jesus' self-understanding of his mission:

> The spirit of the Lord God is upon me,
> because the Lord has anointed me;
> he has sent me to bring good news to the oppressed,
> to bind up the brokenhearted,
> to proclaim liberty to the captives,
> and release to the prisoners;
> to proclaim the year of the Lord's favor.

The connection between Isa 52:7 and 61:1-2a hinges on two points. The "me" of the text appears to be the "servant" (*ebed*) of Isa 40–55. Verse 1 uses the verb "anointed" (*mashakh*) to describe the vocational call and empowerment of the servant. Since anointing was used primarily for the installation of kings, we have here already the blending of the traditions of kingship and servant, an illuminating perspective to Jesus' baptism. Significantly, the verb *basser* is used to describe the servant's mission. The Lord has anointed the servant to "announce the gospel to the poor" (my trans.).

Christian theology has long recognized the importance of Isa 53 in understanding Jesus and his mission.[3] More recently the church has also recognized the significance of 61:1-2a for Jesus' self-understanding in the mission of his life-and death-ministry. But unfortunately, NT scholars and Christian mission theology have not recognized that 52:7, with its prominent emphasis on peace, forms the third part of Isaiah's influence upon Jesus' own self-understanding and the early church's perception of the significance of Jesus. Linking these three texts together discloses the essence of the Servant of the Lord's mission in Isaiah, and thus provides the three-legged foundation for Jesus' self-understanding and our authentic perception of Jesus' mission and ours. All these texts express the mission of the Servant's call to "bring forth justice to the nations" (42:1d), to "faithfully bring forth justice" (42:3c), "until he has established justice in the earth" (42:4b).[4] The threefold strategy of gospelizing peace; self-sacrifice (living for others); and bringing good news to the poor, release to the captives, sight to the blind, with Jubilee practice—all this is Jesus' means—and ours—of proclaiming the kingdom of God.

This key phrase "kingdom of God" in Matthew's, Mark's, and Luke's portrayal of Jesus' proclamation is crucial. The origin of the phrase is puzzling since it is virtually absent from the OT (and intertestamental) writings.[5] The very last phrase of Isa 52:7 (in NRSV) is "Your God reigns." Based upon study of the Isaiah scroll found in Qumran (over a century before Jesus), Bruce Chilton discovered that four texts in Isaiah were rendered in the Aramaic translation of the Hebrew text by the clause "The kingdom of God shall be (is) revealed."[6] In all four Isaiah texts the phrase "the kingdom of God" and the passive form of the verb "reveal" occur in either the present or future tense. *What* or *who* here does the revealing? In Isa 52:7 it is "the one announcing gospel." "The one announcing" reveals the kingdom of God. This provides a significant perspective for understanding Jesus and his mission. For *kingdom of God* and *gospel of peace* are linked in this foundational verse, together with *the messenger*, the *evangel* (English derivative from the Greek *euangel* and stem of the word *preacher* of the gospel: *euangelistēs* as in Acts 21:8 for Philip; Eph 4:11 to designate one grace-gift ministry; 2 Tim 4:5 to describe Timothy).

It is instructive to see the precise phrases in these Isaiah texts (NRSV) rendered in Aramaic by "the kingdom of God shall be (is) revealed":

24:23c. "for the Lord of hosts will reign"
31:4e. "so the Lord of hosts will come down"
40:9. "Behold your God" (RSV; after "herald of good tidings" 2x)
52:7e. (who says to Zion), "Your God reigns"

These four citations from Isaiah are in Zion theology texts. Zion theology is royal theology, related to the Davidic kingship tradition, but consisting essentially of its proclamation of God's own kingship and sovereign rule in Israel. Ben Ollenburger has persuasively shown that Zion is to be distinguished from Davidic kingship. Zion denotes God's rule, and Davidic kingship and its policies may indeed come under Zion's judgment. Even after Jerusalem falls and there is no Davidic heir on the throne, Zion continues.[7] It is a foundational metaphor for "reign of God" in justice and steadfast love. It is also a metaphor that calls for radical trust in God's sovereignty, a point Jesus often makes in his teaching (e.g., Matt 6:19-34).

The kingdom of God lies at the heart of the missionary message, as John Driver has amply shown in his essay in Wilbert Shenk's book *The Transfiguration of Mission*.[8] Indeed, the kingdom proclamation is deeply interconnected with christology as shown in the sequence of Mark 8:38 (Son of Humanity) and 9:1 (kingdom come in power). The Proclaimer, God's messianic messenger Jesus, *and* the Proclaimed, the kingdom of God, are indissoluble and dialectically one whole. The kingdom does not come without the Messiah; the Messiah does not come without the kingdom.

Driver's essay as a whole corrects errant emphases in defining and envisioning the kingdom of God. He rightly emphasizes a balance, even dialectic, between the present and the future, and emphasizes the formation of new community as sign of the kingdom. In his first footnote Driver appeals to Chilton's essay on the kingdom of God, and rightly values his view that kingdom of God means "God come in strength" or "God revealed in consummating strength."[9] Driver rightly contends that this view protects one from aligning the kingdom with an "apocalyptic regime, or as a political movement, or as a program for social improvement. . . . [Rather,] the essential element in the messianic proclamation of the evangel is 'Your God reigns' (Isa 52:7)."[10]

New Testament Citations and Significance

The most widely known NT citation of Isa 52:7 occurs in Eph 2:14, 17 (Pauline). These verses explicitly use the Isaiah phrase "proclaiming the gospel of peace." Verse 14 says "For he is our peace" (*Autos gar estin he eirēnē*), a bold claim in describing Jesus Christ and his significance for the redeemed community. Verse 17 is more textually dependent on Isaiah in saying, "And he came preaching/proclaiming peace" (my trans.). This is linked with "both those far and near," a phrase derived from Isa 57:19. This phrase, "he came proclaiming peace" (a direct rendering of 52:7 LXX, *euangelizomenos eirēnēn*) has inspired two seminal writings, an article by Marlin E. Miller[11] and a book title by John H. Yoder.[12]

This text (Eph 2:13-17) uses the word "peace" (*eirēnē*) four times and also uses the notion of "both becoming one" four times:

> But now in Christ Jesus you who once were *far off* have been brought *near* by the blood of Christ. For he is our **peace**; in his flesh he has made *both groups into one* and has broken down the dividing wall, that is, the hostility between us. He has abolished the law with its commandments and ordinances, that he might create in himself *one new humanity in place of the two*, thus making **peace**, and might *reconcile both groups* to God in *one body* through the cross, thus putting to death that hostility through it. So he came and proclaimed **peace** to you who were *far off* and **peace** to *those* who were *near*. (emphasis added)

It is clear that the fundamental message of the gospel is here understood as making peace between formerly alienated peoples (Jew and Gentile). Miller observes that this perception and proclamation goes beyond the OT understanding of shalom, which already encompassed a wide range of meaning: wholeness in personal and social dimensions both as a *state* of life-conditions and *relationships*, including above all relationship to God. But here a further step is taken:

> The peace established by Jesus as Messiah thus retains and even goes beyond the Hebraic understanding of shalom as including the social relations among God's people and between the people and God. It includes the realization of reconciliation and community unattainable by human efforts and therefore relegated to a utopian future age. What was considered utopian had now through the cross become present reality[13]

Paul regards the united believers to be "one new humanity" (Eph 2:15b). Such a realization of present utopian hope subverts Roman imperial claims and constitutes a counter social, economic, and political order of life. This new order unmasks Rome's so-called Pax Romana, and by contrast shows its oppressive structuring and ordering of society. As Gorman aptly describes it:

> The peace over which the emperor presided was, for many others, oppression, nothing less than raw power. Imperial power meant the power to crush opposition, to expand borders, to colonize, to enslave, and to crucify. It is no wonder, then, that enemies of the imperial power developed and sometimes found expression in outright revolt, as in the Jewish war of 66-70 and the revolt of 135.[14]

In the context of Pax Romana's peace-through-oppression, Paul proclaims a counterpeace, a peace that repudiates domination over others (see Mark 10:42-45) and unites people of diverse backgrounds into the Christ-bond of peace. It exhorts believers to welcome one another as brothers and sisters in Christ, overcoming hierarchical societal structures. The proof of this new order is manifested in Paul's mission strategy to collect monetary resources from the wealthier newly founded churches, to help the poor in Jerusalem. This is Paul's alternative peace-gospel, a subversive power in the empire, inaugurating a new order of society, birthing a new socioeconomic, political creation.[15]

A second crucial text citing Isa 52:7 is Acts 10:34-39a:

> Peter began to speak to them: "I truly understand that God shows no partiality, but in every nation anyone who fears him and does what is right is acceptable to him. You know the message he sent to the people of Israel, *preaching peace by Jesus Christ—he is Lord of all.* That message spread throughout Judea, beginning in Galilee after the baptism that John announced: how God anointed Jesus of Nazareth with the Holy Spirit and with power; how he went about doing good and healing all who were oppressed by the devil, for God was with him. We are witnesses to all that he did both in Judea and in Jerusalem. (emphasis added)

In this sermon, on the occasion of Cornelius' admission into the new Way covenant community, Peter sums up the message of Jesus as that of "preaching the gospel of peace." This quotation from Isa 52:7 (LXX), *euangelizomenos eirēnē*, is linked here to *dia Iēsou Christou* (Acts 10:36). Again, "peace" is the object of "preaching the good news" (*euangelizomenos*). The joining of Jews and Gentiles into one messianic fellowship is *peace*. The boundaries drawn for centuries are overcome by a new oneness that unites rival ethnic parties by joining diverse peoples into a common faith. This does not mean that ethnicity is done away with. Rather, it means that a new and more powerful reality transcends the differences and creates a new messianic identity, to which the ethnic diversities richly contribute. Peace between formerly separated and alienated peoples is the fruit of preaching the gospel; it is the coming of the kingdom of God that preoccupies the query of the disciples in 1:6, which 1:8 answers.

Third, this new reality has been brought about through

Jesus Christ, and "this one is Lord of all" (*houtos estin pantōn kyrios*). The lordship of Jesus Christ, declared in 2:36, is now reaffirmed precisely at this point where Jews welcome Gentiles into the household of faith. Overcoming the divisions arising from life in this world of nations, races, and tribes attests to the lordship of Jesus Christ. We should not overlook that Cornelius is a representative of the empire, not normally esteemed by Jews. With all the sociological and political significance this development entails, Cornelius' conversion symbolizes Rome, with the Pax Romana it sought to achieve, kneeling before the lordship of Jesus Christ. Something greater than even Solomon or the Roman Empire has come into historical existence.

A third text quoting Isa 52:7 is Eph 6:15, in the middle of the notable NT text (6:10-17) on Christian warfare against evil, specifically the principalities and powers, *not* people. The armor is derived or adapted mostly from Isaiah, where it earlier described God's battle against chaos and evil:

Eph 6:14	belt of truth around waist	Isa 11:5a
v. 14	breastplate of righteousness	59:17
v. 15	shoes for your feet . . . make ready to proclaim gospel of peace	52:7
v. 16	shield of faith	7:9b
v. 17	helmet of salvation	59:17
v. 17	sword of the Spirit,	11:4
	which is the word of God	Isa 49:2

The key phrase in Eph 6:15 connects to Isa 52:7 by mentioning specifically the "feet of the messenger" (*hypodēsamenoi tous podas*) and "the gospel of peace" (*euangeliou tēs eirēnēs*). Most striking, the warfare metaphor of the larger text is juxtaposed with and indeed subverted by the definitive description "gospel of peace" for this specific part of the "armor." It beckons us to look for the true meaning of the text not in the military gear of the Roman soldier, but in the moral attributes of God and the believer: truth, righteousness, gospel-peace, faith, salvation, word of God. These are the sources of empowerment that enable believers to withstand the "wiles of the devil" and to stand firm "on that evil day" (when Satan's attack is strong).

Put succinctly, the *battle is peacemaking*, seemingly an oxymoron. But the blending of war and peace imagery occurs also in Rom 16:20: "The God of peace will shortly crush Satan under your feet."[16] The messianic peace extends God's warfare against evil that lay at the heart of the biblical story. Yet never is it human military warfare, but a dependence upon God's victory. It is not some anticipated result (*end*) of literal warfare, but rather "standing against" evil through the power of the prophetic word. The *moral attributes* of the armor are the *means* to peace. At baptism, yes,[17] believers are enlisted in the warfare of peacemaking.

Indeed, this is not military warfare. If it were, the gospel of Jesus Christ would not be a missionary gospel. Too often people have distorted the mission of the church and denied it by aligning the gospel with some form of national imperialism. Rather, these divine attributes are mighty in power against all that challenges or defies God's sovereignty. The passage begins with key emphases that permeate the whole: "Finally, be strong in the Lord and in the strength of *his power*. Put on the whole *armor of God*, so that you may be able to stand against the wiles of the devil" (6:10-11, emphasis added). Most important, it is *God's* battle in which believers enlist, but we always trust in God for victory, for it is *God's* armor. Only by clothing ourselves with *God's* armor are we able to withstand in the struggle, "not against enemies of blood and flesh, but against the rulers, against the authorities, against the cosmic powers of this present darkness, against the spiritual forces of evil in the heavenly places" (6:12-13).

This description of the foes indicates clearly that this is not a military battle, in which one group of people exerts domination through war against another group (nation, ethnic group, or ideologically grouped forces). Clinton Arnold puts this spiritual warfare text into the context of the Ephesian believers' past religious allegiances to the Artemis cult, with its various forms of magic and astrology, and to other mystery cults, in all of which great fear of demonic powers played a major role.[18] Hence Christ's victory is a conquest of these powers; the believers are called to stand against them with the divine armor: "Victory over the 'powers' is not assured apart from the appropriation of the power of God. Failure to resist allows the devil to reassert his dominion."[19]

This text is prone to gross misunderstanding unless set within Paul's larger emphasis of Christ's victory over the powers (as explained in chap. 5 above) and informed by the divine warfare theology of the OT, culminating in the NT kingdom-peace-gospel combating evil.[20] Only then can we understand rightly what it means to put on the *armor of God.* Often commentators observe that all parts of the armor except the sword of the Spirit are defensive. The point is good to the extent that it guards against misconstruing this text as a call to some Christian crusade. In this view, the sword, the word of God, is offensive, since it is the means of evangelism, of rescuing people from the bondage of evil and gathering them into Christ's kingdom.[21]

This view, however, merits careful reconsideration. While the parts of armor, except the sword, are primarily defensive, yet the spiritual attributes they denote have both an offensive and defensive side to them.[22] A certain tension thus exists between the tenor of the metaphor (belt, breastplate, shoes, etc.) and the Christian virtue or action it signifies. Truth, righteousness, salvation, gospel of peace, and faith are powerful in confronting and disarming the enemy. In the Christian life the offensive and defensive blend together. As believers are empowered with these attributes derived from God's character in combating evil, they are able to withstand the evil one. The danger of stressing only the defensive stance lies in its fostering what Yoder Neufeld describes as becoming a church that keeps to itself, rather than confronting evil. "The church's true existence consists of the active and bold actualization of gospel truth, justice, peace, and liberation in human relationships."[23] The active call to peacemaking, so clear in Eph 2:13-17, is not to be lost but is to empower believers in this call to arms, putting on only the divine armor, and *standing* against evil by these peacemaking virtues.

Other texts[24] pertinent to a complete discussion of connecting *peace* to gospel and the kingdom of God are Matt 5:9, the well-known "Blessed are the peacemakers," and the extensive emphasis in Luke on peace as an integral expression of the gospel that the messianic evangel brings to earth (2:10-14). These portions are examined in depth in my volume *Covenant of Peace*, chapters 3 and 5. In that study I observe and document in Appendix 1 that much of NT theology and ethics has neglected this key emphasis as essential in understanding the NT writings. This neglect has tragic consequences, for it allows one to construe NT theology without grasping that its call to mission is essentially also the proclamation of the peace of Jesus Christ. The evangel thus goes forth with an abortive and distorted message of salvation. Given this deficiency, the mission lacks the ecclesiological vision that enables new churches to overcome ethnic divisions and warfare. I cite Wilbert Shenk's *Thesis 14* in his 2004 revised lecture on "Christological Foundations for Evangelizing in a Pluralist Society": "When it is modeled on that of Jesus Christ, the church's witness will always be without coercion—whether physical, psychological, social, or political—and out of compassionate love for the other."[25]

As we witness in life and word to people of other religious traditions, we will encounter their historical, communal memory. Indelibly etched on the Muslim psyche is the history of the Crusades, military campaigns by European Christians from the eleventh to fourteenth centuries in an attempt to wrest control of Palestine from the Arabs, mostly Muslims. In spite of the fact that the majority of Muslims in today's world live in countries never touched directly by the Crusades, this "Christian" (?) action a thousand years ago continues to hamper Christian witness. The current Iraq war only deepens Islamic animosity toward Christianity associated with the West. Similarly, Christian mistreatment of Jews, extended through so many centuries, presents an enormous obstacle to Christian witness. Such historical events profoundly discredit our witness to Jesus Christ. Other people-groups have also suffered horribly, notably Native Americans as white tribes occupied North America. Shameful as this history is, the answer is not to abandon our God-given responsibility. Rather, we must dedicate ourselves anew to a witness that truly reflects Jesus Christ's gospel of peacemaking and reconciliation in the power of the Holy Spirit.

The Prince of Peace: A Song Cycle on the Words of Menno Simons*

Music by James Clemens

This Example We Have in Christ

If we wish to save our neighbor's soul by the help of the Spirit and Word of our Lord, or if we see our neighbors in need or in danger, driven forth for the Word of the Lord, then we should not close our doors to them.

We should receive them in our houses and share our food, aid them, and comfort and assist them in their troubles.

We should risk our lives for our brethren, even if we know beforehand that it will be at the cost of our own lives.

This is the example we have in Christ, who for our sakes did not spare himself, but willingly gave up his life, in order that we might live through him.

Believe the Gospel

Believe the gospel, that is, believe the joyful news of divine grace through Jesus Christ. Cease from sin; show repentance for your past lives; submit obediently to the Word and will of the Lord.

If you walk according to the Spirit and not according to the flesh, then you will become companions, citizens, children and heirs of the new and heavenly Jerusalem.

* These selected texts from Menno Simons were assembled and translated into English by Jan Gleysteen for the "Menno Simons: Image, Art & Identity" Exhibit, produced by the Kaufman Museum in Newton, Kansas. The exhibit showed in the Umble Center at Goshen College, Jan. 10–Feb. 16, 1996. Text used with permission from Jan Gleysteen. For a celebration service at Goshen College, James E. Clemens set the text to music titled, "The Prince of Peace: A Song Cycle on the Words of Menno Simons," published now in *A Field of Voices: Hymns for Worship*, by James E. Clemens and David Wright (Table Round Press, 2007).

A Genuine Christian Faith

A genuine Christian faith cannot be idle, but it changes, renews, purifies, sanctifies and justifies more and more. It gives peace and joy. Happy is the person who has it and keeps it to the end.

The Prince of Peace

The Prince of Peace is Jesus Christ.

We who were formerly no people at all, and who knew of no peace, are now called to be a church of peace.

True Christians do not know vengeance. They are children of peace. Their hearts overflow with peace. Their mouths speak peace, and they walk in the way of peace.

The Glory of Christ

We preach as much as possible, both by day and by night, in houses and in fields, in forests and in wastes.

We preach as much as possible, hither and yon, at home or abroad, in prisons and in dungeons, in water and in fire, on the scaffold and on the wheel, before lords and princes, through mouth and pen, with possessions and blood, with life and death.

We have done this these many years, and we are not ashamed of the gospel of the glory of Christ.

CHAPTER TEN

Peacemaking and Mission Empowered by Worship

No peace, no mission; no mission, no peace.
No worship, no mission and no peace.
—Willard Swartley

> Now the eleven disciples went to Galilee, to the mountain to which Jesus had directed them. When they saw him, *they worshiped him*; but some doubted. And Jesus came and said to them, "All authority in heaven and on earth has been given to me. Go therefore and make disciples of all nations, baptizing them in the name of the Father and of the Son and of the Holy Spirit, and teaching them to obey everything that I have commanded you. And remember, I am with you always, to the end of the age." (Matt 28:16-20. emphasis added)

In this chapter I bring my work on peace and peacemaking, both in this book and in *Covenant of Peace*, to an intersection with the seminal, superb, and important work of Larry Hurtado,[1] who has shown that worship of Jesus is prominent in the NT. Further, he persuasively argues that worship practices reflecting devotion to Jesus were present in the earliest layers of Christian faith (Hurtado's claims refute the early twentieth-century view of W. Bousset that this emphasis emerged within Hellenistic Christianity under influence from pagan cults).

My contribution joins Hurtado's at the point where he addresses two important questions: "How on Earth Did Jesus Become a God? Approaches to Jesus-Devotion in Early Christianity" and "To Live and Die for Jesus: Social and Political Consequences of Devotion to Jesus in Early Christianity."[2] One of the critiques put to Hurtado in his 2004 Theological Lectureship at the Associated Mennonite Biblical Seminary (which applies also to his *Lord Jesus Christ* book) was his silence on the political significance of worship of Jesus as Lord, given the context that at least five of the Roman emperors in the first century claimed the deity title "Son of God." These "Son of God" emperors demanded worship from their citizens and subjects. Hurtado's response was that one cannot do everything in one book, and that this matter is addressed in his next book, then already at the press.[3]

I will return to our intersection later in this chapter. My main purpose in this chapter is to pursue the textual task of showing how important this matter is in key selections from the NT in its canonical form. I begin with Matthew.

Matthew

The Gospel of Matthew is well-known for its call to peacemaking and to proclaim the God-sent Jesus-gospel to all people. It ends with the great commission opening the kingdom of heaven, which Jesus proclaimed, to all people. This emphasis connects to the first Gospel narrative after Jesus' birth, the Magi coming from the East. Together, these two Gospel vignettes form an inclusio on the theme of the gospel for all people.

Even though many have understood Matthew to be the Jewish Gospel of the canonical four, it in truth is fully two-sided, for both Jews and Gentiles; hence it more truly is for all people. Two texts make this clear:

> Jesus went throughout Galilee, teaching in their synagogues and proclaiming the good news of the kingdom and curing every disease and every sickness among the people. So his fame spread throughout all Syria, and they brought to him all the sick, those who were afflicted with various diseases and pains, demoniacs, epileptics, and paralytics, and he cured them. And great crowds followed him from Galilee, the Decapolis, Jerusalem, Judea, and from beyond the Jordan. (Matt 4:23-25)

> Many crowds followed him, and he cured all of them, and he ordered them not to make him known. This was to fulfill what had been spoken through the prophet Isaiah:
>
>> Here is my servant, whom I have chosen, my beloved, with whom my soul is well pleased. I will put my Spirit upon him, and he will proclaim justice to the Gentiles. He will not wrangle or cry aloud, nor will anyone hear his voice in the streets. He will not break a bruised reed or quench a smoldering wick until he brings justice to victory. And in his name the Gentiles will hope. (Matt 12:15b-21)

Three place designations in 4:23-25 denote Gentiles: Syria, Decapolis, and "beyond the Jordan." Galilee also was home of many Gentiles as well as Jews. This description of the scope of the impact of Jesus' ministry comes early in Matthew, perhaps as a preview of what readers are going to hear in the pages that follow. And so it is: the healing of a centurion's son in 8:5-13, with praise for his faith, found "in no one in Israel" (v. 10); the healing of the Canaanite woman's demon-oppressed daughter in the area of Tyre and Sidon (15:21-28); and the provocative judgment, "Therefore I tell you, the kingdom of God will be taken away from you and given to a people that produces the fruits of the kingdom" (21:43).

The chapter 12 text twice specifies Gentiles as the recipients of Jesus' servant ministry, fulfilling prophetic-servant texts from Isa 42:1-4. But Matt 10:5b-6 limits Jesus' sending of his Twelve to Israel: "Go nowhere among the Gentiles, and enter no town of the Samaritans, but go rather to the lost sheep of the house of Israel." As Dorothy Jean Weaver[4] and other scholars have shown, this restrictive text, together with 10:23b, must be funneled through the final narrative of the Gospel, the unto-all-nations great commission. In my reading of Matthew's narrative, the quotations from Isaiah in chapter 12 already break the restriction by twice mentioning Gentiles. This inclusion of Gentiles was indeed signaled in 4:23-25, quoted above.

Just as God's gospel mission is a widely recognized theme in Matthew, so is Jesus' call to peacemaking: "Blessed are the peacemakers, for they will be called children of God" (5:9). As I have shown in *Covenant of Peace*,[5] this verse is linked to the "love of enemies" command in 5:43-48, which identifies also those who practice this love and "pray for those who persecute you" as "children of God" (5:44-45). Elsewhere I have developed Matthew's peacemaking theme, showing its presence in the larger emphases of the Sermon on the Mount, its impact on the Gospel's christological portrait of Jesus, and its prominence in the passion events, especially the triumphal entry (21:1-16) and the Last Supper and Gethsemane scenes (26:26-56).[6]

To these mission and peace themes in Matthew we must add *worship*, and perhaps somewhat shockingly, *worship of Jesus*! This emphasis correlates with Matthew's inclusion of Gentiles, at two levels. First, worship of Jesus is mentioned both in the Gospel's finale, the great commission to "all nations" (28:16-20), and in the Magi's visit to Jesus (2:1-12). Significantly, then, *worship of Jesus* appears in this inclusio that marks Jesus' entrance into and departure from this world.

> Wise men from the East came to Jerusalem, asking, "Where is the child who has been born king of the

> Jews? For we observed his star at its rising, and have come to pay him homage." . . .
>
> [Herod] sent them to Bethlehem, saying, "Go and search diligently for the child; and when you have found him, bring me word so that I may also go and *pay him homage*." . . .
>
> When they saw that the star had stopped, they were overwhelmed with joy. On entering the house, they saw the child with Mary his mother; and they knelt down and *paid him homage*. Then, opening their treasure chests, they offered him gifts of gold, frankincense, and myrrh. (Matt 2:1-2, 8, 10-11, emphasis added)

The Greek word for all these instances (2:2, 8, 11; 28:17) is the same term (*proskyneō*),[7] which means, literally, "to bend the knee" in homage, or worship. That this emphasis occurs early in the Gospel and at the very end is hardly happenstance. Matthew intends it: it is God's gospel announcement. In the Magi narrative a miraculous guiding star brings these "wise men from the East" to Jesus, to fall down and worship, an act of great devotion that contrasts to Herod's mocking use of the phrase about "homage." From crib to crown, from Jesus as a vulnerable baby (especially in light of Herod's evil intent) to Jesus as the resurrected and exalted Son of God on the *mountain*[8]—Jesus receives worship. This emphasis matches Matthew's ubiquitous *royal* christology, one that nevertheless transforms Jewish expectations for a militant, violent Messiah.[9]

In another way the Gospel implicitly portrays worship of Jesus: in the naming of Jesus: through Joseph's dream (1:20-23). Not only is the newborn to be named "Jesus, for he will save his people from their sins," but also "they shall name him Emmanuel," meaning "God is with us." Saving from sin is God's prerogative, and *Emmanuel* tells it plainly: Jesus is God come to earth, surprisingly, in a *royal* baby born with no earthly father, but by the Holy Spirit coming upon Mary, thus God as Father![10]

Put this in tandem with the closing scene of the Gospel. Jesus' final word, after instructing the disciples on what to do, is a promise: "Remember, I am with you always, to the end of the age" (28:20b). The divine presence will abide with them. How or why is Jesus worthy of worship? In these oracles, from the angel addressing Joseph in a dream, to Jesus' promise of his abiding presence, Jesus is God's gospel-face.

Hence, my thesis: worship of Jesus empowers both the mission assigned to Jesus' followers, to proclaim the gospel to all nations, and also the call to peacemaking, living out our new identity as God's children. Falling at Jesus' feet in worship provides the humility and the strength to do what is humanly impossible: love enemies and share the gospel with all people.

Mother Teresa exemplifies the point. Her devotion to Jesus, I believe, empowered her humble sharing of her life with the poor. She incarnated the gospel, proclaiming it in person and deed, and indeed making peace with all people. She has become an icon of what Matthew calls us to, as Jesus' faithful followers.

If *worship of Jesus* remains in doubt, look at two other scenes in the Gospel, where disciples, male and female, worship Jesus! The first is on target at the midpoint of the Gospel, forming the climax of Matthew's narration of Jesus walking on the water and Peter's failed attempt to do the same (14:22-33). Matthew ends the narrative thus: "And those in the boat worshiped him, saying, 'Truly you are the Son of God'" (v. 33). The same Greek word (*proskyneō*) is used here, as in the earlier texts cited.

The second disciple response is that of the women who come to the tomb on Easter morning, startled by an earthquake and then an angel (28:1-2). After they receive the commission to go and tell the male disciples that Jesus will meet them in Galilee, Jesus appears to them and says, "Greetings!" Their response? "And they came to him, took hold of his feet, and *worshiped him*. Then Jesus said to them, 'Do not be afraid; go and tell my brothers to go to Galilee; there they will see me'" (28:9b-10, emphasis added).

This emphasis on *worship of Jesus* is crucial to Matthew's christology. When viewed in the context of emperor worship, this Gospel calls us to an alternative loyalty. God has sent Jesus as true Son of God. To believe in Jesus and accept him as Prophet, Savior, Messiah is to acknowledge him as truly Son of God,[11] who is worthy to receive our worship. Jesus, not Caesar and not Satan,[12] is the divine One whom Jesus' followers worship. To go forth to the nations and proclaim the gospel that Jesus is the true royal Son of God counters and exposes the imperial deity-claims. The peacemaking that Jesus calls his followers to practice counters and exposes also the pretenses of the Pax Romana. *Worship of Jesus* thus fuels both peacemaking and mission. When our zeal for peacemaking and mission flags, we need again to fall at Jesus' feet, and through that worship become recharged, empowered to be missional, peacemaking people.[13]

Mark

My chapter on Mark in *Covenant of Peace* develops Mark's unique narrative craft of portraying Jesus as Messiah who fulfills the peaceable strands of OT messianic hope. Jesus' instructs his disciples as they walk on the way (*en tē hodō*, as in 8:27) explicating the way of peace that eventually leads not only to Jerusalem but also to the kingdom of God. Jesus calls his followers to be at peace with one another (9:50), in contrast to their rivalry with one another over who gets top seats in the kingdom (9:33-34; 10:35-37).[14]

Mark's mission emphases are also uniquely developed, in such small details as Jesus saying when cleansing the temple, "My house shall be called a house of prayer for all nations" (11:17; the last three words, only in Mark among the Gospels, appear in Isa 56:7, which Jesus quotes). A similar phrase occurs in 13:10: "And the good news must first be proclaimed to all nations," and again, memorably, about the woman who "has done a good thing:" "Truly I tell you, wherever the good news is proclaimed in the whole world, what she has done will be told in remembrance of her" (14:9).

Mark's inclusion of "outsiders" is explicit in several places (5:1-20; 7:24-30). But his emphasis on "the gospel for all nations" is more subtle in the Gospel's narrative. Peter's confession of Jesus as Messiah is the Gospel's pivotal point (8:27-30). This is the moment of messianic disclosure. For the first time those who would be Jesus' followers grasp this truth. The disclosure occurs as sequel to the feedings of the multitudes. Those feedings, intended to be signs of messianic disclosure, accomplish their purpose.[15]

Jesus elicits the messianic confession in the far north of Galilee, on the border between Israel and the nations, not in Jerusalem. The location is significant, disclosing Mark's central emphasis: Jesus is Messiah *for all people*, just as the double bread-feeding on both sides of the sea (Jewish and Gentile) has already signified. We have heard it said: No Christ, no mission. But Mark's point is even more striking. By including Gentiles as recipients of God's manna-blessings *before* Jesus is confessed to be the Messiah, Mark's Gospel says: No mission, no Christ.

This location for divine revelation and Jesus' subsequent teaching that the Son of Man *must* suffer and be killed clashes with popular Jewish messianic understandings. The hopes for a military conqueror have to be transformed from the core outward. A suffering Messiah is so counter to many (but not all) Jewish expectations of the Messiah that Jesus' identity during his ministry is rightly shrouded in secrecy. Mark intensifies this point by showing further that what the Jewish leaders rejected, the Gentiles received. The Gospel's dual points of climax in 15:38 and 39 make the point. Immediately after Jesus draws his last breath, the veil of the temple is torn in two, and a *Gentile* centurion acclaims Jesus as Son of God.

Verse 38 is Mark's last word on the destiny of the temple.

What does it mean? Was the curtain the one between the holy place and the holy of holies? Or was it the curtain at the entrance to the temple? While commentators differ on this, the end result is the same. Mark is saying that the partitions that have controlled hierarchical access into God's presence are done away with. The end of the temple's function has come! Now all people, including Gentiles, are invited to affirm Jesus and worship God. Jesus is the Messiah for the world, for all nations.

In chapter 13 the end (of the temple) is not to come until the gospel is preached "to all nations" (13:10). But here in 15:38 the temple's functional end is declared in and through Jesus' death. How are both these points true? Mark carefully uses two different words for temple. In chapters 11–13 he uses *hieron*, which designates the physical structure, the building. In chapters 14–15 he uses *naos*, which designates the sanctuary, the place where God and humans meet (14:58; 15:29, 38; *except* 14:49, referring to the setting in chaps. 11–13). Jesus' death, then, is the end of the *naos*, the old sanctuary. But, the *hieron*, the building, continued into Mark's time while the gospel had been and continued to be preached to all nations (13:10).

But is the *naos*, the sanctuary destroyed, never to rise again? What about 14:58 and 15:29? "In three days I will *build another*"; in John (2:20), "*raise it up*!" (emphasis added). What else, according to Mark's Gospel, is to happen "in three days"? Do you remember? Do you understand!? The passion predictions are also resurrection predictions: "*In three days* I will rise again." By connecting the events that will occur "in three days," Mark subtly but forcefully proclaims the resurrected Jesus as the rebuilt temple—but located where?[16]

"But after I am raised up, I will go before you to Galilee" (14:28). And now for the second last verse of the book:[17] "Go, tell his disciples and Peter that he is going ahead of you to Galilee; there you will see him, just as he told you" (16:7).

What is the meaning of Galilee? Matthew (4:15), by quoting Isa 9:1, connects Galilee to the nations. And Mark infers the same. This provides the clue to indicate that the temple to be built without hands (Mark 14:58) will welcome the worship of the nations.[18]

In Mark, Galilee represents Palestine's open door to the nations of the world.[19] This call to world mission, inferred by Mark, is proclaimed openly by Matthew (28:16-20).

Mark's distinctive contribution lies in his correlation of the Gospel's major themes with Jesus' call to mission:

1. Jesus is confessed to be Messiah of the kingdom only when Gentiles as well as Jews have been fed the messianic bread. Only then is the secret disclosed, with its truth protected from nationalistic hope and anchored in following on the way, the way of the cross to God's kingdom, a way—for all nations!
2. It is significant that in three days the temple will be rebuilt (14:58) *and* the crucified Messiah will be raised. Further, the resurrected Jesus will meet his disciples in Galilee. Hence, worship[20] will be through Jesus, the new *naos*-temple, who meets those who come to Galilee, the open door to all nations. Mark hereby signals the call to make disciples of all nations. The new temple-community is built in the midst of the nations affirming Jesus as Messiah.
3. Jesus as Messiah died on a cross, disappointing much Jewish political hope and offending disciples then and now who want only a sweet Jesus. Through such a death, that of a political criminal, a Gentile soldier affirms Jesus to be true Son of God, in his obedient suffering and death (15:39).[21] What a scandal! God disclosed—on the cross. This is the offense of the gospel, through which both Jews and Gentiles enter the kingdom. Indeed, this is the moral muscle of mission. The cross too is God's wisdom in Jesus Christ, whom we

worship. Emperors who claimed "Son of God" deity required worship. This climactic confession invites readers to regard Jesus worthy of the same.

> COME . . .
> die to the old,
> WORSHIP . . .
> Through the new,
> PROCLAIM . . .
> to all nations!

Luke-Acts

In chapters 4 and 5 of *Covenant of Peace*, I exposit at length Luke's keen interest in and development of *peace* (*eirēnē*), occurring fourteen times in the Gospel and seven times in Acts. These many distinctive uses (most not found in Mark and Matthew) are clearly intentional, so that Luke sets forth a peace theology. Here I do not repeat what is available in *Covenant of Peace*, but I cite only my modified summary, combined with a synopsis of mission emphasis as well. Chapter 8 above also explicates Luke's mission emphasis.

> Luke's presentation of peace challenges us to find new categories of understanding the gospel in relation to the world powers and its peace rhetoric. A strong liberationist and transformational emphasis permeates both volumes. Luke's peace manifesto arises consistently from the side of the gospel's own agenda and its encounter with diverse peoples. None of the prevailing models of gospel and politics fit the Luke-Acts reality. Hence, we need a conceptual transformation to grasp the reality of Luke's narrative as it presents the "spreading flame"[22] of Jesus' gospel in Palestine and into the Roman world. Might it be identified as "an alternative subversive messianic establishment of true righteousness/justice and peace"? Perhaps Luke intends to present Jesus as the fulfillment of both the Jewish messian-

ic hope of true righteousness and peace (Isa 11; passim) and of the pregnant Greco-Roman hope for a millennial age of peace, which as Virgil's *Fourth Eclogue* anticipated, would be inaugurated by a miraculous birth of a royal son.[23]

In this coming age, now announced as come in Jesus Christ, shalom finds expression in the new *laos* community of the Spirit, in which a fundamental reversal of values guides the community into bold witness in the name of Jesus. They proclaim the gospel to the ends of the earth and are not intimidated by the political authorities (Jewish or Roman). They are accused of seeking to turn the world upside down (in Acts 17:6b from ruffians in Thessalonica framed by Jewish opponents), not through any violence but by the bold public proclamation of the kingdom-gospel of peace. This Way community also cared for each other in every way. . . .

Luke's story of the gospel's expansion into the world depicts also encounter with the demonic in the magic of the day (Simon in 8:9-24; Elymas [Bar-Jesus] in 13:6-12; and a slave girl fortune-teller in 16:16-18) and in idolatry as well (in Athens in 17:16-31 and in Ephesus in 19:23-41). These confrontations portray the peace-gospel challenging the economic systems dependent upon these magical and idolatrous practices, the intellectual philosophical worldview with its multiple gods and goddesses—linked into the political structure, as becomes evident in Paul's preaching that undermined the god/goddess business of Demetrius in chapter 19. Paul and Silas' imprisonment in Philippi and the mob's uproar in Ephesus have nothing to do with Jews inciting the opposition. Rather, local citizens of Rome's Pax Romana are threatened by the proclamation of this gospel precisely because it calls for a new life order under the sovereign lordship of Jesus Christ. Economically, culturally, and politically, the gospel means a "stop" to fashioning god-images out of wood or clay, but owning the crucified and risen Jesus Christ as God's revelation of God's self,

> and reckoning with the truth that a day of reckoning, judgment, is coming.
>
> The peace of this gospel is revolutionary; it ends one world and begins another. No longer does ethnic identity lead to rivalry.
>
> No longer does economic livelihood depend upon magic and idolatry.
>
> No longer does the community acknowledge Caesar as Lord.
>
> A new world begins where Jesus the vindicated Righteous One is Savior and Lord, where the Holy Spirit turns old Babel into Pentecostal multi-ethnic fellowship love, and where the new kingdom-peace-gospel turns all things upside down: overcoming internal and external conflicts, transforming violent Saul into a gospel peacemaker, welcoming Cornelius into The Way community, and seating people formerly hostile to one another at the Lord's banquet table.[24]

Luke mentions worship only three times in the Gospel. The first two occurrences appear in the temptation narrative (4:4-8; par. Matt 4:9-10). Only once does worship of Jesus occur, in Luke's final verses immediately following his mission charge (24:48-49). The text with these two emphases is:

> Then he opened their minds to understand the scriptures, and he said to them, "Thus it is written, that the Messiah is to suffer and to rise from the dead on the third day, and that repentance and forgiveness of sins is to be proclaimed in his name to all nations, beginning from Jerusalem. You are witnesses of these things. And see, I am sending upon you what my Father promised; so stay here in the city until you have been clothed with power from on high."
>
> Then he led them out as far as Bethany, and, lifting up his hands, he blessed them. While he was blessing them, he withdrew from them and was carried up into heaven. And

> *they worshiped him*, and returned to Jerusalem with great joy; and they were continually in the temple blessing God. (Luke 24:45-53, emphasis added)

Only here does Luke use *proskyneō* to denote the disciples' worship of Jesus (24:52), in his climactic portrait of Jesus, who was just carried up to heaven. With this sequence of implied ascension (see Acts 1:9-11), it appears that Luke connects worship of Jesus with Jesus' exaltation to lordship at God's right hand. This same point occurs again in Acts, in the climax of Peter's Pentecost sermon: "Know with certainty that God has made him both Lord and Messiah, this Jesus whom you crucified" (2:36).

Two other features complement Luke's emphasis of worship of Jesus. Luke's Gospel is toned with repeated use of words that belong to worship:

- "Praise" (*aineō*): four times (2:13, 20; 19:37; 24:53).
- "Glorify" (*doxazō*): nine times (2:20; 4:15; 5:25, 26; 7:16; 13:13; 17:15; 18:43; 23:47). The noun *glory* (*doxa*) occurs ten times (2:9, 14, 32; 9:31, 32; 12:27; 14:10; 17:18; 19:38; 24:26).
- "Bless" (*eulogeō*): thirteen times (1:28, 42, 64; 2:28, 34; 6:28; 9:16; 13:35; 19:38; 24:30, 50, 51, 53).

God receives the praise, glory, and worship, but it is Jesus, his birth, deeds of power, and teachings that astound and prompt praise, glory, blessing, and worship.

Second, while Luke uses a plethora of titles for Jesus (Messiah-Christ, Son of humanity, Son of God, and several times even Savior) his most distinctive appellation is Lord, both for God (33 times) and for Jesus (42 times in Luke, 50 in Acts). This speaks volumes regarding Luke's view of Jesus' exalted status, worthy of worship! *Lord* has a long history in Hebrew Scripture: it is the English rendering of the Septuagint (Greek) *kyrios*, which renders the sacred Tetragrammaton

(YHWH), going back to Exod 3:13-17. Much more could be said,[25] but the picture is clear: Jesus as Lord welcomes our worship, and thus we continue the work of the apostles *in the name of Jesus* (see Acts 3–4). Mission and peacemaking follow, inherent in God's calling.

John

The peace and mission themes in John are developed in chapter 11 of my *Covenant of Peace* book,[26] and that need not be repeated here. Peace/peacemaking and mission are linked to worship in the story of Jesus and the Samaritan woman (the verb *proskyneō* appears nine times—twice each in John 4, vv. 20, 22, 23, 24, and once in v. 21—and the noun once, in v. 23) and in John 20:19-23, 28, key texts in my study.

Jesus' encounter with the Samaritan woman in John 4 is a prototype story for peacemaking, mission, and worship—for Jesus' first disciples and for us today. In 20:19-31 peace, mission, and worship are blended, with Thomas' confession, "My Lord and my God," poignantly climaxing encounter with Jesus, overcoming doubt.

In the middle of the Gospel, another point, not addressed in my essay, also emerges. On this point the Gospel leitmotif "My hour has not yet come" (as in 2:4) *turns* to "My hour has now come" (cf. 12:23). Greeks come to Jerusalem to *worship* (12:20), saying to Philip, "Sir, we wish to see Jesus" (12:21). This inquiry, reported to Jesus, like an alarm clock *rings* the hour for Jesus' glorification. As in Mark, only when the Gentiles, here represented by Greeks, receive the blessings of the Messiah can the full disclosure of Jesus' life purpose unfold and move relatively swiftly to *glorification*, which in John is both being lifted up on the cross and being exalted not only as Son but also God of God: John 1:1, 18[27] and 20:28 form the christological inclusio of the Gospel.

John's emphasis on *glorification*, his view of "being lifted up," reminds us that both mission and peacemaking stand in the service of true worship of God. Chiastic structuring of the John 4 peacemaking event regularly puts verse 24, "worship in spirit and truth," at the center of the chiasm. The empowering *must* (*dei*) of Jesus' journey into "enemy" land—sent from the heart of God—culminates in this Samaritan woman's testimony to her fellow Samaritans that Jesus is Messiah, who gives living water. Her townsfolk then confess Jesus to be the Savior of the world. This opens the door to true worship and glorification of God, in which neither Jerusalem nor Gerizim is prescriptive. The story is rich with its mission, peacemaking, and worship wrapped together: God's Christmas gift has come in Jesus. Jesus, the Logos of life and light, ends the worship wars, making "in spirit and in truth" the means and criteria of true worship.

John 20:19-28 also wraps peace, mission, and worship together as Jesus' gift to his distraught disciples. The "Peace be with you" greeting (at the end of vv. 19, 21, 26) heals the disciples' stress, renewing hope and opening the future. Jesus commissions his disciples: "As the Father has sent me, so I send you." Jesus then breathes on them, saying: "Receive the Holy Spirit. If you forgive the sins of any, they are forgiven; if you retain the sins of any, they are retained." Thomas missed this healing encounter. A week later he too hears "'Peace be with you'" and is healed from his doubt and despair in his own particular way—invited to touch Jesus' nail-prints in his hands and spear-wound in his side. His response? The worship climax of the Gospel, "My Lord and my God!" joins and extends Mary Magdalene's announcement, "I have seen the Lord" (20:18).

One other key text in John where worship of Jesus occurs is 9:38. When the man born blind comes to perceive that Jesus who healed him is indeed "the Son of Man," he falls at Jesus' feet and worships him. In symbolic theology so characteristic of this book, the synonomous parallel of *seeing* the light and *worship of Jesus* cannot be missed.

Paul

Paul uses the word "peace" forty-four times in different contexts, and to indicate at least four dimensions: relational peace with God, relational peace with fellow humans, inner peace, and corporate sociopolitical peace that contrasts to Rome's Pax Romana. Most significant is Paul's coining the appellation "God of peace," which he uses seven times, (see chart in chap. 3 above). This frequent appellation is unmatched by any similar description, such as "God of love" (used only in 2 Cor 13:11 with "God of peace") or "God of truth." Peace permeates Paul's epistles and is surely a key to his theology as a whole, a point that has been marginalized in scholarly work in NT theology and ethics.

Mission too is at the heart of Paul's writings. His "conversion" call is to be an apostle to the Gentiles. He spends his entire Jesus-as-Messiah life seeking to win people for Christ, both Jew and Gentile. He finally gives his life by taking a relief gift to Jerusalem to demonstrate through material aid the unity of the believing Gentiles and Jews in Christ Jesus (Rom 15:25-27)—one church, one faith, one *Lord*.

With these strong emphases on peacemaking and mission, Paul also extols Jesus Christ in worship. Two noted scholars, Richard Bauckham and Larry Hurtado, have done much in the last decade to show that in the earliest written NT sources, Jesus is viewed as sharing in the *identity* of God (Bauckham at St. Andrews) and was worshipped by earliest Christians (Hurtado at Edinburgh). To appreciate Paul's contribution, I will incorporate much from Bauckham.[28] Bauckham's approach describes two characteristic, identifying features of Israel's one God: creator and ruler. Most of God's activity in the OT falls within these two overarching categories: creating and ruling, which includes redeeming, covenant-making, giving Torah, ordering, and promising.

I introduce these emphases by asking a key question: What does "Everyone who calls on the name of the Lord shall be saved" mean? Romans 10:13 quotes this phrase from the

OT (Joel 2:32). Peter also quotes this text in Acts 2:21 with extended exposition on Jesus' death and resurrection. As we saw in Luke above, this sermon culminates with "Therefore let the entire house of Israel know with certainty that God has made him both Lord and Messiah, this Jesus whom you crucified" (2:36). God is Lord, Jesus is Lord, and "the Lord is the Spirit" (2 Cor 3:17). Bauckham's well-argued thesis is this: "'The Father, the Son, and the Holy Spirit' *names* the newly disclosed identity of God, revealed in the story of Jesus the Gospel has told" (emphasis added).[29]

The earliest postresurrection reflection on Jesus presents and proclaims a "high christology" (contra those who puzzle over "How did Jesus become God?"). This is a consistent picture. Bauckham's approach, wisely chosen, is to think not in terms of function and ontology (our modern Western impositions) but in terms of identity. This means that the identity features of God/Lord (YHWH) in the OT are also the identity features of Jesus in the NT. Jesus' identity is described in terms that match God's identity in Israel's Scripture and the NT as well.

In five complementary emphases I set forth key points in Bauckham's and Hurtado's arguments that this high christology is fully monotheistic, with points 2 and 3 my own formulations. The claims made for Jesus do not view Jesus in some rival or independent "God" position. Rather:

1. *God is Creator; Jesus is agent of creation.* This portrayal of Jesus appears in six NT Scriptures: John 1:1-5; Col 1:15-17; 1 Cor 8:6; Heb 1:2-3, 10-12; Rev 3:14 (here Jesus Christ is the *origin* of creation). The Colossians text merits quotation (I include verses 18-20 also because they speak of both mission and peace):

> He [Jesus Christ] is the image of the invisible God, the firstborn of all creation; for in him all things in heaven and on earth were created, things visible and invisible,

> whether thrones or dominions or rulers or powers—all things have been created through him and for him. He himself is before all things, and in him all things hold together. He is the head of the body, the church; he is the beginning, the firstborn from the dead, so that he might come to have first place in everything. For in him all the fullness of God was pleased to dwell, and through him God was pleased to reconcile to himself all things, whether on earth or in heaven, by making peace through the blood of his cross.

Although this text does not explicitly mention worship of Jesus, it does present Jesus' identity features in accord with what God does. Jesus participates in God's creation work.[30] He is one with God in both creation and salvation in this text, and thereby worthy of worship.

First Corinthians 8:6 is especially striking because it shows a carefully formulated parallelism between God as creator and Jesus as creator:

> To us there is but one God, the Father,
> of whom are all things, and we in him;
> and one Lord Jesus Christ,
> by whom are all things, and we by him. (KJV)

Paul is responding to a situation of Corinthian believers eating meat sacrificed to idols and participating in pagan temple banquets. His reply is a Christ-filled Shema combined with a version of Rom 11:36. "From him and through him and to him are all things." This verse echoes the well-known Shema: "Hear, O Israel: The Lord our God *is* one Lord" (Deut 6:4 RSV).

Bauckham holds that Paul has arranged the words here in such a way as to produce an affirmation that God the Father–the Lord Jesus Christ is one. He notes also an implicit reference to Christ as Word or Wisdom in Paul's incisive and profound grasp of Jesus the Christ's identification with

YHWH the one God—from the beginning—before the world was created.[31] Remember that Paul is a good Jew, who like Jesus repeats the Shema twice daily, at least.

This interlocking of the Shema's monotheism with the identity of Jesus Christ as included in the one God's identity shows the NT face: Jesus is one with God and God-Jesus is one. The divine identity of Jesus does not compete in any way with robust monotheism. Including Jesus in God's identity as Creator means that Jesus is included within the divine cosmic sovereignty. Further, we might note that this inclusion of Jesus Christ in the divine identity of Creator implicitly affirms Jesus' preexistence, a point that is explicit in John 1:1-4.

2. *God saves, Jesus saves.* This answers my key question: What does "Everyone who calls on the name of the Lord shall be saved" mean? "Calling on the name of the Lord to be saved" can be put straightforwardly: God saves, Jesus saves. "Lord" is used to denote God as especially revealed to Moses (Exod 3:13-15; 6:2b). "Lord" in its YHWH identity and Jesus identity[32] is savior, redeemer, deliverer, and protector from evil. "Healer" also describes this saving, delivering activity.

Throughout the OT the major portrait of God is God's saving deeds for Israel. This is the core of the salvation-history (*Heilsgeschichte*). Jesus delivers us from the powers of evil. Jesus casts out demons. Jesus saves us from our sins, through his compassion and forgiveness (a mark of divine identity) and restores us to right relationship with God. Paul's mission is to proclaim this gospel of salvation to the whole world (Rom 1:15-17).

Similarly, John's portrayal of Jesus' work as God's work dominates the discourses in John 5; 7; and 8. Jesus' prayer in John 17 also shows the inseparable identity of Jesus and God. Interdependence and reciprocity of love mark the Father and the Son in John. Further, the relation is one of "mutual indwelling": the Father in the Son and the Son in the Father. Into this mutual divine indwelling, Jesus calls believers also, so that they may be one even as Jesus and the Father are one (17:21, 23). Divine love flows from the Father and Son in self-donation on the cross, for the life of the world (6:51).

3. *God of peace; Jesus Christ is our peace.* One of my students observed from study of my book *Covenant of Peace* that Paul's contribution in identifying God as "God of peace" seven times, together with identifying Jesus Christ as our peace (several times in Eph 2:14-18 and implicit elsewhere), is another pillar for this portrait of including Jesus in the identity of God (see n. 31). Jesus' birth evokes the messianic hope for "peace on earth" (Luke 2:14). Acts 10:36 sums up Jesus' work as "preaching the gospel of peace." The phrase stems from Isa 52:7 (cf. Nah 1:15): "How beautiful upon the mountain are the feet of the messenger who brings good news, who announces" the good news (gospel) of "peace" (on Isa 52:7 see chap. 9 above). Jesus' seventh Beatitude, "Blessed are the peacemakers, for they will be called children of God," makes the same identity link between Jesus and God. This is affirmed again in Matt 5:45, where those who obey Jesus' command to love enemies show their identity as children of God.

4. *Humiliation and exaltation characterize God/YHWH's and Jesus' means to save.* Bauckham puts in parallel the texts of Phil 2:6-11 and Isa 52:13–53:12; 45:22-23. Note the two stages: humiliation and exaltation, in both the Paul and Isaiah texts (where it is the Servant of the Lord who *pours himself out*, etc.).[33]

As noted in John's Gospel, these two stages are fused in the double meaning of "lift up": Jesus' suffering on the cross and glorification through the giving of his life for the life of the world. The glorified/exalted aspect of Jesus' identity is ascribed in John also through the frequent use of "I AM," with parallels to God's self-claim in Isa 40–55: "I am God/the Lord; there is no other," "I am . . . " (at least seven times in Isa 40–55 and nine times in John).

Textual Demonstration

Philippians 2:6-11 (Bauckham's trans.)	Isaiah 52–53; 45
[Christ Jesus], though he was in the form of God, did not regard equality with God as something to be used for his own advantage,	
but *poured himself out,* taking the *form* of a slave, being born in human *likeness;* and being found in human *form,* he *humiliated* himself, becoming obedient *to the point of accepting death—*	53:12: because he poured himself out . . . (52:14; 53:2: form . . . appearance) (53:7: he was brought low)
even death on a cross.	53:12: . . . to death.
Therefore also God *exalted him to the highest place* and conferred on him the Name that is above every name,	53:12: Therefore . . . . 52:13: he shall be exalted and lifted up and shall be very high.
[10]so that at the name of Jesus *every knee should bend,* in heaven and on earth and under the earth, [11]*and every tongue should acknowledge* that Jesus Christ is Lord, to the glory of God the Father.	45:22-23: Turn to me and be saved, all the ends of the earth! For I am God, and there is no other. By myself I have sworn, from my mouth has gone forth in righteousness a word that shall not return: "To me every knee shall bow, every tongue shall swear."[34]

A similar parallel in Revelation is striking. The Seer's vision grasps humiliation and enthronement in one image: "humiliation" in the image of the slain "Lamb" (Isa 53:7//Rev 5:6; "Lamb" denotes Jesus 28 times in Revelation) *and* the enthroned "Lamb" (5:13). The parallel use of "the Alpha and the Omega" as identities for God (1:8) and Jesus (22:13) is also striking. Thus:

5. *God and Jesus are worthy of worship*. Bauckham mentions this point but does not develop it. Here recall Matthew's inclusio in which worship of Jesus is explicit, early from the Magi, and later (chap. 28) from the disciples, first female[35] and then male. According to Matthew, Luke, John, and Paul, early Christians worshipped Jesus.[36] In Revelation, both God and the Lamb share the throne and receive worship. Further, worship of Jesus is early, as attested in the pre-Pauline hymn of Phil 2:6-11 and the preserved Aramaic *Marana tha*, "Our Lord, come" (1 Cor 16:22b; cf. Rev 22:20). The Aramaic testifies that this address to Jesus, a prayer-shout, originated with Aramaic, likely Palestinian, Christians.

This fivefold portrait of Jesus' identity is the lens to see Jesus' inclusion into God's identity: "'The Father, the Son, and the Holy Spirit' names the newly disclosed identity of God, revealed in the story of Jesus the Gospel has told."[37]

Hurtado's approach emphasizes "devotion to Jesus" and often appeals to christological titles to enhance his key points that early Christians engaged in devotional practices, with Jesus as recipient. He enumerates six:

> (1) hymns about Jesus sung as part of early Christian worship; (2) prayer to God "through" Jesus and in Jesus' name, and even direct prayer to Jesus himself, particularly the invocation of Jesus in the corporate worship setting; (3) "calling upon the name of Jesus," particularly in Christian baptism and in healing and exorcism; (4) the Christian common meal enacted as a sacred meal where the risen Jesus presides as "Lord" of the gathered community; (5) the practice of ritually "confessing" Jesus in the context of Christian worship; and (6) Christian prophecy as oracles of the risen Jesus, and the Holy Spirit of prophecy understood as also the Spirit of Jesus.[38]

Although Hurtado speaks briefly about the political consequences of regarding Jesus as Lord in the context of imperial claims to deity and lordship over all its citizens and slaves,[39] that conflict is pervasive in almost all the NT writings, as I emphasize in *Covenant of Peace*: in Matthew, Mark, Luke-Acts, Paul, Pastorals, John, 1 Peter, Revelation.[40]

In this respect the early church's mission, peacemaking, and worship of Jesus are deeply intertwined. Living for Jesus meant finding wisdom and strength not to bow to Caesar but to witness boldly before authorities, be subject but not necessarily obedient, and to put one's hope not in the empire but in heavenly citizenship, where and when Jesus' lordship will be manifest and uncontested. Dying for Jesus meant risking and experiencing martyrdom, refusing to give even "a pinch of incense to the Emperor in worship," as Peter Davids put it.[41]

William R. Farmer rightly proposes that the books that made it into the canon did so because they nurtured and empowered Christians amid suffering. It is striking how prominent that theme is in virtually all the NT writings.[42] Noting the correlation between emerging lists of books and persecution in several early "canon-type" listings, Farmer concludes: "That the reality of Christian martyrdom in the early church and the selection of Christian writings for the NT canon stand in some vital relationship to one another is as certain as anything that can be conjectured on this complex historical question."[43] Revelation (see next chapter) is a shining example.

Conclusion

What does "calling on the name of the Lord mean"? It means worship of the Lord—God, yes, *and* Jesus Christ. For Jesus is Prophet-Servant, Messiah, Savior, Son of humanity, Son of God, and Lord. In his lordship, peace, mission, and worship are inextricable. The Portuguese praise song "Cantai ao Senhor" makes the point well. Each of four stanzas speaks an aspect of praise, each repeated three times: "O Sing to the Lord,

O sing God a new song, O sing to the Lord"; then, "By his holy power the Lord has done wonders"; third, "So dance for the Lord and blow all the trumpets"; and fourth, "O shout to the Lord, who gave us the Spirit." A fifth stanza then declares, "For Jesus is Lord! Amen! Alleluia!" I recently sang this praise song with gusto, for it affirms Jesus is Lord, whom we praise in worship. Thanks be to God!

A Christian Pledge of Allegiance

I pledge allegiance to Jesus Christ,
And to God's kingdom for which he died—
One Spirit-led people the world over,
Called to peace, mission, and worship of
God—Jesus Christ,
In Spirit and Truth,
Indivisible,
With love and justice for all.[*]

[*] To catch the emphasis of this chapter, I have added several additional lines to the pledge proposed by J. Nelson Kraybill and June Alliman Yoder, *The Mennonite*, August 3, 2004, 11.

CHAPTER ELEVEN

Revelation: A Worship Service of Peace and Mission

The blood of the martyrs is the seed of the church.
—Tertullian, *Apology* 50

Revelation, a vision received "on the Lord's day" (1:10), is a rich resource for worship. The many hymns in Revelation climax the respective visions of judgment. In this service they are "choirs" of praise. Revelation was written in political circumstances of persecution and/or threatened persecution. The word "peace" is used only twice, first in the introit, also a salutation (1:4). Its second use is in 6:4, where as the apocalyptic chaos begins, peace is taken from the earth. The community endures in faith through its perseverance and its fervency in worship of God Almighty and the Lamb. This is the church's faith-resistance to the idolatry of the emperor deity cult. The community of faith does not presently experience shalom in its fullest sense. But the great hymns of worship that punctuate the vision of Revelation proclaim the triumph of God's shalom. This triumph is also the consummation of the church's mission, in which people from every tribe and nation join in majestic praise to God and the Lamb for victory over evil. The singing saints worship God and the Lamb on the throne! "Throne" is used forty-six times; "Lamb" appears twenty-eight times and is the main identity-mark of Jesus Christ in Revelation.[1]

The worship resource below is taken directly from the book of Revelation. It works well for a presentation of forty-five minutes to an hour. It needs eight people, each with a copy of the service, to assist the worship leader, who carries the part of John. These are a narrator, two people for angel voices (male and female), two voices for elders (male and female), the voice of Jesus, the voice of God, and a voice designated simply in the text as voice or loud voice. A trumpeter, if available, might sound forth at several crucial places in the drama. The two elders and two angels fall down and worship where the text indicates. Select a person to lead the congregational hymns (a full choir could be used for specific sections from *The Messiah* oratio at the appropriate places).

John is the leader throughout this worship drama. The congregation can be divided into creatures, elders, or angels, either by seating arrangement or by selected clues. The leader, John, signals by raised hand and number of fingers: one for creatures; two for elders; three for angels; and five (open hand) for all at the appropriate time for "repeating" what he says. When the worship leader (John) raises an open hand, the creatures, elders, and angels respond together. The form of response is lining out, in which the leader delivers a brief line, and the respective group repeats it immediately after the leader. The worship leader (John) reads the brief line first (each / means stop); the respective group (note number in left margin) repeats it immediately. The leader gives the intonation and the vitality.

This service might be done on a regular basis in the congregation, at the same time each year to celebrate a given event within the Christian calendar. It is a fitting celebration for the Easter season or the Fourth of July, when as believers in the United States we loyally reaffirm our allegiance to Jesus as our Lord.

The Service of Worship

The text of Revelation is based on the NRSV with occasional wording from RSV, NIV, or my own translation.

Narrator: The revelation of Jesus Christ, which God gave to John to show God's servants what must soon take place; God made it known by sending an angel to God's servant John, who testified to the word of God and to the testimony of Jesus Christ, even to all that he saw.
Blessed is the one who reads aloud the words of the prophecy. (1:1-3a)

John or Choir of eight: *Processional* [chanted by participants as they walk to the front]:

Grace to you and peace from God
  who is and who was and who is to come.
"I am the Alpha and the Omega,"
  says the Lord God,
who is and who was and who is to come,
  the Almighty. (1:4b, 8)

John: I, John, your brother who share with you in Jesus the persecution and the kingdom and the patient endurance, was on the island called Patmos because of the word of God and the testimony of Jesus.
I was in the spirit on the Lord's day, and I heard behind me a loud voice like a trumpet saying, (1:9-10)

Voice: "Write in a book what you see and send it to the seven churches." (1:11a)

John: Then I turned to see whose voice it was that spoke to me, and on turning I saw seven golden lampstands, and in the midst of the lampstands I saw one like the Son of Man, clothed with a long robe and with a golden sash across his chest. His head and his hair were white as white wool, white as snow; his eyes were like a flame of fire, his feet were like burnished bronze, refined as in a furnace, and his voice was like the sound of many waters. In his right hand he held seven stars, and from his mouth came a sharp, two-edged sword, and his face was like the sun shining with full force. When I saw him, I fell at his feet as though dead. But he placed his right hand on me, saying, (1:12-17b)

Voice of Jesus: "Do not be afraid; I am the first and the last, and the living one.
I was dead, and see, I am alive forever and ever;
and I have the keys of Death and of Hades.
Now write what you have seen, what is, and what is to take place after this.
As for the mystery of the seven stars that you saw in my right hand,
and the seven golden lampstands:
the seven stars are the angels of the seven churches,
and the seven lampstands are the seven churches." (1:17c-20)

Act I

[*To keep the service to 45 minutes I've omitted several churches: Pergamum, Thyatira, and Sardis. For a longer service, these may be added, read from your Bible.*
If so, I suggest that you ask another person to share reading, alternating voices with the churches.]

Narrator: In Act I the glorified Jesus addresses the seven churches (chaps. 2–3). The exiled apostle hears the message of the revealed Jesus to the seven churches. Each message is a call to faithfulness and perseverance in the faith. Each call and admonition ends with a promise.

John: To the angel of the church in Ephesus, write: "I know your works, your toil, and your patient endurance, I know that you cannot tolerate evildoers; . . . I also know that you are enduring patiently and bearing up for the sake of my name, and that you have not grown weary. But I have this against you, that you have abandoned the love you had at first. Unless you repent, I will remove your lampstand. Yet this is to your credit: you hate the works of the Nicolaitans, which I also hate. Let anyone who has an ear listen to what the Spirit is saying to the churches. To everyone who conquers, I will grant to eat of the tree of life that is in the paradise of God." (2:2-7)

To the angel of the church in Smyrna, write: "I know your affliction and your poverty, even though you are rich. . . . Do not fear what you are about to suffer. Beware, the devil is about to throw some of you into prison so that you may be tested. . . . Be faithful until death, and I will give you the crown of life. Let anyone who has an ear listen to what the Spirit is saying to the churches. Whoever conquers will not be harmed by the second death." (2:9-11).

To the angel of the church in Philadelphia, write: . . . "Look, I have set before you an open door, which no one is able to shut. I know that you have but little power, and yet you have kept my word and have not denied my name. I will make those of the synagogue of Satan . . . come and bow down before your feet, and they will learn that I have loved you. Because you have kept my word of patient endurance, I will keep you from the hour of trial that is coming on the whole world to test the inhabitants of the earth. I am coming soon; hold fast to what you have, so that no one may seize your crown. If you conquer, I will make you a pillar in the temple of my God; you will never go out of it. I will write on you the name of my God, and the name of the city of my God, the new Jerusalem that comes down from my God out of heaven, and my own new name. Let anyone who has an ear listen to what the Spirit is saying to the churches." (3:7-114)

To the angel of the church in Laodicea, write: . . . "I know your works; you are neither cold nor hot. I wish that you were either cold or hot. So, because you are lukewarm, and neither cold nor hot, I am about to spit you out of my mouth. For you say, 'I am rich, I have prospered, and I need nothing.' You do not realize that you are wretched, pitiable, poor, blind, and naked. Therefore I counsel you to buy from me gold refined by fire so that you may be rich; and white robes to clothe you and to keep the shame of your nakedness from being seen; and salve to anoint your eyes so that you may see. I reprove and discipline those whom I love. Be earnest, therefore, and repent. Listen! I am standing at the door, knocking; if you hear my voice and open the door, I will come in to you and eat with you, and you with me. To the one who conquers I will give a place with me on my throne, just as I myself conquered and sat down with my Father on his throne. Let anyone who has an ear listen to what the Spirit is saying to the churches." (3:14-22)

Pause (before chap. 4)

After this I looked, and there, in heaven a door stood open! And the first voice, which I had heard speaking to me like a trumpet, said, (4:1a)

Voice: "Come up here, and I will show you what must take place after this." (4:1b)

Trumpet:

John: At once I was in the spirit, and there in heaven stood a throne, with one seated on the throne! And the one seated there looks like jasper and carnelian, and around the throne is a rainbow that looks like an emerald. Around the throne are twenty-four thrones, and seated on the thrones are twenty-four elders, dressed in white robes, with golden crowns on their heads. Coming from the throne are flashes of lightning, and rumblings and peals of thunder, and in front of the throne burn seven flaming torches, which are the seven spirits of God; and in front of the throne there is something like a sea of glass, like crystal.

Around the throne, and on each side of the throne, are four living creatures, full of eyes in front and behind: the first living creature like a lion, the second living creature like an ox, the third living creature with a face like a human face, and the fourth living creature like a flying eagle. And the four living creatures, each of them with six wings, are full of eyes all around and inside. Day and night without ceasing they sing, (4:2-8a)

1: "Holy, holy, holy, / the Lord God the Almighty, /
who was and is / and is to come!" (4:8b)

John: And whenever the four living creatures give glory and honor and thanks to the one who is seated on the throne, who lives for ever and ever, the twenty-four *elders fall down* before the one who is seated on the throne and *worship* the one who lives for ever and ever; they cast their crowns before the throne, singing, (4:9-10)

2: "You are worthy, our Lord and God /
to receive glory / and honor and power, /
for you created all things, /
and by your will they were created and have their being." (4:11)

Act II

Narrator: In Act II the slain Lamb appears as the One who holds the destiny of history. (5:1-14)
We now worship the one who emerges from the right hand of the One seated on the throne, the One worthy to open the scroll.

John: Then I saw in the right hand of the one seated on the throne a scroll written on the inside and on the back, sealed with seven seals; and I saw a mighty angel proclaiming with a loud voice (5:1-2a),

Angel voice: "Who is worthy to open the scroll and break its seals?" (5:2b)

John: And no one in heaven or on earth or under the earth was able to open the scroll or to look into it. And I began to weep bitterly because no one was found worthy to open the scroll or to look into it.

Then one of the elders said to me, (5:3-5a)

Elder voice: "Do not weep.
See, the Lion of the tribe of Judah, the Root of David, has conquered,
so that he can open the scroll and its seven seals." (5:5b)

John: Then I saw between the throne and the four living creatures and among the elders a Lamb standing as if it had been slain, having seven horns and seven eyes, which are the seven spirits of God sent out into all the earth. He went and took the scroll from the right hand of the one who was seated on the throne.
When he had taken the scroll, the four living creatures and the twenty-four elders fell before the Lamb, each holding a harp and golden bowls full of incense, which are the prayers of the saints. They sing a new song, (5:6-9a)

1 and 2: "You are worthy to take the scroll /
and to open its seals, /
because you were slain /
and by your blood
you redeemed people for God /
from every tribe and language /

and people and nation /
    and you made them a kingdom /
and priests serving our God, /
    and they shall reign on earth." (5:9b-10)

John: Then I looked, and I heard around the throne and the living creatures and the elders the voice of many angels, numbering myriads of myriads and thousands of thousands, saying with a loud voice, (5:11-12a)

3: Worthy is the Lamb who was slain /
    to receive power / and wealth and wisdom / and might and honor / and glory and blessing!" (5:12b)

John: And I heard every creature in heaven and on earth and under the earth and in the sea, and all that is in them, singing, (5:13a)

5: "To the one who is seated on the throne /
and to the Lamb /
    be blessing and honor / and glory and might /
      for ever and ever!" (5:13b)

John: And the four living creatures said, (5:14a)

1: "Amen!"

John: And the *elders fell down and worshiped* (5:14b)

Congregational Hymns:
"Let the Whole Creation Cry," *HWB* #51, verse 1
Or Choir: *The Messiah*, "Worthy Is the Lamb Who Was Slain"

Act III

Narrator: In Act III the martyrs disclose the meaning of history (chaps. 6–7).
As the seven seals are opened, each opened seal describes an aspect of the tribulation of God's saints and martyrs in history. With the fifth seal there is an outcry from the martyrs from under the altar:

Two elder voices: Sovereign Lord, holy and true, how long will it be before you judge and avenge our blood on the inhabitants of earth? (6:10)

John: Then each of them was given a white robe and told to rest a little longer, until the number of their fellow servants and their brothers and sisters who were to be killed as they had been was completed.

I looked, and there came a great earthquake; the sun became black as sackcloth, the full moon became like blood, and the stars of the sky fell to the earth as the fig tree drops its winter fruit when shaken by a gale. The sky vanished like a scroll rolling itself up, and every mountain and island was removed from its place.

Then the kings of the earth and the magnates and the generals and the rich and the powerful, and everyone, slave and free, hid in the caves and among the rocks of the mountains, calling to the mountains and rocks, "Fall on us and hide us from the face of the one seated on the throne and from the wrath of the Lamb; for the great day of their wrath has come, and who is able to stand?"

After this I saw four angels standing at the four corners of the earth, holding back the four winds of the earth so that no wind could blow on earth or sea or against any tree. I saw another angel ascending from the rising of the sun, having the seal of the living God, and he called with a loud voice to the four angels who had been given power to damage earth and sea, saying, (6:12–7:2)

Angel: "Do not damage the earth or the sea or the trees, until we have marked the servants of our God with a seal on their foreheads." (7:3)

John: And I heard the number of those who were sealed, one hundred forty-four thousand, sealed out of every tribe of the people of Israel. (7:4)

[*Pause*]

John: After this I looked, and there was a great multitude that no one could count, from every nation, from all tribes and peoples and languages, standing before the throne and before the Lamb, robed in white, with palm branches in their hands. They cried out in a loud voice, (7:9-10a)

2: "Salvation belongs to our God /
who is seated on the throne, /
and to the Lamb!" (7:10b)

John: And all the angels stood around the throne and around the elders and the four living creatures, and they fell on their faces before the throne and worshiped God, singing, (7:11)

3: "Amen! / Blessing and glory and wisdom /
and thanksgiving and honor /
and power and might /
be to our God for ever and ever! / Amen." (7:12)

John: Then one of the elders addressed me, saying, (7:13a)

Elder (male): "Who are these, robed in white, and where have they come from?" (7:13b)

John: "Sir, you know." (7:14a)

Elders: "These are they who have come out of the great ordeal;
they have washed their robes
and made them white in the blood of the Lamb.
For this reason they are before the throne of God,
and worship him day and night within his temple,
and the one who is seated on the throne will shelter them.

They will hunger no more,
and thirst no more;
the sun will not strike them,
nor any scorching heat;
for the Lamb at the center of the throne will be their shepherd,
and he will guide them to springs of the water of life,
and God will wipe away every tear from their eyes." (7:14b-17)

Act IV

Narrator: In Act IV God is victorious in history: the seven trumpets blow (chaps. 8–11)

John: With the opening of the seventh seal, there is silence in heaven for about half an hour.

Silence [1-3 minutes].

Then seven trumpets are given to the seven angels.

6 blasts: With each trumpet blast, God's battle against evil rages more fiercely and the victory blast sounds stronger.

With the seventh trumpet blast, the victory cry bursts forth in full crescendo.

7th blast:

The seventh angel blew his trumpet, and there were loud voices in heaven, saying, (11:15a)

3: "The kingdom of the world /
has become the kingdom of our Lord /
and of his Christ, / and he shall reign for ever and ever." / (11:15b)

John: Then the twenty-four elders who sit on their thrones before God fell on their faces and worshiped God, singing, (11:16:17a)

2: "We give you thanks, Lord God Almighty, /
who are and who were, /
for you have taken your great power /
and begun to reign. /
The nations raged, but your wrath has come, /
and the time for judging the dead, /
for rewarding your servants, /

the prophets and saints, /
and all who fear your name, /
both small and great, /
and for destroying those who destroy the earth." (11:17-18)

John: Then God's temple in heaven was opened, and the ark of God's covenant was seen within God's temple; and there were flashes of lightning, rumblings, peals of thunder, an earthquake, and heavy hail. (11:19)

Act V

Narrator: In Act V the struggle in history continues; God rescues the Saints (chaps. 12–14; 15:2-4). Another picture of God's combat against evil emerges.

John: A woman clothed with the sun bears a child, whom the dragon seeks to destroy. After warring in heaven, the dragon is cast down to earth, and I heard a loud voice in heaven saying,

Loud Voice: "Now have come the salvation and the power
and the kingdom of our God
and the authority of God's Messiah,
for the accuser of our comrades has been thrown down,
who accuses them day and night before our God.
But they have conquered the accuser by the blood of the Lamb
and by the word of their testimony,
for they did not cling to life even in the face of death.

Rejoice then, you heavens and those who dwell in them!
But woe to the earth and the sea,
for the devil has come down to you with great wrath,
because the devil knows that the time is short!" (12:10-12)

Narrator: The dragon then turns upon the seed of the child, making war on the saints through the beast. The faithful, those who conquer the beast and its image, are delivered. One like the Son of Man appears with a sickle in his hand to gather the harvest and throw the grapes into the great winepress of the wrath of God.
As seven angels with seven plagues dispense the bowls of God's wrath, *the saints*, those who have kept the commandments of God and the faith of Jesus, who have conquered the beast and its image, stood beside a sea of glass with harps of God in their hands. (12:13–15:2)

John: And they sing the song of Moses, the servant of God, and the song of the Lamb, saying, (15:3)

2: "Great and amazing are your deeds, /
Lord God the Almighty! /
Just and true are your ways, /
King of the nations! /
Lord, who will not fear and glorify your name? /
For you alone are holy. /
All nations will come and worship before you, /
for your judgments have been revealed." (15:3b-4)

Act VI

Narrator: In Act VI God judges evil: the seven bowls of wrath are poured out (15:5–18:24)

John: God's wrath is poured out upon the harlot, the city set on seven hills, the great mother of harlots. The angel of the water testifies to the justice of God's judgment:

Angel of Waters: "You are just, O Holy One, /
who are and were, /
for you have judged these things; /
because they shed the blood of saints and prophets, /
you have given them blood to drink. /
It is what they deserve!" (16:5b-6)

John: And I heard the altar respond, (16:7a)

2: "Yes, O Lord God, the Almighty, /
your judgments are true and just!" (16:7)

John: When the sixth angel poured his bowl on the river Euphrates the forces of the unholy trinity, the beast, the dragon, and the false prophet assembled demonic spirits to perform signs and deceive the kings of the whole world, assembled for the great battle at Harmagedon (16:12-16), then the seventh angel poured his bowl into the air, and a loud voice came out of the temple, from the throne, saying, (16:17)

Voice: "It is done!" (16:17d)

John: And there came flashes of lightning, rumblings,

peals of thunder, and a violent earthquake, such as had not occurred since people were upon the earth, so violent was that earthquake. (16:18)

[*Pause*]

John: One of the seven angels showed me the judgment of the great whore seated on many waters, a woman on whose forehead was written, "Babylon the great, mother of . . . earth's abominations. In her, Babylon/Rome, was the blood of the saints and the blood of the witnesses to Jesus. (17:1-6) The angel revealed to me that this woman, i.e., Babylon-Rome with its seven kings, will make war on the Lamb, and the Lamb will conquer them, for he is Lord of lords and King of kings, and those with him are called and chosen and faithful. (17:7, 14) After this I saw another angel coming down from heaven, having great authority; and the earth was made bright with the angel's splendor. The angel called out with a mighty voice: (18:1)

5: "Fallen, fallen is Babylon the great!" /
"Alas! Alas! the great city, /
Babylon, the mighty city! /
For in one hour your judgment has come." /
(18:2b, 10b)

Rejoice over it, O heaven, /
you saints and apostles and prophets! /
For God has given judgment for you against it!"
(18:20)

John: In it was found the blood / of prophets and saints, /
and of all who have been slain on earth."
(18:24)

Act VII

Narrator: In Act VII God's purpose triumphs; a new heaven and new earth appear, and God's dwelling place is with God's people. (chaps. 19–22)

John: After this I heard what seemed to be the loud voice of a great multitude in heaven, saying, (19:1a)

5: "Hallelujah! / Salvation and glory and power /
belong to our God, /
for God's judgments are true and just; /
God has judged the great harlot /
who corrupted the earth with its fornication, /
God has avenged on her the blood of God's servants." (19:1b-2)

John: Once more they cried,

5: "Hallelujah! / The smoke from it
goes up for ever and ever." (19:3)

John: And the twenty-four elders and the four living creatures fell down and worshiped God who is seated on the throne, saying, /

1 and 2: "Amen. Hallelujah!" (19:4)

John: And from the throne came a voice crying,

Angel voice: "Praise our God, all you God's servants,
and all who fear God, small and great." (19:5)

John: Then I heard what seemed to be the voice of a great multitude, like the sound of many waters and like the sound of mighty thunder peals, crying out, (19:6a)

5: "Hallelujah! / For the Lord our God the Almighty reigns. /
Let us rejoice and exult /
and give God the glory, /
for the marriage of the Lamb has come, /
and the Lamb's Bride has made herself ready; / (19:6b-7)

"Hallelujah! / Salvation, / glory /
and power / belong to our God. /

John: And the angel said to me,

Angel voice: "Write this: Blessed are those who are invited to the marriage supper of the Lamb." (19:9)

Communion begins [*optional: will lengthen service*]

Congregational Hymns: *HWB* #121, "Holy God, we praise thy name"
HWB #285, "All hail the power of Jesus' name"

John: The angel who invited us to this marriage supper of the Lamb said to me,

Angel: "These are the true words of God." (19:9d)

John: Then I fell at the angel's feet to worship, but the angel said to me,

Angel: "You must not do that! I am a fellow servant with you and your comrades who hold the testimony of Jesus. *Worship God*. For the testimony of Jesus is the Spirit of prophecy." (19:10)

Loud voice: "Behold, the dwelling of God is with humanity.
God will dwell with them,
and they will be God's people,
    and God will be with them;
God will wipe away every tear from their eyes.
    Death will be no more;
    mourning and crying and pain will be no more,
    for the former things have passed away."
    (21:2b-4)

John: And the one who sat upon the throne said,

God's voice: "Behold, I make all things new."

John: Then the one on the throne said to me,

God's voice: "It is done! I am the Alpha and the Omega,
    the beginning and the end!
To the thirsty I will give water as a gift from the spring of the water of life. Those who conquer will inherit these things, and I will be their God and they will be my children. But as for the cowardly, the faithless, the polluted, the murderers, the fornicators, the sorcerers, the idolaters, and all liars, their place will be in the lake that burns with sulfur, which is the second death." (21:6-8)

John: I saw no temple in the city, for its temple is the Lord God the Almighty and the Lamb. And the city has no need of sun or moon to shine on it, for the glory of God is its light, and its lamp is the Lamb. The nations will walk by its light, and the kings of the earth will bring their glory into it. Its gates will never be shut by day—and there will be no night there. People will bring into it the glory and the honor of the nations. But nothing unclean will enter it, nor anyone who practices abomination or falsehood, but only those who are written in the Lamb's book of life.

Then the angel showed me the river of the water of life, bright as crystal, flowing from the throne of God and of the Lamb through the middle of the street of the city. On either side of the river is the tree of life with its twelve kinds of fruit, producing its fruit each month; and the leaves of the tree are for the healing of the nations. Nothing accursed will be found there any more. But the throne of God and of the Lamb will be in it, and God's servants will worship God; they will see God's face, and God's name will be on their foreheads. And there will be no more night; they need no light of lamp or sun, for the Lord God will be their light, and they will reign forever and ever. (21:22–22:5)

And the angel said to me,

Angels: "These words are trustworthy and true, for the Lord, the God of the spirits of the prophets, has sent God's angel to show God's servants what must soon take place." (22:6)

Jesus' voice: "Behold, I am coming soon."

Angel's voice: "Blessed are those who keep the words of the prophecy of this book."

John: "I John am he who heard and saw these things. And when I heard and saw them, I fell down to worship at the feet of the angel who showed them to me; but the angel said to me, (22:8-9a)

Angel's voice: "You must not do that! I am a fellow servant with you and your comrades the prophets, and with those who keep the words of this book. Worship God."

John: And the angel said to me,

Angel's voice: "Do not seal up the words of the prophecy of this book, for the time is near. Let the evildoer still do evil, and the filthy still be filthy, and the righteous still do right, and the holy still be holy." (22:10)

Jesus' voice: "Behold, I am coming soon, bringing my recompense, to repay every one for what they have done. I am the Alpha and the Omega, the first and the last, the beginning and the end." (22:12)

John: The Spirit and the Bride say, "Come."
And let everyone who hears say, "Come."
Let everyone who is thirsty come,
let those who wish take the water of life as a gift. (22:17)

The one who testifies to these things, says,

Jesus: "Surely, I am coming soon."

Cong.: Amen. Come Lord Jesus.

Antiphon:

John: The grace of the Lord Jesus Christ be with all God's people.

Cong.: Amen.

Antiphon:

John or Choir of eight: *Recessional* [Participants recess, chanting or singing]

"I am the Alpha and the Omega,
the first and the last,
the beginning and the end." (22:13)

Finale

Send forth your light and your truth;
let them lead me;
let them bring me to your holy hill and to your dwelling.

Then I will go to the altar of God,
to God my exceeding joy;
and I will praise you with the harp,
O God, my God.

CONCLUSION

The intertwining of peace and mission is evident in all eleven chapters of this book. Both themes are inherently united also in the biblical understanding of salvation. Perry Yoder has shown that the biblical understanding of shalom is integrally tied to its view of salvation, peace, and justice.[1] Biblically, mission is interconnected as well, in light of God's promise to Abraham to make him a blessing to the nations and the recurring prophetic and Psalms motif that all people shall come to know the name of the Lord. As shown in chapter 9, Isa 52:7-10 links shalom-peace and mission together with the word salvation. This is the gospel to be announced. The church in the last century has separated these emphases: it has done so at its peril.

Worship also is intertwined with peace and mission, as chapters 10 and 11 demonstrate. In chapter 10 I have shown this threefold thematic relationship in all the main NT writings. In Revelation the church's mission is to proclaim through its worship Jesus' lordship in repudiation of Caesar's claims to divine status and imperial demand for worship.

The challenge facing the church in the twenty-first century is to proclaim and live a holistic gospel in which peace, mission, and worship are perceived and valued as interconnected—each mutually supportive of the other. If this does not happen, the church will readily ally itself with the dominant ideology of its time, which in the United States of America includes its imperialism. Mission then inadvertently extends Western culture, decadent as it is. Worship is co-opted to peddle forms of civil religion in which God's power and the country's military might are allied recipients of praise and worship (even though the latter is not acknowledged). In this scenario people of other religions, notably Islam with its varied cultural and national faces, increasingly hate the imperial West—and Christianity indirectly.

Churches that have commingled God and Caesar must repent and renounce syncretistic worship. In this repentance, we will value peacemaking that shows clearly whom we worship: God and the Lamb. In this repentance we will commit to mission that is God-sent, Spirit-empowered, and worship-grounded. Because peace, mission, and worship are interdependent, we will be empowered in our Sunday-to-Sunday worship to recommit to mission and peacemaking.

We now see more clearly that the salvation we profess through Jesus Christ our Lord bears true gospel-fruit in peacemaking, mission, and worship—that each leg of this tripod is ever dependent on the other two.

Sending

Go into the world fired with longing,
to speak of God's saving love
in the words of those who would hear, . . .
to bring healing and hope to those living in despair.

May the God who breathed life into creation delight you;
may Christ Jesus give life to your dreams,
and may the Holy Spirit enflame and empower you
with a passion for peace, [mission, and worship].

Go in the power of the Spirit to love and serve the Lord.*

* From *Leader: Equipping the Missional Church* (Mennonite Publishing Network), Spring 2006, 46; used with permission.

APPENDIX

Anabaptist Basis and Example for Witness to Christ's Lordship over Government

Michael Sattler, from his Trial and Martyrdom Record, addressing the civil authorities (1527)

> Eighthly, if the Turks should come, we ought not to resist them. For it is written [Exod 20:13; Matt 5:21]: Thou shalt not kill. We must not defend ourselves against the Turks and others of our persecutors, but are to beseech God with earnest prayer to repel and resist them. But that I said that, if warring *were* right, I would rather take the field against so-called Christians who persecute, capture, and kill pious Christians than against the Turks was for the following reason. The Turk is a true Turk, knows nothing of the Christian faith, and is a Turk after the flesh. But you who would be Christians and who make your boast of Christ persecute the pious witnesses of Christ and are Turks after the spirit!
>
> In conclusion, ministers of God, I admonish you to consider the end for which God has appointed you, to punish the evil and to defend and protect the pious [Rom 13:3-6]. Whereas, then, we have not acted contrary to God and the gospel, you will find that neither I nor my brethren and sisters have offended in word or deed against any authority.
>
> —From *Spiritual and Anabaptist Writers*[1] (141)

Menno Simons, from *The Complete Writings of Menno Simons*[2]
From *Foundation of Christian Doctrine* (1539), Part III. "Appeals For Toleration," Section A. "Exhortation to the Magistrates"

> Therefore, dear sirs, take heed; this is the task to which you are called: namely, to chastise and punish, in the true fear of God with fairness and Christian discretion, manifest criminals, such as thieves, murderers, Sodomites, adulterers, seducers, sorcerers, the violent, highwaymen, robbers, etc. Your task is to do justice between a man and his neighbor, to deliver the oppressed out of the hand of the oppressor; also to restrain by reasonable means, that is, without tyranny and bloodshed, manifest deceivers who so miserably lead poor helpless souls by hundreds of thousands into destruction. Whether the deceivers are priests, monks, preachers, baptized or unbaptized, it is your task to restrain them so that they may no longer detract from the power of the almighty majesty of God, our only and eternal Saviour, Christ Jesus, the Holy Ghost, and the Word of grace; nor introduce such ridiculous abuses and idolatry under semblance of truth as has been done until now. In this way, in all love, without force, violence, and blood, you may enlarge, help, and protect the kingdom of God with gracious consent and permission, with wise counsel and a pious, unblamable life. . . .
>
> O highly renowned, noble lords, believe Christ's Word, fear God's wrath, love righteousness, do justice to widows and orphans, judge rightly between a man and his neighbor, fear no man's highness, despise no man's littleness, hate all avarice, punish with reason, allow the Word of God to be taught freely, hinder no one from walking in the truth, bow

to the scepter of him who called you to this high service. Then shall your throne stand firm forever. (193)

O my dear sirs, what are you doing? Where in the world is the sword of righteousness, of which you boast, given and entrusted to you? You have to acknowledge that you have put it in the sheath, and in its stead you have drawn the sword of unrighteousness. Yes, dear sirs, men carry on so (may God have pity) that the prophets may well write and exclaim, My princes are rebellious and companions of thieves; everyone loveth gifts, and followeth after rewards: they judge not the fatherless, neither doth the cause of the widow come unto them. Therefore saith the Lord, the Lord of hosts, the Mighty One of Israel, Ah, I will ease me of mine adversaries, and avenge me of mine enemies [Isa 1:23-24]. (196)

Therefore, dear sirs, take heed wisely, rightly to execute your responsible and dangerous office according to the will of God. For alas, I fear that many of you as yet have paid but little attention to it, and as a result Anti-christ with his wickedness is exalted, and Christ with His righteousness is rejected. Ponder if only for once that which is written, Keep thee far from a false matter; and the innocent and righteous slay thou not; for I will not justify the wicked, says the Lord. [Exod 23:7]. (197)

O illustrious, noble lords and princes, be pleased to receive in love and humility the simple, plain, but nevertheless true, instruction of your poor servant. Do not despise that wherewith I have so thoroughly and well meaningly admonished your worthy highnesses.

Do not dwell on my weakness nor on my unlearnedness, but look intently at Christ, his Word, Spirit, and example which I have here set forth and taught in good faith to you and to all men according to my small gift.

Repent sincerely with a repentance acceptable to God, wail and weep with David, put on sackcloth and raiments of hair, scatter ashes upon your head; humble yourselves with the king of Nineveh, confess your sins with Manasseh; die unto your ambitious flesh and pride. Fear the Lord your God with all your powers; judge in all wisdom with fear and trembling; help the oppressed; grieve not the distressed; promote the cause of widows and orphans in their right; protect the good; punish the evil in a Christian manner; perform your God-given duties correctly; seek the kingdom and country that will endure forever; and remember that here on earth you are but pilgrims and sojourners in a strange land, no matter how much held in honor.

Hear, believe, fear, love, serve, and follow your Lord and Saviour, Jesus Christ, for He it is before whom every knee shall bow; God's eternal Word, Wisdom, Truth, and Son. Seek his honor and praise in all your thoughts, words, and actions, and you shall reign forever. (206)

From Section B. "To the Learned Ones"

With this I leave all lords and princes in the Lord's hand together with all the magistracy and rulers below them. (207)

From *The True Christian Faith* (ca. 1541)

Captains, knights, foot soldiers, and similar bloody men risk body and soul for the sake of gain, and swear with uplifted fingers that they are ready to destroy cities and countries, to take citizens and inhabitants, to kill them and take their possessions, although these have never harmed them nor given them so much as an evil word. O God, what cursed, wicked abomination and traffic: And they call that protecting the country and the people, and assisting in justice! (368)

From *A Pathetic Supplication to All Magistrates* (1552)

Be pleased, in godly fear, to ponder what it is that God requires of your Highnesses. It is that without any respect of persons you judge between a man and his neighbor, protect the wronged from him who does him wrong, even as the Lord declares, Execute judgment and justice, Assist, against the violent, him that is robbed, Abuse not the stranger, the widow, the orphan, Do violence to no man, and shed no innocent blood, so that your despised servants and unhappy subjects, having escaped the mouth of the lion, may in your domain and under your paternal care and gracious protection, serve the Lord in quietness and peace, and piously earn their bread, as the Scripture requires. (526)

Noble sirs, we are not joking. Nor do we play with words. What we write we mean from the bottom of our hearts, as our grievous trials, heavy chains, life and limb, testify and declare.

May the great and merciful Lord Jesus, who is a Lord of lords and a King of kings, grant your Noble Highness and Honorable Excellences, altogether rightly to know the truth, faithfully to walk in it, piously to rule your cities and provinces in happy peace, to the praise of your God and the salvation of many souls! This we wish with all our hearts. Amen.

Blessed are the merciful, for they shall obtain mercy [Matt 5:7]. Be merciful even as your Father is merciful.

Verily I say, what you have done to one of the least of my brethren you have done unto me [Matt 25:40].

Your Noble Highnesses and Honorable Excellences' faithful and obedient subjects, which we are able to be by the will of God and through His grace. (530-31)

From *Epistle to Martin Micron* (1556): Menno's word on capital punishment, speaking about rulers and the God-given limits of their authority

> Seven. It is also manifest that you encourage and strengthen the rulers in their impenitent lives not a little by your writing; rulers who are usually quite obdurate, proud, ambitious, puffed up, self-conceited, pompous, selfish, earthly, carnal, and often bloodthirsty. And that you may gain their favor and praise the more therewith I, miserable man, must be your blind and imprisoned Samson as a spectacle and derision, although I never in my life spoke an insulting word against the rulers or against their office and service.
>
> I have from the beginning of my ministry fraternally warned them in my writings in faithful, unadulterated truth from my soul against the destruction of their souls, admonishing them to a godly, penitent, Christian life, pointing them with the Scriptures to the perfect Spirit, Word, commandment, prohibition, ordinance, and example of Christ. And when you proposed your pharisaical, Herod-like question concerning the magistracy, I said nothing more to you than that it would hardly become a true Christian ruler to shed blood. For this reason, If the transgressor should truly repent before his God and be reborn of Him, he would then also be a chosen saint and child of God, a fellow partaker of grace, a spiritual member of the Lord's body, sprinkled with his precious blood and anointed with His Holy Ghost, a living grain of the Bread of Christ and an heir to eternal life; and for such an one to be hanged on the gallows, put on the wheel, placed on the stake, or in any manner be hurt in body or goods by another Christian, who is of one heart, spirit, and soul with him, would look somewhat strange and unbecoming in the light of the compassionate, merciful, kind nature, disposition, spirit, and

example of Christ, the meek Lamb—which example He has commanded all His chosen children to follow.

Again, if he remain impenitent, and his life be taken, one would unmercifully rob him of the time of repentance of which, in case his life were spared, he might yet avail himself. It would be unmerciful to tyrannically offer his poor soul which was purchased with such precious treasure to the devil of hell, under the unbearable judgment, punishment, and wrath of God, so that he would forever have to suffer and bear the tortures of the unquenchable burning, the consuming fire, eternal pain, woe, and death. Never observing that the Son of Man says: Learn of me, I have given you an example, Follow me, I am not come to destroy souls, but to save them. . . .

That the office of the magistrate is of God and His ordinance I freely grant. But him who is a Christian and wants to be one and then does not follow his Prince, Head, and Leader Christ, but covers and clothes his unrighteousness, wickedness, pomp and pride, avarice, plunder, and tyranny with the name of magistrate, I hate. For he who is a Christian must follow the Spirit, Word, and example of Christ, no matter whether he be emperor, king, or whatever he be. For these following admonitions apply to all alike: Let this mind be in you which was also in Christ Jesus [Phil 2:5]. He that saith he abideth in him, ought himself also so to walk, even as he walked [1 John 2:6]. (920-22)

Elsewhere (1043) Menno (in 1555) acknowledges that some crimes are worthy of capital punishment, but he does not thereby justify the art, particularly by magistrates who nominally profess to be Christian.

Conclusion

I doubt that the Anabaptists ever thought of a cleavage between the personal and social dimensions of Christian witness. I do not think they could think in terms of evangelism alone versus social concerns alone. Our wish to dichotomize these two betrays a misunderstanding of the gospel and infidelity to the central proclamation of the Christian faith:

JESUS IS LORD OF ALL

NOTES

Introduction

1. The story of Bill Beck, pastor of Hopewell Mennonite Church, Kouts, Ind., is also salutary. It accentuates the mission aspect of a traditional Mennonite church in welcoming him when he visited the church to hear his Mennonite girlfriend, Sherry, sing, while he was home from basic training. Some years later when his own denomination waffled in what it believed on abortion, he remembered the Mennonites. What he regarded earlier as their weaknesses he now saw as their strength, courage "to withstand scorn and ridicule from members of their [local] community." As he studied the teachings of Jesus and the example of Christ (1 Cor 11:1), he realized that he could not imagine Jesus "in battle-dress uniform." He pondered what Jesus meant in commanding "Love your enemies" and "Turn the other cheek." Finally, he says, "I chose to become a 'real' Mennonite. I intentionally chose the way of Jesus—the way of discipleship and peace." See *Gospel Evangel: A Newsletter of Indiana-Michigan Mennonite Conference*, January/February 2006, 4-5.

1. Shalom-Jubilee: Biblical Call to Peacemaking

1. Claus Westermann, "Peace [*Shalom*] in the Old Testament," in *The Meaning of Peace*, ed. Perry B. Yoder and Willard M. Swartley, rev. ed. (Elkhart, IN: IMS, 2001), 49. For a more extensive treatment of the meaning of *shalom* in the OT, see Willard M. Swartley, *Covenant of Peace: The Missing Peace in New Testament Theology and Ethics* (Grand Rapids: Eerdmans, 2006), 28-34.

2. Kremer, Jacob. "Peace—God's Gift: Biblical-Theological Considerations," in P. Yoder and W. Swartley, *Meaning of Peace*, 21-35.

3. For these contextual concepts of justice/righteousness, see Chris Marshall, *The Little Book of Biblical Justice* (Intercourse, PA: Good Books, 2005), 10-21. I've added "eschatological hope" and the subpoints under "atonement."

4. These emphases appear in John Howard Yoder's *Politics of Jesus*, rev. ed. (Grand Rapids: Eerdmans, 1994), 60-75. I extend these in my study of Luke in *Covenant of Peace*, 137-40.

5. See Willard M. Swartley, "Biblical Sources of Stewardship," in

The Earth Is the Lord's, ed. Mary Evelyn Jegen and Bruno Manno (New York: Paulist Press, 1978), 32-34.

6. José Miranda, *Marx and the Bible: A Critique of the Philosophy of Oppression*, trans. John Eagleson (Maryknoll, NY: Orbis Books, 1974), 93-95.

7. Abraham J. Heschel, *The Prophets* (New York: Harper & Row, 1962), 3-4.

8. See the helpful treatment of justice in Luke by Joseph A. Grassi, *Peace on Earth: Roots and Practices from Luke's Gospel* (Collegeville, MN: Liturgical Press, 2004); W. Swartley, *Covenant of Peace,* 123-44.

9. See W. Swartley, *Covenant of Peace*, 41-42, for discussion.

10. For fuller treatment of "Peace," Hebrew *Shalom* and Greek *Eirene*, see W. Swartley, *Covenant of Peace*, 27-52 (chap. 2), and my article on "Peace" in *The Westminster Theological Wordbook of the Bible*, ed. Donald E. Gowan (Louisville: Westminster John Knox, 2003), 354-60.

11. *Confession of Faith in a Mennonite Perspective*, authorized by the General Board of the General Conference Mennonite Church and the Mennonite Church General Board (Scottdale, PA: Herald Press, 1995).

2. Jesus on Peace and Violence

1. See my work on the formation and structure of the Synoptic Gospels: Willard M. Swartley, *Israel's Scripture Traditions and the Synoptic Gospels: Story Shaping Story* (Peabody, MA: Hendrickson, 1994).

2. William R. Farmer, presenting a minority view persuasive in my judgment, proposes that encouragement in suffering was a characteristic of the books accepted into the canon. This theme appears in virtually all the NT writings: *Jesus and the Gospel: Tradition, Scripture, and Canon* (Philadelphia: Fortress, 1982), 177-221. Showing the correlation between emerging lists of accepted books and persecution, Farmer concludes: "That the reality of Christian martyrdom in the early church and the selection of Christian writings for the New Testament canon stand in some vital relationship to one another is as certain as anything that can be conjectured on this complex historical question" (221). See also Farmer and Denis M. Farkasfalvy, *The Formation of the New Testament Canon: An Ecumenical Approach* (New York: Paulist, 1983), 7-95.

3. W. Swartley, *Covenant of Peace*, makes this point in greater detail.

4. Donald B. Kraybill, *The Upside-Down Kingdom*, rev. 3rd ed. (Scottdale, PA: Herald Press, 2003).

5. These people are called "church" (*ekklesia*) in Matt 16:16-19. The local city (*polis*) assembly was called by the same name. Jesus' new community was thus an alternate, in many ways a contrast, community to the dominant society in the broader culture.

6. The statement in Matt 5:43, "It was said, . . . 'Hate your enemy,'" is controversial for nowhere does Jewish Scripture make that point. It occurs in the Dead Sea Scrolls, and it may have been a practical version of some of the Psalm texts that speak about hatred of enemies, as in Ps 139:19-22.

7. Ulrich Mauser, *The Gospel of Peace*, SPS 1 (Louisville: Westminster/John Knox, 1992), 36.

8. For this reason it is certainly an authentic word of Jesus, even by analysis of critical scholars in the well-known Jesus Seminar group.

9. For the etching, titled "Dirk Willems Saving His Captor's Life," see p. 72.

10. William Klassen, "The Novel Element in the Love Commandment of Jesus," in *The New Way of Jesus*, ed. William Klassen (Newton, KS: Faith & Life Press, 1980), 100-14, esp. 110.

11. Ibid., 111.

12. David Flusser, *Jesus* (Jerusalem: Magnes Press. 1998), 88.

13. The literature is vast on the love commands generally. See Victor Paul Furnish's good study, *The Love Command in the New Testament* (Nashville: Abingdon, 1972).

14. Marius Reiser, "Love of Enemies in the Context of Antiquity," *NTS* 47 (2001): 411-27.

15. Gordon Zerbe, *Non-retaliation in Early Jewish and New Testament Texts: Ethical Themes in Social Context*, Journal for the Study of the Pseudepigrapha: Supplement Series 13 (Sheffield: JSOT Press, 1993), 171-72. For fuller reporting and analysis of this helpful work, see my review, *Critical Review* (1995): 328-30; or *MQR* 69 (July 1995): 410-12. Flusser's position above concurs with Reiser and Zerbe.

16. Alan Kirk, "'Love Your Enemies, the Golden Rule, and Ancient Reciprocity," *JBL* 122 (2003): 677-86.

17. Several collections of peace stories show how nonresistant love expresses itself in positive actions toward enemies, how Jesus' peace children live out their calling; Elizabeth Hershberger Bauman, *Coals of Fire* (Scottdale, PA: Herald Press, 1954); Cornelia Lehn, *Peace Be with You* (Newton. KS: Faith & Life Press, 1980). Both collections of stories, written for children, are also instructive to adults. A wider set of stories and cases is presented more recently by Eileen Egan, *Peace Be with You: Justified Warfare or the Way of Nonviolence* (Maryknoll, NY: Orbis Books, 1999).

18. Klassen, "Love Your Enemy: A Study of New Testament Teaching on Coping with the Enemy," in *Biblical Realism Confronts the Nation*, ed. Paul Peachey (Scottdale, PA: Herald Press distributing for Church Peace Mission / Fellowship Publications, 1963), 162-68. Klassen also shows how Paul in Rom 12–13 applies this teaching to the

Christian's relationship to political power. The themes of *love* and the *good* "are intimately interwoven." "*Agape* love is transparent in its rejection of the evil, and in its alignment with *to agathon* (the good, 12:9)." This perspective guides the argument of 13:1-7, in which the authority's function is to approve the good (170-71).

19. John Ferguson, *The Politics of Love: The New Testament and Non-violent Revolution* (Greenwood, SC: Attic Press. n.d.), 4-5. Clarence Bauman, late AMBS professor and specialist in Sermon on the Mount studies, also proposes "Do not resist by (with) evil" as the better translation of the Greek text. See Clarence Bauman, "Response to Moltmann's 'The Lutheran Doctrine of the Two Kingdoms and Its Use Today,'" in *Politics of Discipleship and Discipleship in Politics: Jürgen Moltmann Lectures in Dialogue with Mennonite Scholars*, ed. Willard M. Swartley (Eugene, OR: Cascade Books / Wipf & Stock, 2006), 88-89. This translation proposal is significant, for it eliminates the key NT textual basis supporting a passive response to evil.

20. Guy F. Hershberger, *War, Peace, and Nonresistance* (Scottdale, PA: Herald Press, 1953), 50-60. John E. Lapp's manual *Studies in Nonresistance: An Outline for Study and Reference* (Scottdale, PA: Peace Problems Committee of the Mennonite General Conference, 1948) also illustrates this point. See also the Mennonite statement in Donald F. Durnbaugh, ed., *On Earth Peace: Discussions on War/Peace Issues Between Friends, Mennonites, Brethren, and European Churches, 1935-1975* (Elgin, IL: Brethren Press, 1978), 50.

21. Walter Wink, "Neither Passivity nor Violence: Jesus' Third Way," *SBL 1988 Seminar Papers* (Atlanta: Scholars Press, 1988), 24. Also in his revised version of this essay, in *Love of Enemy and Nonretaliation in the New Testament*, ed. Willard M. Swartley (Louisville: Westminster/John Knox, 1992), 107.

22. Wink, "Neither Passivity nor Violence," in W. Swartley, *Love of Enemy*, 104-11.

23. For fuller evaluation of Wink, see Swartley, *Covenant of Peace*, 64.

24. Luise Schottroff, "'Give to Caesar What Belongs to Caesar and to God What Belongs to God': A Theological Response of the Early Christian Church to Its Social and Political Environment," in W. Swartley, *Love of Enemy*, 223-57, esp. 232. She correlates this teaching with Paul's in Romans under the topic "Make Room for God's Wrath: Romans 12:14-21" and takes up a study of Rom 13:1-7. She presents a persuasive case that Matt 5:38-48 and Rom 12–13 are entirely compatible and represent a consistent pattern of early Christian response to evil (similar emphases occur in 1 Peter).

25. John Paul Lederach, *Journey Toward Peacemaking* (Scottdale, PA: Herald Press, 1999), 25-44.

26. John Howard Yoder, "The Way of the Peacemaker," in *Peacemakers in a Broken World*, ed. John A. Lapp (Scottdale, PA: Herald Press, 1969), 116-18. Ferguson says that the Greek word *teleios* may mean (1) "perfect," (2) "all-embracing," (3) "absolute," and/or (4) "mature." All shades of meaning should be included here (*Politics of Love*, 5-6).

27. Ronald J. Sider, *Christ and Violence* (Scottdale, PA: Herald Press, 1979), 26.

28. Ibid., 27, 32ff.

29. C. H. C. Macgregor, *The New Testament Basis of Christian Pacifism* (Nyack, NY: Fellowship Publications, 1954), 32-33. See p. 108 for his collections of verses on the love ethic. Culbert G. Rutenber in *The Dagger and the Cross: An Examination of Pacifism* (Nyack, NY: Fellowship Publications, 1950) similarly connects the love command to God's love in Christ: "This love can never be mere vague goodwill, or absence of a will-to-harm. It is always as positive and outgoing as the love of God himself. . . . This is not a passive principle of supine submission, but the active effort to express the divine love by seeking the enemies' good" (37-38).

30. Gordon D. Kaufman, "Nonresistance and Responsibility," in *Nonresistance and Responsibility, and Other Mennonite Essays* (Newton, KS: Faith & Life Press, 1979), 64-78, esp. 65. In his volume's next essay, "Christian Decision Making," Kaufman proposes four considerations that inform how one decides on such a matter as participation in war. These are justice, promises, and commitments we have made, together with the role one plays in society, redemptive love for the sinner, and the knowledge of oneself as sinner (86-91). After observing that justice may conflict with redemptive love, Kaufman argues for the moral and religious right of Mennonites as a "believers church" subcommunity to hold its position of nonparticipation in war (91-98).

31. Elsewhere I have written more extensively on this section: *Mark: The Way for All Nations* (Eugene, OR: Cascade Books / Wipf & Stock, 2000), chaps. 7–8; idem, *Israel's Scripture Traditions*, 98-102, 111-15; and "Discipleship and Imitation," in *Violence Renounced: René Girard, Biblical Studies, and Peacemaking*, ed. Willard M. Swartley (Telford, PA: Pandora Press; Scottdale, PA: Herald Press, 2000), 230-34.

32. In John 6:15, Jesus fed the multitude of 5,000; the crowd wanted to make Jesus king by force, but he escaped through their midst.

33. Richard B. Hays, *The Moral Vision of the New Testament* (HarperSanFrancisco, 1996), 333. Hays also comments on other texts often used to support violence: Jesus' cleansing of the temple and soldiers in the NT. He rightly argues that neither provides normative moral guidance (334-36).

34. Jean Lasserre, *War and the Gospel*, trans. Oliver Coburn (Scottdale, PA: Herald Press, 1962), 65-66.

35. Jesus overcame the third temptation (Matt 4:8-10), rejected Peter's view of messiahship (Mark 8:27-33), refused to call down fire upon the Samaritans (Luke 9:51-55), entered Jerusalem on a donkey (Matt 21:1-9); and commanded Peter to sheathe the sword (John 18:10-11), on which Rev 13:10 makes the same point. See Ferguson, *Politics of Love*, 24-26.

36. Ibid., 26.

37. Rutenber, *Dagger and the Cross*, 47.

38. Jesus' cleansing of the temple is often misused as a biblical argument to support the Christian's use of violence in war. Jesus' action was thoroughly prophetic, depending on the power of the word. Even though some translations of John 2:15 portray Jesus using the whip of cords against people, an alternative exegesis (reflected in NIV, NEB, GNB) takes the phrase "with the sheep and oxen" to be explanatory of the "all" (*pantas*) that Jesus drove out with a whip. Verse 16 supports this interpretation in saying that Jesus, after driving *all* out, spoke to those who had been selling the pigeons.

39. For alternative exegesis see Swartley, *Covenant of Peace*, 112, n. 44.

40. Donald Senior, *Matthew,* Abingdon NT Commentaries (Nashville: Abingdon, 1998), 31.

41. For further study of this matter, see W. Swartley, *Covenant of Peace*, 68-72, esp. n. 52. Jesus' parables in Matthew depicting final judgment with violent retributive imagery are also problematic. Does this undermine his portrayal of God's mercy in 5:45? As humans we must leave judgment to God, for only God can do what both justice and mercy require. For scholarly treatment of this dilemma, see David J. Neville, "Toward a Teleology of Peace: Contesting Matthew's Violent Eschatology," *JSNT* 70 (2007) forthcoming.

42. An excellent "Litany of Repentance" with a plea for forgiveness is No. 691 in *HWB*. The litany comes from *Adventurous Future*, ed. Paul H. Bowman (Elgin, IL: Brethren Press, 1959).

43. J. R. Burkholder, "The Politics of Jesus," in *A Peace Reader*, ed. E. Morris Sider and Luke Keefer Jr. (Nappanee, IN: Evangel Press, 2002), 37. J. R. Burkholder here reflects on J. H. Yoder's *Politics of Jesus*. The Sider and Keefer book describes well the pacifist perspective. It includes two chapters on the OT, four on the NT, and numerous chapters on church historical and contemporary practical perspectives. Two other similar important books recently published are Dale W. Brown, *Biblical Pacifism*, rev. ed. (Nappanee, IN: Evangel Publishing House; Scottdale, PA: Herald Press, 2003); and John D. Roth,

Choosing Against War: A Christian View; A Love Stronger Than Our Fears (Intercourse, PA: Good Books, 2002).

3. Paul on Peacemaking

1. William Klassen, "Pursue Peace: A Concrete Ethical Mandate (Romans 12:18-21)," in *Ja und Nein: Christliche Theologie im Angesicht Israels* (FS Wolfgang Schrage), ed. Klaus Wengst and Gerhard Sass (Neukirchen-Vluyn: Neukirchner Verlag, 1998), 195-207. Diagram used with permission.

2. See W. Swartley, *Covenant of Peace*, 208-11, for discussion of the import of this appellation, and n. 52 for sources contributing to the discussion. Here I mention only Mauser, *Gospel of Peace*, 105-9.

3. The text here reads: "Each of you speak truth clearly to his neighbor, and do not fall into wrath and troublemaking, but be at peace, holding to the God of peace. Thus no conflict will overwhelm you."

4. The occurrence in Heb 13:20 is also in a benediction.

5. Mauser, *Gospel of Peace*, 105. In the manuscript form of his book (133), Mauser identified also "the Lord/God of wisdom" (*1 Enoch* 63:2; Josephus, *Jewish Antiquities* 11.64 [11.6.11]) and "the Lord/God of righteousness" (1QM 18.8; Tob 13:6).

6. See Num 6:24-26. Paul frequently uses "grace" (*charis*) with "peace" in his salutations. For discussion of its origins, see Mauser, *Gospel of Peace*, 107-8. John E. Toews regards the "grace and peace" salutation as "a specifically Pauline creation"; *Romans*, BCBC (Scottdale, PA: Herald Press, 2004), 42.

7. Mauser, *Gospel of Peace*, 106.

8. Whether the text should read "We have peace" (indicative) or "Let us have peace" (hortatory subjunctive), reflecting a textual variant, is discussed well and fully by Erich Dinkler, "*Eirēnē*—the Early Christian Concept of Peace," in P. Yoder and W. Swartley, *Meaning of Peace*, 99-101 (cf. Westminster/John Knox, 1992 ed., 182-83); see nn. 108-10.

9. Krister Stendahl, *Paul Among Jew and Gentile* (Philadelphia: Fortress, 1976), 1-40.

10. J. H. Yoder, *Politics of Jesus* (Grand Rapids: Eerdmans, 1972), 231-32; rev. ed. (1994), 226.

11. Perry B. Yoder, *Shalom: The Bible's Word for Salvation, Peace, and Justice* (Newton, KS: Faith & Life Press, 1988; repr., Nappanee, IN: Evangel Press, 1997), 71-84. In this respect his view is similar to that of J. G. D. Dunn, who argues that the two patterns are more similar than J. P. Sanders perceives; see Dunn, "The New Perspective on Paul," in *Jesus, Paul, and the Law* (Louisville: Westminster/John Knox, 1990), 183-215.

12. John E. Toews regards Abraham's faith as such not the key

emphasis, but rather his trust, "faithing" God, which leads Paul to appeal to Abraham, in accord with Jesus' own faithfulness (*Romans*, 120-24, 375-80).

13. Sider, *Christ and Violence*, 33-35.

14. See this same chiasm in George Shillington's *2 Corinthians*, BCBC (Scottdale, PA: Herald Press, 1999), 127. Shillington has an excellent discussion of this passage, setting it within the wider letter context.

15. J. H. Yoder, *Politics of Jesus*, 123-30 (1994:120-27).

16. Ibid., 134 (1994:131).

17. Vernard Eller, *War and Peace from Genesis to Revelation* (Scottdale, PA: Herald Press, 1981), 140-43.

18. Ibid., 145-52.

19. Ibid., 168-72. Ferguson's description of "The Way of Christ" for his followers focuses similarly on love, the cross, and the Christian's life in Christ: "Christ showed us a new way, a way of life, a way of changing the world. It was politically relevant. It was *in its own way* revolutionary. It was the way of love, the way of the Cross, the way of non-violence, the way of Truth-force, Soul-force, Love-force. It is still the way. He seeks to fulfill it in us" (*Politics of Love*, 115). For fuller treatment of Revelation's "Lamb Christology"—faithful following Jesus—see Swartley, *Covenant of Peace*, 330-39.

20. J. H. Yoder, *Politics of Jesus,* 150-51 (1994:147-48).

21. Ibid., 153 (1994:150); on 155 (1994:152) Yoder quotes J. H. Oldham's statement to the 1948 WCC Amsterdam Assembly to illustrate the distinctive task of the church: "The church is concerned with the primary task of re-creating a true social life . . . through . . . its primary functions of preaching the Word and . . . its life as a worshipping community. . . . There is nothing greater that the church can do for society than to be a center in which small groups of persons are together entering into this experience of renewal and giving each other mutual support in Christian living and action in secular spheres."

22. Ibid., 161 (1994:157).

23. Ernest D. Martin, *Colossians and Philemon*, BCBC (Scottdale, PA: Herald Press, 1993), 113.

24. Klaus Wengst, *Pax Romana and the Peace of Jesus Christ.* trans. John Bowden (Philadelphia: Fortress, 1987), 17.

25. Wengst, *Pax Romana*, 52, from Tacitus, *Agricola* 30, 3-31, 2.

26. For treatment of the peace theology in these books, see W. Swartley, *Covenant of Peace*, 254-75, 323-43, and chap. 11 below.

27. Hays, *Moral Vision*, quoting from 331, 314, 343-44 respectively.

28. Glen H. Stassen, "The Fourteen Triads of the Sermon on the Mount," *JBL* 122 (2003): 267-308 (diagram on 296); Stassen and David P. Gushee, *Kingdom Ethics: Following Jesus in Contemporary Context*

(Downers Grove, IL: InterVarsity Press, 2003), 126. See also the discussion in Stassen, *Just Peacemaking: Transforming Initiatives for Justice and Peace* (Louisville: Westminster/John Knox, 1992), 36-88 (diagram on 44-45); and my treatment of this in *Covenant of Peace*, 65-66.

29. "Brief and Clear Confession, 1544," p. 423 in Wenger, *Complete Writings.*

30. "The Cross of the Saints, ca. 1554," p. 603 in Wenger, *Complete Writings.*

31. "Letters and Other Writings," pp. 1034-35 in Wenger, *Complete Writings.*

4. Peacemakers: Salt of the Earth, Light of the World

1. See here Toews' excellent treatment of these passages in *Romans.*

2. In novel genre, Walter Wangerin Jr. makes this point memorably, in *Jesus: A Novel* (Grand Rapids: Zondervan, 2005), 71-74.

3. Philip Yancey, "Exploring a Parallel Universe," *Christianity Today*, November 2005, 128.

4. D. Kraybill, *The Upside-Down Kingdom*, 33-83. Kraybill helpfully sets these temptations within their contemporary cultural realities: Satan's bid for Jesus to become a messianic military ruler within the political upheaval of the time, the lure to become a religious holy hero within the piety of the temple cult, and the wilderness bread temptation within the context of the peasant masses living in poverty.

5. Jeffrey B. Gibson, *The Temptations of Jesus in Early Christianity*, JSNTSup 112 (Sheffield: Sheffield Academic Press, 1995), esp. 110 and the summaries for every chapter. Even "the testing" connected with the divorce controversy involves the same issue, for to speak against divorce jeopardizes Jesus' security under Herod's political control, since Herod has notoriously violated the prohibition (285-87).

6. George Shillington, "Salt of the Earth? (Mt 5:13/Lk 14:30f.)," *Expository Times* 112, no. 4 (January 2001): 120-21. Alan Kreider earlier proposed a similar interpretation: "Salt and Light," *The Third Way* 11 (September 1988): 14-16; with a sequel on "Light" (October 1988): 14-16; see also Kreider, "Salty Discipleship," *The Other Side* 25 (March-April 1989): 34-37; and *Journey Toward Holiness* (Scottdale, PA: Herald Press), 222-24, 238, n. 1. Through research into nineteenth-century farmers' cyclopedias, Kreider learned that in Britain at that time farmers used salt in limited quantity as a fertilizer, a practice plausible also in the time of Jesus.

7. Mark A. Noll observes and laments that so often when the church enters the political sphere, the cross and its ethic of suffering are pushed aside, and believers emphasize righteousness and duty: *Adding Cross to Crown: The Political Significance of Christ's Passion* (Grand Rapids: Baker Books, 1996), 27.

8. Michael Sattler, "On Two Kinds of Obedience," in *The Legacy of Michael Sattler*, trans. and ed. John H. Yoder, (Scottdale, PA: Herald Press, 1973) 121-25. Sattler's distinction reminds one of Jesus' distinction between "servant" and "friend" in John 15:14-15.

9. This contrasts with Martin Luther's two-kingdom doctrine, in which the Christian lives and functions as both "Christ-person" and "world-person." See Jürgen Moltmann, "The Lutheran Doctrine of the Two Kingdoms and Its Use Today," in W. Swartley, ed., *Politics of Discipleship*, 3-18; his critique, 17-18; and his chapter "Following Jesus Christ in an Age of Nuclear War," 51-57. See also Clarence Bauman's "Response to Moltmann's 'Two Kingdoms,'" in *Politics of Discipleship*, 88-91.

10. Another significant OT stream of thought is the prophets' oracles against the foreign nations. For the most part these oracles are in forms of judgment against foreign nations. Whether they were ever sent or delivered to the nation's headquarters is unclear. But one thing is certain: the prophets were concerned about the moral responsibility of all the nations. Numerous chapters in Isaiah, Jeremiah, and Ezekiel consist of oracles addressed to the foreign nations. This indicates that no power stands outside accountability to God's ethical will for people.

11. See the collection of essays *The Bible and Law*, ed. Willard M. Swartley, Occasional Papers 3 (Elkhart, IN: IMS, 1983); also Toews, *Romans*, 194-216, and esp. his essay on "Law," 389-94.

12. Myron Augsburger, "Beating Swords into Plowshares," *Christianity Today* 20 (November 21, 1975), 196.

13. Myron Augsburger, "Facing the Problem," in *Perfect Love and War*, ed. Paul Hostetler (Nappanee, IN: Evangel Press, 1974), 15.

14. Augsburger, "Beating Swords," 197.

15. See the various essays in Robert L. Ramseyer, ed., *Mission and the Peace Witness* (Scottdale, PA: Herald Press, 1979), especially Ramseyer's, "Mennonite Missions and the Christian Peace Witness," 114-34; also Samuel Escobar and John Driver, *Christian Mission and Social Justice* (Scottdale, PA: Herald Press, 1978).

16. Fernando Enns, "Public Peace, Justice, and Order in Ecumenical Conversation," in *At Peace and Unafraid*, ed. Duane Friesen and Gerald Schlabach (Scottdale, PA: Herald Press, 2005), 241-59, esp. 252.

17. Stassen and Gushee, *Kingdom Ethics*, 25-31.

18. W. Swartley, "Mutual Aid Based in Jesus," in *Building Communities of Compassion: Mennonite Mutual Aid in Theory and Practice*, ed. Willard M. Swartley and Donald B. Kraybill (Scottdale, PA: Herald Press, 1998), 32.

19. See my fuller description of mutual aid practices in ibid. and in chap. 7 of my *Covenant of Peace*, 219-21.

20. Paul Alexander, like Tom Oliver, came to this commitment to be a peacemaker, refusing participation in war, through extended study of the Scriptures. For Alexander's story see June Krehbiel, "Focus on Jesus: Pentecostal Pacifist to Speak for Joint Worship at San José Mennonite Convention," *The Mennonite*, May 15, 2007, 14-15. http://www.mennoniteusa.org/news/news/april-june0704_13_07.htm

5. Christian Witness to Christ's Lordship over the Powers

1. In two cases in Isaiah—24:23c, "for the Lord of hosts will reign"; and 31:4e, "so the Lord of hosts will come down"—the Aramaic translation, which Jesus likely used, renders it as "the kingdom of God shall be (is) revealed." See chap. 9 (below) on this point and its significance for Jesus' proclamation of the gospel.

2. In Isa 6:3, "Holy, holy, holy, is the Lord of hosts," the word *Sabaoth* is carried over into the Greek text, not translated, thus indicating its special significance in relation to the holy.

3. Yahweh Sabaoth is clearly connected to the ark (first at Shiloh), then to the temple, where Yahweh's kingship and sovereignty are denoted by "Zion" as a theological symbol. "Zion" symbolizes God's security and defense of the covenant people: God coming from Zion to protect and defend permeates numerous Psalms (20; 48; 50:1-6; 76) and Isaiah. In Isaiah 1–6 "Lord of hosts" occurs ten times and "Zion" occurs eight times. See 1:24 and 27 for parallel uses and 37:32 and 51:15-16 where the two terms occur together. God as "the Holy One" and "Zion" are linked in 5:16, 24; 6:3; 54:5. Many of the Zion texts emphasize both security and God's/Yahweh's defeat of enemies, protecting from chaos, and crushing military weapons and foes. See Ben C. Ollenburger for his treatment of key texts in both Psalms and Isaiah: *Zion, City of the Great King: A Theological Symbol of the Jerusalem Cult* (Sheffield: Sheffield Academic Press, 1987), esp. 46-80, 107-29, 144-62.

4. For these passages in Daniel, I am using Theodotian's revision of LXX or of some older Greek translation.

5. One aspect not developed here, but in chap. 10 below, is Jesus' identity with God. Thus early Christians worshipped him. The numerous aspects of this correlation go beyond the limits of this study, but chap. 10 is a beginning.

6. In W. Swartley, *Covenant of Peace* (239-41), I list over a half dozen texts in each of three columns that view government power negatively, positively, and what I call normatively—Christ's victory over the powers.

7. Walter Pilgrim, *Uneasy Neighbors: Church and State in the New Testament* (Minneapolis: Fortress, 1999), 7-36. The first column of Scriptures in his n. 1 identify seven texts that view government negatively.

8. For current thinking on the values that Christian believers in the peace church tradition would witness to in relation to matters of public order and security, see articles in Friesen and Schlabach, *At Peace and Unafraid*: Duane Friesen, "In Search of Security: A Theology and Ethic of Peace and Public Order," 37-82, esp. 68-75; "Appendix to Part I: Peace Theology: A Visual Model with Narrative Explanation," 153-64, diagram on 153; Fernando Enns, "Public Peace, Justice, and Order in Ecumenical Perspective," esp. paragraphs b, c, and d on 252-53; Gerald Schlabach, "Just Policing and the Christian Call to Nonviolence," 405-21; and the two articles by Daryl Byler and Lisa Schirch, 179-94, 423-44.

9. The same emphases appear in 1 Peter. In 3:8-17 the dominant contrast is between "evil" (*kakos*), appearing seven times (vv. 9 [twice], 10, 11, 12, 13, 17), and "good" (*agathos*), six times (vv. 10, 11, 13, 16 [twice]), 17), sometimes in a verbal form. In 2:14-15, 18-25 similar contrasts occur. Again, following love (3:8-9), seeking peace (3:11), and maintaining a good conscience (3:16) are correlative ethical directives. See also 1 Thess 5:15. The divine basis for the authority of government in Rom 13 is complemented by the phrase "human creation" (*anthrōpinē ktisei*) in 1 Pet 2:13. Note also that in 1 Tim 2:1 kings stand in grammatical apposition to "all men"; they are no more and no less.

10. In the models of Christian relation to and responsibility for government presented by Moltmann, this view follows the Anabaptist model, not the two-person Lutheran view, noted above. See Moltmann, "Following Jesus Christ in an Age of Nuclear War," in W. Swartley, ed., *Politics of Discipleship*, 52-56.

11. In fact, the violent end of the continuum extends still further, to global lethal violence (cosmocide) in which both the people and the environment are destroyed. Adherents to the just-war position draw their line of acceptable intervention short of the unacceptable extreme of "indiscriminate" and "disproportionate" killing, as does Oliver O'Donovan, *In Pursuit of a Christian View on War* (Bramcote, UK: Grove Books, 1977). However, Christians should regard *all* killing to be an unacceptable extreme.

12. I discuss this more fully in my chapter on Luke in *Covenant of Peace*, 124-25.

13. For a careful study of Revelation's critique of Rome's economic imperialism, see J. Nelson Kraybill, *Imperial Cult and Commerce in John's Apocalypse*, JSNTSup 132 (Sheffield: Sheffield Academic Press, 1996).

14. I provide a longer list of negative assessments of government officials in chap. 8 of *Covenant of Peace,* 228-34.

15. See the Lutheran, Reformed, and Anabaptist solutions to this dilemma in Jürgen Moltmann's presentations. In W. Swartley, ed. *Politics of Discipleship*, part 1, chaps. 1–4.

16. See the arguments I earlier set forth in *Slavery, Sabbath, War, and Women: Case Issues in Biblical Interpretation* (Scottdale, PA: Herald Press, 1983), 112-49.

17. For critique of Niebuhr, see John Howard Yoder, *Reinhold Niebuhr and Christian Pacifism*, Heerewegen Pamphlet 1 (Zeist, Netherlands: [Mennonite Conference and Peace Center], 1954); repr., *MQR* 29 (April 1955): 101-17; Richard Hays, *Moral Vision*, 215-25.

18. Lydia Harder, "Seeking Wisdom in the Face of Foolishness: Toward a Robust Peace Theology," in *At Peace and Unafraid*, ed. Friesen and Schlabach, 117-52.

19. A description of these events recently came to light, together with the publication of a letter from Jacob Swartley, John and Magdalena's son, to John Herr of the Reformed Mennonites in Lancaster: "Letter to Bishop John Herr in 1819," *Pennsylvania Mennonite Heritage* 30 (January 2007): 20-22. Jacob apparently belonged to the "Funkites," who sided with the Continental Congress and paid the Revolutionary War tax, contra the Franconia Mennonite position.

20. John L. Ruth, *'Twas Seeding Time: A Mennonite View of the American Revolution* (Scottdale, PA: Herald Press, 1976), 40, 138. As Ruth puts it, "There is friendship and respect in the midst of the chaos of a war, and the soldiers, having drunk to the health of the newlyweds, leave without taking so much as a chicken."

21. Friesen and Schlabach, *At Peace and Unafraid*, 153-63 (diagram on 153). In my judgment the six facets of wisdom-witness lack an important seventh: the ongoing relief and development work of Mennonite Central Committee, which is itself a demonstration to the powers that Pax Christi achieves what Pax Americana cannot (cf. Eph 3:9-10), but rather does exactly the opposite by imperial power, which causes war, loss of lives, famine, refugees, widows, orphans, and widespread destruction, from which it will take decades to recover.

22. For the testimony of a former Lockheed missile engineer who left his job for Christian reasons, see Robert C. Aldridge, "The Courage to Start," in *The Risk of the Cross: Christian Discipleship in the Nuclear Age*, ed. Christopher Grannis, Arthur Laffin, and Elin Schade (New York: Seabury, 1981), 46-50.

23. Chris Sugden, *A Different Dream: Non-violence as Practical Politics* (Bramcote, UK: Grove Books, 1976); Richard K. Taylor, *Blockade: A Guide to Non-violent Intervention* (Maryknoll, NY: Orbis Books, 1977); Peter D. Bishop, *A Technique for Loving: Non-Violence in Indian and Christian Traditions* (London: SCM Press, 1981). For the inspiring story of how, during the Second World War, a French congregation through nonviolent resistance saved the lives of over 2,000 Jews, see Philip Hallie, *Lest Innocent Blood Be Shed* (New York: Harper & Row, 1979).

24. See 1 Tim 2:1-2; Jim Wallis, "The Work of Prayer," *Sojourners* 8 (March 1979): 3-5; Henri Nouwen, "Letting Go of All Things," *Sojourners* 8 (March 1979): 5-6.

25. For such a miracle in our time, see Sarah Corson, "Welcoming the Enemy: A Missionary Fights Violence with Love," *Sojourners* 12 (April 1983): 29-31 (http://www.sifat.org/about_us/True%20Stories/welcoming%20the%20enemy.htm). See also David Jackson, *Dial 911: Peaceful Christians and Urban Violence* (Scottdale, PA: Herald Press, 1981); and John H. Yoder, *What Would You Do? A Serious Answer to a Standard Question*, expanded ed. with Joan Baez, Tom Skinner, Leo Tolstoy, et al. (Scottdale, PA: Herald Press, 1992).

26. Two special problems that arise are use of force in disciplining children and in restraining a thief or rapist. For the former, the good of the child and love for the child require the clear expression of parental authority; the discipline must be guided not by anger and revenge but by genuine love and concern for the child's well-being (Eph 6:1-4). In the latter case, diversionary tactics and the *word*-weapon of reprimand should be our foremost responses. Force as an expression of care for the one to whom it is applied may be used so long as no permanent physical harm is done; yet we must remember that force evokes more force. For stories of nonviolent resistance in such situations, see E. H. Bauman, *Coals of Fire*; Lehn, *Peace Be With You*; A. Ruth Fry, *Victories Without Violence* (London: Dennis Dobson, 1957); and Egan, *Peace Be with You*.

27. Jean-Michel Hornus, *It Is Not Lawful for Me to Fight*, trans. Alan Kreider and Oliver Coburn (Scottdale, PA: Herald Press, 1980), 158, 163, 243.

28. This happened in 1981 to Superior Court Judge William Bontrager in Elkhart, IN, USA, as reported in *Newsweek*, Dec. 2, 1981, 1259-60.

29. John Howard Yoder, *The Christian Witness to the State* (Elkhart, IN: IMS; Newton, KS: Faith & Life Press, 1964); 3rd printing with updated notes, Faith & Life Press, 1977; 2nd ed., Scottdale, PA: Herald Press, 2002.

30. See here chap. 3 in W. Swartley, *Covenant of Peace*, 60-61; and also such arguments in idem, *Slavery, Sabbath, War, and Women*, 101; and for extensive treatment of the scholarly evasion over the last several centuries, Clarence Bauman, *The Sermon on the Mount: The Modern Quest for Its Meaning* (Macon, GA: Mercer University Press, 1985).

31. George D. McClain, *Claiming All Things for God: Prayer, Discernment, and Ritual for Social Change* (Nashville: Abingdon, 1998), 120-25.

32. For more background information and a longer historical perspective of the witness leading up to these six weeks, see Jürgen Moltmann, "Foreword," in W. Swartley, *Politics of Discipleship*, xiii-xiv. Moltmann reports that church membership numbered 300,000; over the preceding weeks many of these people showed up with candles and prayers for the reunification of Germany.

33. Willard M. Swartley, "Biblical Faith Confronts Evil Spiritual Realities," 38-39, and "Reflections on Deliverance Ministry," 109-13, in *Even the Demons Submit: Continuing Jesus' Ministry of Deliverance*, ed. Loren L. Johns and James R. Krabill (Elkhart, IN: IMS; Scottdale, PA: Herald Press, 2006).

34. Thomas H. McAlpine, *Facing the Powers: What Are the Options?* (Monrovia, CA: MARC, 1991).

35. McAlpine's description (ibid.) of this category is too restrictive. It should include a broader use of exorcism in the ministry of the church. Peter Wagner's theory and strategy regarding territorial powers is only one emphasis, and a disputed one among scholars and practitioners of deliverance ministry. See Clinton Arnold, *Crucial Questions About Spiritual Warfare* (Grand Rapids: Baker Books, 1997); idem, *Powers of Darkness: A Study in Principalities and Powers in Paul* (Grand Rapids: Zondervan, 1992). See also McClain, *Claiming All Things for God*, for ritual use of exorcism to free social and political systemic power from demonic control.

36. Willard M. Swartley, "Jesus Christ, Victor Over Evil," in *Transforming the Powers: Peace, Justice, and the Domination System*, ed. Ray Gingerich and Ted Grimsrud (Minneapolis: Fortress, 2006), 96-112.

37. See my articles "Biblical Faith Confronts Evil Spiritual Realities," 24-40, and "Reflections on Deliverance Ministry," 108-13, in *Even the Demons Submit* (n. 33 above).

38. As was his custom, J. H. Yoder would give articles or copies of files that he thought would be of special interest to a given colleague, in light of that person's field of study and interest. Hence, in the late 1970s I was recipient of his file of correspondence with John R. Stott. Both taught a course at Regent College in the summer of 1976, but in separate terms. On leaving, Stott left a note for Yoder, raising questions about his work on the powers. The key points identified above are Yoder's summary of Stott's note of concern.

39. I have summarized the main points of the ensuing correspondence to clarify these points in dispute, representative of an ongoing debate between various Christians seeking to be faithful to their Christian calling to expose and witness against evil as it shows itself in our world today. This summary is available upon request.

40. On this see chap. 1 in Wink's *The Powers That Be: Theology for a New Millennium* (New York: Doubleday, 1998), 13-36.

41. For Wink's new worldview proposal see Walter Wink, "The New Worldview: Spirit at the Core of Everything," in *Transforming the Powers: Peace, Justice, and the Domination System*, ed. Ray Gingerich and Ted Grimsrud (Minneapolis: Fortress Press, 2006) 17-28. I responded to his presentation of this given at Eastern Mennonite University: "Response to Walter Wink's Paper, 'Your Worldview Determines What You Can Believe'" (unpublished; available in the AMBS Library).

42. My own early publications showing J. H. Yoder's exegetical influence (I was his student in 1960-62) are "Peacemakers: The Salt of the Earth," in J. A. Lapp, *Peacemakers in a Broken World* (1969), 85-100 (from which I draw in chaps. 4 and 5 above); and my paper on "The Christian and Payment of War Tax," first presented in 1975 and later revised (1980) for distribution by several church agencies (published here for the first time as chap. 6).

43. Leo Driedger and Donald B. Kraybill, *Mennonite Peacemaking: From Quietism to Activism* (Scottdale, PA: Herald Press, 1994), 62. Striking to me is John H. Yoder's predominant emphasis on *nonresistance* in chap. 3 of his *The Original Revolution* (Scottdale, PA: Herald Press, 1972), 55-90, an adapted 1954 speech. Did Yoder's emphases also shift? I think so.

44. The insightful article by Mark Thiessen Nation, "Toward a Theology for Conflict Transformation: Learnings from John Howard Yoder," *MQR* 80 (2006): 43-60, may mean that this statement either needs qualification or cannot stand. Nation identifies six prominent emphases in Yoder that are theologically foundational to conflict transformation. Yoder's most notable contribution to resolving conflict within the church is his "Binding and Loosing" article, originally in *Concern*, No. 14, A Pamphlet Series for Questions of Church Renewal (Scottdale, PA: [The Concern Group], February 1967), 2-32; it appears now in briefer form in *Body Politics: Five Practices of the Christian Community Before the Watching World* (Scottdale, PA: Herald Press, 2001), 1-13. Yoder's subtitle suggests that what he outlines here for the church has significance also for the world.

45. *Confession of Faith in a Mennonite Perspective*, 85-88.

46. See also Willard M. Swartley, "Jesus Christ: Victor Over Evil," in Gingerich and Grimsrud, *Transforming the Powers*, 96-112.

47. In his third letter to Stott, J. H. Yoder maintains that the two are not the same, but says no more.

48. Anthony J. Tambasco, "Principalities, Powers, and Peace," in *Blessed Are the Peacemakers: Biblical Perspectives on Peace and Its*

Social Foundations, ed. Anthony J. Tambasco (New York: Paulist Press, 1989), 118-19; Walter Wink, *Naming the Powers* (Philadelphia: Fortress, 1984), 22-35; idem, *Unmasking the Powers: The Invisible Forces That Determine Human Existence* (Philadelphia: Fortress, 1986), 9-107.

49. Willard M. Swartley and Thomas Finger, "Bondage and Deliverance: Biblical and Theological Perspectives," in *Essays on Spiritual Bondage and Deliverance*, ed. Willard M. Swartley, Occasional Papers 11 (Elkhart, IN: IMS, 1988, 10-38; Arnold, *Powers of Darkness*; Gregory A. Boyd, *God at War: The Bible and Spiritual Conflict* (Downers Grove, IL: InterVarsity, 1997). Millard Lind's work on warfare in the OT provided a biblical exegetical basis for J. H. Yoder in their collegiality at AMBS in the 1960s and 1970s, even though Lind's *Yahweh Is a Warrior* (Scottdale, PA: Herald Press, 1980) was not published until after Yoder's *Politics of Jesus* (1972). See now also my articles in notes 36-37 above.

50. Thomas Yoder Neufeld, "*Put on the Armour of God": The Divine Warrior from Isaiah to Ephesians*, JSNTSup 140 (Sheffield, UK: Sheffield Academic Press, 1997); *Ephesians*, BCBC (Scottdale, PA: Herald Press, 2002), 69-85, 87-88, 92-94, 151-54, 290-316.

51. Clinton E. Arnold, *Ephesians, Power and Magic: The Concept of Power in Ephesians in Light of Its Historical Setting*, SNTSMS 63 (Cambridge: Cambridge University Press, 1989), 121.

52. Ragner Leivestad, *Christ the Conqueror: Ideas of Conflict and Victory in the New Testament* (London: SPCK, 1954), 160-63.

53. See Willard M. Swartley, "Smelting for Gold: Jesus and Jubilee in John H. Yoder's *Politics of Jesus*," in *A Mind Patient and Untamed: Assessing John Howard Yoder's Contributions to Theology, Ethics, and Peacemaking*, ed. Gayle Gerber Koontz and Ben C. Ollenburger (Telford, PA: Cascadia Publishing House; Scottdale, PA: Herald Press, 2004), 288-301.

54. J. H. Yoder, *Politics* (1994), 98 // 96.

55. Gibson, *Temptations of Jesus*.

56. For example, Susan R. Garrett sets Jesus' temptations in the broader biblical context of the nature of temptation, and thus sees other dimensions of struggle in the "testings" Jesus encounters: in *The Temptations of Jesus in Mark's Gospel* (Grand Rapids: Eerdmans, 1998).

57. See Yoder Neufeld's works referred to above. For Finger, see his two-volume work, *Christian Theology: An Eschatological Approach* (vol. 1, Nashville: Thomas Nelson, 1985; repr., Scottdale, PA: Herald Press, 1987; vol. 2, Herald Press, 1989), esp. 1:322-33 and chap. 7 in vol. 2; for W. Swartley, see W. Swartley and Finger, "Bondage and Deliverance," as well as W. Swartley, "Exorcism" (285-87) and

"Satan" (791-94), in *The Mennonite Encyclopedia*, vol. 5, ed. C. J. Dyck and D. D. Martin (Scottdale, PA: Herald Press, 1990); idem, "Biblical Faith Confronts Evil Spiritual Realities," 24-40, and "Reflections on Deliverance Ministry," 108-14, in Johns and Krabill, *Even the Demons Submit*.

58. Stephen Dintaman, "The Spiritual Poverty of the Anabaptist Vision," *Conrad Grebel Review* 10 (Spring 1992): 205-8, esp. 207. See also follow-up essays to this article in *Conrad Grebel Review* 13 (Winter 1995): 2-22.

6. Christians and the Payment of Taxes Used for War

1. Clinton Gardner, *The Church as a Prophetic Community* (Philadelphia: Westminster, 1967), 111-12.

2. This is the basis for Israel's refusal of a king: Judg 8:22-23; cf. 1 Sam 8:4-9.

3. S. G. F. Brandon, *Jesus and the Zealots* (New York: Scribner, 1967).

4. For viewing these texts in three parallel columns and further discussion, see W. Swartley, *Covenant of Peace*, 229.

5. For discussion of this intrinsic dual dimension, see Luise Schottroff's article "'Give to Caesar," in W. Swartley, *Love of Enemy and Nonretaliation*, 223-57.

6. Josephus, *Jewish Antiquities* 18.1.1; *Jewish War* 2.8.1.

7. Some scholars, however, hold that the followers of Judas were called Sicarii (dagger-carriers), but not Zealots. They argue that Josephus does not use the latter term as such until AD 66, when Menahem heads the Zealot party to defend the temple. For this view, see Morton Smith, "Zealots and Sicarii: Their Origins and Relation," *Harvard Theological Review* 64 (1971): 1-19. Richard A. Horsley makes much of this point, objecting to viewing Jesus against the Zealot option. See Horsley, *Jesus and the Spiral of Violence: Popular Jewish Resistance in Roman Palestine* (San Francisco: Harper & Row, 1987). The headquarters for this AD 6 revolt was Sepphoris, only three miles north of Nazareth. At this time, Jesus would have been about ten years old.

8. William Lane, *Commentary on the Gospel of Mark* (Grand Rapids: Eerdmans, 1974), 423.

9. Ethelbert Stauffer, *Christ and the Caesars* (London: SCM Press, 1955), 124.

10. Ibid.

11. Ibid., 125.

12. Ibid., 127.

13. C. Milo Connick, *Jesus: The Man, the Mission, and The Message*, rev. ed. (Englewood Cliffs, NJ: Prentice-Hall, 1973), 335.

14. Mark (12:17), however, lacks the introductory "then," which this interpretation almost requires. Luke (20:25) does begin Jesus' answer with "Then." Matthew (22:21) begins Jesus' answer with "Render therefore." Either Luke's or Matthew's version would strengthen this proposed interpretation.

15. See my fuller discussion of this segment in *Mark: The Way*, 49-57.

16. For fuller analysis of Mark 12, see ibid., 171-74.

17. Donald D. Kaufman, *What Belongs to Caesar? A Discussion on the Christian Response to Payment of War Taxes* (Scottdale, PA: Herald Press, 1969; rev. ed., Eugene, OR: Wipf & Stock, 2006), 41-42. See further Kaufman's overall excellent discussion of these various texts, and especially his quotation of C. G. Rutenber on 41.

18. I am indebted to Daryl Schmidt's helpful essay on Luke 23 for these insights: "Luke's 'Innocent' Jesus: A Scriptural Apologetic," in *Political Issues in Luke-Acts*, ed. Richard J. Cassidy and Philip Scharper (Maryknoll, NY: Orbis Press, 1983), 111-21. My article in the same volume, "Politics and Peace (*Eirēnē*) in Luke's Gospel," 18-37, supports also the view, contra much Lukan scholarship, that the peace of Jesus' gospel in Luke is not a political pact with Rome but a new social reality transcending both Judaism and the politics of the empire. In the final analysis Pilate too stood judged by "the King" because he could not comprehend Jesus (especially emphasized in John 18–19). Like the Jewish religious leaders who cried, "Crucify him!" Pilate, though pronouncing Jesus "Not guilty," was judged by Jesus. Thus Jesus' cry, "Father, forgive them; for they do not know what they are doing" (Luke 23:34) extends equally to both peoples involved in this travesty of justice.

19. Oscar Cullmann, *The State in the New Testament* (New York: Scribner, 1956), 48.

20. Victor Paul Furnish, *The Moral Teaching of Paul* (Nashville: Abingdon, 1979), 126.

21. Perry B. Yoder, *From Word to Life: A Guide to the Art of Bible Study* (Scottdale, PA: Herald Press, 1982), 73-75.

22. In this light, Rom 13:1-7 has had an undue influence in discussion about the nature and authority of the state. This has led Christian people to an indiscriminate passivity and obedience toward government. Paul was not spelling out a normative theory of the authority of the state, but using traditional beliefs (Jewish and Hellenistic) to substantiate practical counsel.

23. Suetonius, *Lives of Twelve Caesars, Claudius* 5.25.4, in Loeb Classical Library, vol. 148 (Latin series), trans. J. C. Rolfe (Cambridge,

MA: Harvard University Press, 1959), 53. "Chrestus" is a variant form of "Christus"; it is uncertain whether this refers to Jewish Christians or disputes between Jews and Christians.

24. *Annals of Tacitus* 13, in Loeb Classical Library, vol. 153 (Latin series), trans. John Jackson (Cambridge, MA: Harvard University Press, 1956), 89. On historical reconstruction of the events lying behind Rom 12–13, especially the tax issue, see J. Friedrich, W. Pohlmann, and P. Stuhlmacher, "Zur historischen Situation and Intention von Rom 13.1-7," *Zeitschrift für Theologie und Kirche* 73 (1967): 131-66.

25. Nero did reform the collection of the commission-tax, requiring "a check . . . to be placed on the cupidity of the collectors" and the rates of tax to "be posted for public inspection." Several collectors faced charges of alleged acts of cruelty, but were acquitted by the Caesar. Tacitus, *Annals* 13, Loeb 153: 89, 91.

26. The specific Greek verb used in Acts 5:29 is *peitharchein*, which carries the meaning of "being persuaded towards a given position," thus heeding or obeying that respective source of authority. The verb, *hypakouō*, describes obedient response to a spoken command. The word for subjection (*hypotassō*) literally means "to tie under," thus denoting the accepting of a position in the societal order. See J. H. Yoder, *Politics of Jesus* (1972), 174-75 (1994 ed., 170-72).

27. *The Living Bible* paraphrase of 13:1 plays into this erroneous view: "Obey the government, for God is the one who put it there. There is no government anywhere that God has not placed in power." What an interpretation!

28. See J. H. Yoder, *Politics of Jesus* (1972), 207-9 (1994, 205-7).

29. John Howard Yoder, "The Things That Are Caesars: (Part I)," *Christian Living*, July 1960, 5. C. J. Cadoux points out that numerous church fathers took the view of "double obligation," in which taxes are Caesar's due, but respect and honor are God's due: *The Early Church and the World* (Edinburgh: T&T Clark, 1925), 258, 351, 369-70, 371, 539. Some modern commentators have followed the same view, suggesting that Paul's counsel follows Jesus' words of rendering to both Caesar and God. But Yoder doubts this interpretation, noting that 1 Pet 2:17 assigns honor to the emperor; discrimination is required, rather, in each area: tax, revenue, respect, honor.

30. Wilma Bailey, *"You Shall Not Kill" or "You Shall not Murder"? The Assault on a Biblical Text* (Collegeville, MN: Liturgical Press, 2005).

31. See W. Swartley, *Covenant of Peace*, 208-11, 258-59.

32. For a complete list of texts of Jesus' victory over the powers, see ibid., 229, the "Normative" column.

33. A helpful and important resource bringing together the voices

of those opposing payment of taxes for war is Donald D. Kaufman's *The Tax Dilemma: Praying for Peace, Paying for War* (Scottdale, PA: Herald Press, 1978; repr., Eugene, OR: Wipf & Stock, 2006).

34. If Paul's specific command to pay taxes in the Roman situation of AD 55-58 is not consonant with the basic moral principles enunciated in Rom 12–13, then two options follow: Either 13:1-7 is a later non-Pauline interpolation (held by a few scholars), or Paul makes a pragmatic concession.

35. For further study of the hermeneutical issues involved in this study, I refer the reader to my book *Slavery, Sabbath, War, and Women*, esp. chaps. 1, 3 and 215-34; and my article, "How to Interpret the Bible: A Case Study of Romans 13:1-7 and the Payment of Taxes for War," *Seeds* 3, no. 4 (June 1984): 28-31.

36. Earlier, during the Vietnam War, we refused payment of the telephone tax to express our objection to that war, even though we on principle object to all war (see chap. 5 above addressing this distinction). Just-war theory becomes rationalization of self-interests.

37. The visits of Japan's Prime Minister Koizumi dressed in traditional garb to the Yasukuni Shrine, symbol of former Prime Minister Nakasone's nationalism, prompted this poetic response.

7. The Bible and Israel: Two Interpretations and More

1. Cf. Ollenburger, *Zion, City of the Great King.*

2. The relationship between this Edward Irving and John Nelson Darby form of Dispensationalism and the rise of Zionism is beyond the scope of treatment here. See Stephen Sizer, *Zion's Christian Soldiers: The Bible, Israel, and the Church* (Nottingham, UK: InterVarsity, 2007).

3. For a perceptive and hard-hitting exposure of using Scripture to legitimate violent conquest, appealing to OT land promises and warfare precedents—and even using the Isa 65:17 and Rev 21:1-2 imagery of "new heavens and new earth" to describe Columbus' new world discovery, see Michael Prior, *The Bible and Colonialism: A Moral Critique* (Sheffield, U.K.: Sheffield Academic Press, 1997), 53—but also Chap. 4 on "Colonialism and Palestine" and Chap. 7 "Towards a Moral Reading of the Bible."

4. Barbara R. Rossing, *The Rapture Exposed: The Message of Hope in the Book of Revelation* (Boulder, CO: Westview Press, 2004); Loren L. Johns, *The Lamb Christology of the Book of Revelation: An Investigation into Its Origins and Rhetorical Force* (WUNT[2] 167. Tübingen: Mohr Siebeck, 2003); Richard J. Bauckham, *Climax of Prophecy: Studies on the Book of Revelation* (Edinburgh: T & T Clark, 1993). See my fuller discussion of the theology of Revelation in

Covenant of Peace, Chapter 12, and esp. my reference to Johns and Rossing, 324, note 1.

5. For further treatment of the issue of "Land" in the Bible, see my article in *The Westminster Theological Wordbook of the Bible*, ed. Donald E. Gowan (Louisville: Westminster John Knox, 2003), 281-84.

6. See Willard Swartley, "Bosch and Beyond: Biblical Issues in Mission," *Mission Focus* 11 Supplement (2003): 77-105.

7. Toews, *Romans*, 238-39.

8. David E. Holwerda, *Jesus and Israel: One Covenant or Two?* (Grand Rapids: Eerdmans, 1995), 2.

9. Toews, *Romans*, 254-56.

10. Ibid., 256.

11. Alan F. Segal, *Paul the Convert: The Apostolate and Apostasy of Saul the Pharisee* (New Haven: Yale University Press, 1990), 160.

12. Segal sums up these two ways for Jews to become Christian; ibid., 11-12, 146, 214.

13. In a 2005 Society of Biblical Literature session on "Paul and Supersession," Bruce Longenecker espoused a midrange (on low-high grid) supersession in Paul, claiming three Jewish scholars, including Daniel Boyarin, in support. Douglas Harinck, however, after traversing God's purpose in creation, election of Israel, and the messianic community, contended that "we cannot claim Paul for supersession of any kind." Aside from the term itself, the crucial issue is that the church not be viewed as displacing Israel. In response, Terence Donaldson and Claudia Selzer advised using other terminology to describe the messianic community's relation to Israel, avoiding "church versus Israel." Michael Greenwald observed the dramatic shift in sensitivity and emphasis between pre-World War II and post-WWII in treatment of this topic.

14. See Toews' treatment, *Romans*, 288-90.

15. Holwerda has a helpful brief treatment of various positions on this difficult issue: *Jesus and Israel*, 1-26. He rightly laments Luther's views and is much influenced by the important, notable contributions of Karl Barth and Markus Barth, which he deftly summarizes. He disagrees with Rosemary Ruether, who sacrifices key christological beliefs and embraces a two-covenant approach. Holwerda holds to a promise-fulfillment relationship between the Testaments, a view reflective of NT texts. But care is required that this does not slip into some form of "displacement" theology (see 147-76). N. T. Wright's contribution is quite helpful in presenting Jesus as one with Israel (Jewish) and the in-person fulfillment of Israel and its mission in Jesus' calling, messianic claims, and obedience: *Jesus and the Victory of God* (Minneapolis: Fortress, 1996), 477-539. Wright, however, does not sufficiently guard

his discussion from "displacement" implications.

16. On this I recommend Richard Hays' excellent treatment, "Anti-Judaism and Ethnic Conflict," in *Moral Vision*, 407-43. In *Covenant of Peace* (68-70), however, I diverge from his interpretation that Matthew is anti-Judaic. I regard Matthew's view more positively, seeing harsh critique of "Jews" as referring to hostile Jewish leaders and Jesus' judging statements in the tradition of the OT prophetic critique, such as in Ezek 34, calling God's people to repentance.

17. W. Swartley, *Covenant of Peace*, 69-72, 281-82 (esp. n. 6), 300, 312.

18. Toews, *Romans*, 289-90.

19. Will Herberg, *Faith Enacted as History: Essays in Biblical Theology* (Philadelphia: Westminster, 1976), 44-46.

20. Ibid., 54.

21. This, Herberg (ibid.) notes, is "an unforgettable phrase from Jacques Maritain."

22. Ibid., 90.

23. John Howard Yoder, "'It Did Not Have to Be,'" in *The Jewish-Christian Schism Revisited*, ed. Michael C. Cartwright and Peter Ochs (Grand Rapids: Eerdmans, 2003), 43-68. This book includes a lengthy appendix that narrates a 53-year history (1949-2002) of Mennonite efforts in the Middle East (among Jews and Palestinians) as two significant contexts for the development of Yoder's thought on this topic. Yoder himself, as a Mission Board executive, played a role in this development. Another effort headed by Frits Kuiper, a Mennonite theologian in the Netherlands, was beginning a Christian kibbutz in Galilee, Nes Ammin, an "ensign to/for the peoples," with the hope that here a Jewish-Christian witness might be given to the world. See Jacob Enz, "Judaism and Jews," *Mennonite Encyclopedia* 5: 469.

24. Alain Epp Weaver, "The Power of Diaspora: Seeking the Peace of Palestine-Israel," in *At Peace and Unafraid*, ed. Friesen and Schlabach, 275.

25. Ibid.

26. Daniel Boyarin, *Borderlines: The Partition of Judeo-Christianity* (Philadelphia: University of Pennsylvania Press, 2004), 2: "How and why that border was written and who wrote it are the questions that drive the book."

27. Speaking to Menno Scholars in October 2006, Boyarin acknowledged that his discovery of J. H. Yoder's work gave him the courage to put into print what was long brewing in his mind. He spoke appreciatively of Yoder's work, affirming diaspora existence for God's peoplehood—both Jewish and Christian—as God's good design. However, unlike Yoder, he would not judge the alternative view, need-

ing to possess land for survival, as an expression of unfaithfulness.

28. Daniel Boyarin, "Judaism as a Free Church: Footnotes to John Howard Yoder's *The Jewish-Christian Schism Revisited*," *CrossCurrents* 56 (2007): 14.

29. Laura L. Brenneman, "Further Footnotes on Paul, Yoder, and Boyarin," *CrossCurrents* 56 (2007): 60-69, esp. 67.

30. Alain Epp Weaver, "Further Footnotes on Zionism, Yoder, and Boyarin," *CrossCurrents* 56 (2007): 41-51, esp. 44-49. See also Epp Weaver, ed., *Under Vine and Fig Tree: Biblical Theologies of Land and the Palestinian-Israeli Conflict* (Telford, PA: Cascadia, 2007).

31. For the text of this Declaration, and the history leading to it, see Stephen Sizer, "The Historical Roots of Christian Zionism from Irving to Balfour: Christian Zionism in the United Kingdom (1820-1918), in *Challenging Christian Zionism: Theology, Politics, and Israel-Palestine Conflict*, ed. Naim Ateek, Cedar Duaybis and Maurine Tobin (London: Melisende, 2005), 30.

32. See here two essays: Donald Wagner, "From Blackstone to Bush: Christian Zionism in the United States (1890-2004)," in Ateek, *idem*, 32-44, and Gary Burge, "Theological and Biblical Assumptions of Christian Zionism," in Ateek, *idem*, 45-49.

33. Robert W. Jenson, "Toward a Christian Theology of Judaism," in *Jews and Christians: People of God*, ed by Carl E. Braaten and Robert W. Jenson (Grand Rapids: Eerdmans, 2003): 1-13. Other essays in this volume are also most noteworthy. From the Jewish side, see the helpful article by David Novak, "From Supersessionism to Parallelism in Jewish-Christian Dialogue," *idem*, 95-113.

34. This is emphasized especially by Richard John Neuhaus, "Salation Is from the Jews," *idem*, 71.

35. Herberg, *Faith Enacted as History*, 90.

36. Ibid., 61.

8. Biblical Perspectives on Mission

1. Bruce M. Metzger, *The New Testament: Its Background, Growth, and Content* (Nashville: Abingdon, 1965), 172.

2. Some scholars doubt the connection, pointing out that Erastus was a quite common name: e.g., Justin J. Meggitt, "The Social Status of Erastua (Rom. 16:23)," *Novum Testamentum* 38 (1996): 218-23.

9. The Evangel as Gospel of Peace

1. C. H. Dodd, a pacifist, failed to include this text in his fifteen key texts shaping NT theology, in his seminal book, *According to the Scripture: The Sub-Structure of New Testament Theology* (London: Nisbet, 1952).

2. Peter Stuhlmacher paved the way in showing these connections. See his essay in the volume he edited, *The Gospel and the Gospels* (Grand Rapids: Eerdmans, 1991), 1-25. The definitive work showing the influence of this text upon early Christian writings is Hubert Frankemölle's "Jesus als deuterojesajanische Freudenbote? Zur Rezeption von Jes 52,7 und 61,1 im Neuen Testament, durch Jesus und in den Targumim," in *Vom Christentum zu Jesus* (FS Joachim Gnilka), ed. Hubert Frankemölle (Freiberg: Herder, 1989), 34-67.

3. Hence emphasis rightly has fallen on a sacrificial life, not in the sense that the evangel's life replaces the sacrifice of Jesus, but that one patterns one's life after the self-giving acts of Jesus, both in this ministry and his death on the cross.

4. Matthew's citation of this text (42:1-2) provides the literary clue to broaden from "mission to the Jews only" (10:5-6) to "Go therefore and make disciples of all nations" (28:19), since the Isaiah text (also 11:10) in Matthew twice mentions the nations or Gentiles.

5. The term does occur in 1 Chron 28:5, in speaking of the Lord choosing "Solomon to sit upon the throne of *the kingdom of the Lord* over Israel" (emphasis added). See also Wisd of Sol 10:10, where "kingdom of God" appears. But these two uses are not adequate to explain the dominant role of the motif in the Synoptic Gospels. Some other factors must have influenced this, which I take up in the ensuing discussion. The Lord's kingship, however, is a dominant theme throughout the Hebrew Scripture (Exod 15:18; 1 Sam 8:7; Pss 24:7-10; 47; 48:1-2; 74:12-13; 84:3; 93; 95–99; 145:1, 11-13; Isa 43:15; 44:6). In Exod 19:3-5 (RSV) God's covenant with Israel gives to Israel their kingdom identity: "You shall be to me a kingdom of priests." Hence the basic components of the metaphor "kingdom of God" are indeed present in the OT.

6. This information is accessible in part 2 of Bruce Chilton's *A Galilean Rabbi and His Bible: Jesus' Use of the Interpreted Scripture of His Time* (Wilmington, DE: Michael Glazier, 1984); idem, "Regnum Dei Deus Est," *Scottish Journal of Theology* 31 (1978): 261-70.

7. Ollenburger, *Zion, City of the Great King.*

8. John Driver, "The Kingdom of God: Goal of Messianic Mission," in *The Transfiguration of Mission*, ed. Wilbert R. Shenk (Scottdale, PA: 1993), 83-105. Shenk's ordering of the essays in *Transfiguration* is correct: David Shank's essay, "Jesus the Messiah: Messianic Foundation of Mission" (37-82) precedes Driver's. In introducing these essays, Shenk rightly says that these elements are necessary to grasp "the *missio Dei*, . . . *Jesus the Messiah*, God's anointed one, in whom God's reign is inaugurated in the world and through whom that reign will be fully established; who makes peace by the blood of the cross, reconciles former enemies, and forms of them the messianic community" (31).

9. Driver, "Kingdom of God," 104, n. 1. From Bruce Chilton, *The Kingdom of God in the Teachings of Jesus* (Philadelphia: Fortress, 1984), 126.

10. Ibid.

11. Marlin E. Miller's article, "He Came Preaching Peace," appeared first in the *Gospel Herald*, vol. 76, no. 35 (August 30, 1983): 593-96. A related article, "Gospel of Peace," appeared in *Mission Focus*, vol. 6, no. 1 (September 1977): 1-5. Both are now available in Miller's *Theology of the Church: Writings by Marlin E. Miller*, ed. Richard A. Kauffman and Gayle Gerber Koontz, Text-Reader Series no. 7 (Elkhart, IN: IMS, 1997): 3-20.

12. John H. Yoder's book *He Came Preaching Peace* (Scottdale, PA: Herald Press, 1985) contains twelve essays, all related to this theme.

13. Miller, *Theology of the Church*, 7.

14. Michael J. Gorman, *Cruciformity: Paul's Narrative Spirituality at the Cross* (Grand Rapids: Eerdmans, 2001), 270. For fuller description of the Pax Romana's oppressive strategies, drawing on Klaus Wengst's work, see W. Swartley, *Covenant of Peace*, 38-40.

15. For fuller description, see W. Swartley, *Covenant of Peace*, 219-21.

16. For treatment of this text see ibid., 210-11.

17. Yoder Neufeld emphasizes this point: baptism is enlistment in this new-creation army of love and peacemaking: *Ephesians*, 311-12, 316.

18. Arnold, *Ephesians, Power and Magic*, 14-41.

19. Ibid., 121.

20. Jesus' exorcisms are the prototype of this warfare against the evil powers. See W. Swartley, *Covenant of Peace*, 95-100, 138-40.

21. Arnold represents well this view in *Powers of Darkness*, 154-58.

22. See Yoder Neufeld, *Ephesians*, for the same point. He criticizes both H. Berkhof and J. H. Yoder, saying they "downplay the offensive nature of the church's struggle much more than does Ephesians" (315).

23. Ibid., 315.

24. One might consider Rom 10:15, which completely quotes the first two phrases of Isa 52:7, but the more reliable manuscripts do not contain "of peace," but stops with "the good news." In light of Paul's theology as a whole, it is correct to assume that he understood the gospel as a gospel of peace, but here his emphasis falls on responding to or refusing the good news. In light of the division such alternative response brings (see Luke 12:51-53), Paul does not emphasize here the *peace* that the gospel produces, as he does in Ephesians.

25. Wilbert R. Shenk, "Christological Foundations for Evangelizing in a Pluralist Society," in a two-lecture series, "Christian Witness In A Religiously Plural World," 11 (Manuscript available in Associated Mennonite Seminary Library, Elkhart, Indiana).

10. Peacemaking and Mission Empowered by Worship

1. Larry W. Hurtado, *Lord Jesus Christ: Devotion to Jesus in Earliest Christianity* (Grand Rapids: Eerdmans, 2003).

2. These topics are chaps. 1 and 3 respectively in Larry Hurtado's later book titled, *How on Earth Did Jesus Become a God? Historical Questions About Earliest Devotion to Jesus* (Grand Rapids: Eerdmans, 2005).

3. Ibid.

4. Dorothy Jean Weaver, *Matthew's Missionary Discourse: A Literary-Critical Analysis*, JSNTSup 38 (Sheffield: JSOT Press, 1990).

5. W. Swartley, *Covenant of Peace*, 56-58.

6. Ibid., 60-90, 179-81, 185-87.

7. I will be restricting my analysis to use of *proskyneō* in relation to Jesus. For use of other terms to indicate homage, as well as *proskyneō*, see Hurtado, *How on Earth?* 139-51.

8. There are seven mountains in Matthew, with this last mountain in chap. 28 signifying royalty. For exposition of this point, see W. Swartley, *Israel's Scripture Traditions*, 228-32.

9. I develop this at length in my *Covenant of Peace*, 77-90.

10. God as "my Father (in heaven)" occurs often in Matthew, complemented with "your Father (in heaven)." See ibid., 81-84.

11. In ibid., I discuss Robert Mowery's contribution in showing that Matthew's unique grammatical form of this phrase *theou huios* (in 14:33; 27:43, 54), which matches the form used of/by five Roman emperors, is clearly a challenge to the imperial world.

12. Two additional uses of *proskyneō* occur in relation to Satan's ploy, tempting Jesus to worship him (4:9, 10). Satan promises Jesus the kingdoms of the world if Jesus falls down and worships Satan. Jesus' response denounces his claim: "Worship the Lord your God and serve only him." Satan's temptation parallels, perhaps represents, the two alternative "Son of God" (*theou huios*) realities: Emperor *or* Jesus Christ! This parallel between Satan and emperor-claiming-deity is reflected in another of Matthew's uses of *proskyneō*: 20:20, where the mother of James and John asks Jesus to give her sons top seats in the coming kingdom. Jesus hears this request as the extension of the Satan-temptation and transforms the messianic expectation through his answer, repudiating how the rulers of the Gentiles lord it over them (v. 25).

13. Perhaps *healing* should be added to this triad, for in Matt 8:2; 9:18; and 15:25 those who cry for healing—and are healed—come to Jesus and kneel at his feet (*proskyneō*). The remaining single use is in a parable, in 18:26, where the servant pleading for forgiveness of debt (sins as well?) likewise kneels. In all these cases people come to Jesus as One with divine power to transform their lives.

14. See W. Swartley, *Covenant of Peace*, 100-112.

15. For fuller exposition of the feedings and Mark's distinctive way of disclosing Jesus' identity, see my book *Mark: The Way for All Nations*, 110-26.

16. For a list of commentators who have understood "the rebuilding of the temple" to refer to the Christian community, see Donald Juel, *Messiah and Temple* (Missoula, MT: Society of Biblical Literature, 1977), 145, and see his discussion on 143-58.

17. According to the majority of the earlier and more reliable manuscripts, Mark's Gospel ends with 16:8.

18. It is odd and perhaps intentional that the only other place Mark uses the term "three days" is in 8:2, to describe how long the multitude on the east side of the Sea of Galilee waits for the bread of the Messiah. The feeding on the east side of the sea, with *seven* loaves for *four* thousand and *seven* baskets left over signifies Gentile multitude! However, the phrase "and in three days I will raise another made without hands," found in a few less reliable manuscripts at the end of 13:2, cannot be regarded as part of the original text.

19. For a summary of the scholarly work on the Gentile significance of Galilee, see G. H. Boobyer, "Galilee and Galileans in St. Mark's Gospel," *Bulletin of John Rylands Library* 35 (1953): 334-38; and T. A. Burkill's essay on "Galilee and Jerusalem" in *Mysterious Revelation* (Ithaca, NY: Cornell University Press, 1963), 252-57.

20. Mark uses the Greek word for "worship" (*proskyneō*) only twice. To understand his uses, we must also be aware of Mark's frequent use of irony, where in this case the voices who speak *worship* are those from the negative side of the D & D (demonic and divine) voices. In my *Mark* book I develop how christological disclosure in Mark emerges from what the demons and the divine voice speak. Mark's first use of *proskyneo* is in 5:6, where the Gerasene demoniac *falls down at Jesus' feet* and laments Jesus' coming: "'What have you to do with me, Jesus, Son of the Most High God? I adjure you by God, do not torment me!'" The second use is 15:18-19, where the soldiers mock Jesus: "Hail, King of the Jews!" and then *fall down* in pretend worship. What the demons and the soldiers say, ironically, is the *truth*! Cf. 1:24, 34; 3:11; 15:26, 29, 32.

21. If the Gentile soldier's "confession" was a statement of disgust (not normally assumed by scholarship, but not impossible), then it functions as irony, as do Mark's two uses of *proskyneō* (see previous note). In that case, it is nonetheless *the truth*, from Mark's Gospel's point of view. Given Mark's pervasive means of including Gentiles in the gospel's saving power, I take the soldier's word at the cross as a true confession.

22. *The Spreading Flame*, the title of F. F. Bruce's study of Acts and

the growing church (Grand Rapids: Eerdmans, 1953); subtitle: *The Rise and Progress of Christianity.*

23. See Helmut Koester's 1991 SBL address in which he describes this Greco-Roman hope: "Jesus the Victim," *JBL* 111 (1992): 2-15, esp. 11. The vision for this eschatological hope is developed in Virgil's *Aeneid*, and it includes two notable features in relation to the NT Jesus-kingdom account: the birth of a divine child and fulfillment of "the promises and the righteousness of the primordial time."

24. These paragraphs are modified slightly from my *Covenant of Peace*, 171-73.

25. See my extensive work with this topic and the sources cited there: *Israel's Scripture Traditions*, 240-42 and the larger section.

26. That essay may also be found in *Beautiful Upon the Mountains: Biblical Essays on Mission, Peace, and the Reign of God*, eds. Mary H. Schertz and Ivan Friesen (Elkhart, IN: IMS; Scottdale, PA: Herald Press, 2004), 161-82.

27. It seems to me that the manuscripts of John 1:18 reading "It is God the only God who . . ." are the most persuasive, based on both external (manuscript evidence) and internal considerations.

28. Richard A. Bauckham, *God Crucified: Monotheism and Christology in the New Testament* (Grand Rapids: Eerdmans, 1998).

29. Ibid., 76.

30. As Sheila Klassen Wiebe puts it in discussing Col 1:15-20 (Uniform Series: *Adult Bible Study*, Winter 2006–7 [Scottdale, PA: Faith & Life Resources, December 3, 2006], 5), "Jesus Christ, who is the image of God, represents God to us. . . . This [first] stanza [of the Colossian hymn] also affirms Christ's supremacy over all creation in rank and time, for he is 'firstborn of all creation' (v. 15) and 'before all things' (v. 17)."

31. In this paragraph and the integrating of the three Scriptures, see Paula Killough's paper, "Is/Was Jesus God?" November 28, 2006 (available in the AMBS Library); based also on Bauckham, *God Crucified*, 37-38.

32. See here the engaging article by R. Kendall Soulen, "Hallowed Be Thy Name! The Tetragrammaton and the Name of the Trinity," in *Jews and Christians: People of God*, ed. Carl E. Braaten and Robert W. Jenson (Grand Rapids: Eerdmans, 2003) 14-40.

33. In addition to Bauckham's discussion of this passage in *God Crucified*, see Hurtado, *How on Earth?* 83-107.

34. Bauckham, *God Crucified*, 59.

35. Noted by Janet Rasmussen in New Testament Theology and Ethics class, Fall 2006.

36. See Larry Hurtado, *Lord Jesus Christ*, 134-216.

37. Bauckham, *God Crucified*, 76.

38. Larry W. Hurtado, *How on Earth?* 28. The term Hurtado frequently uses is "Binitarian worship," which he sees in evidence also in the Pastoral Epistles, such as "King of kings and Lord of lords" (1 Tim 6:15). See Hurtado, *Lord Jesus Christ*, 512-18.

39. Hurtado, *How on Earth?* 77-78.

40. Swartley, *Covenant of Peace*, 83-88, 112-20, 133-34, 145-46, 164-73, 245-53, 264-73, 284-89, 324-42.

41. See my lengthy quote (in ibid., 272-73) from Peter Davids, *The First Epistle of Peter*, NICNT (Grand Rapids: Eerdmans, 1990), 104.

42. Farmer, *Jesus and the Gospel*, 177-221.

43. Ibid., 221. See also Farmer and Farkasfalvy, *Formation of the New Testament Canon*, 7-95.

11. Revelation: A Worship Service of Peace and Mission

1. For fuller analysis of the setting of Revelation and its theology, christology, and ethics, see chapter 12 in my *Covenant of Peace*. That chapter ends with a shorter version of the worship resource and fits within a half-hour service.

Conclusion

1. Perry B. Yoder, *Shalom*.

Appendix

1. George Huntston Williams and Angel M. Mergal, eds., *Spiritual and Anabaptist Writers: Documents Illustrative of the Radical Reformation* and *Evangelical Catholicism as Represented by Juan de Valdés* (Philadelphia: Westminster, 1957).

2. J. C. Wenger, ed., *The Complete Writings of Menno Simons, c. 1496-1561*, trans. Leonard Verduin (Scottdale, PA: Herald Press, 1956).

BIBLIOGRAPHY

Aldridge, Robert C. "The Courage to Start." In Grannis, et al., *The Risk of the Cross*, 46-50.

Arnold, Clinton. *Crucial Questions About Spiritual Warfare.* Grand Rapids: Baker Books, 1997.

———. *Ephesians, Power and Magic: The Concept of Power in Ephesians in Light of Its Historical Setting.* SNTSMS 63. Cambridge: Cambridge University Press, 1989.

———. *Powers of Darkness: A Study in Principalities and Powers in Paul.* Grand Rapids: Zondervan, 1992.

Ateek, Naim, Cedar Duaybis and Maurine Tobin, eds. *Challenging Christian Zionism: Theology, Politics, and Israel-Palestine Conflict.* London: Melisende, 2005.

Augsburger, Myron. "Beating Swords into Plowshares." *Christianity Today* 21 (Nov. 21, 1975): 195-97.

_____. "Facing the Problem." In *Perfect Love and War*, ed. Paul Hostetler, 11-20. Nappanee, IN: Evangel Press, 1974.

Bailey, Wilma. *"You Shall Not Kill" or "You Shall Not Murder"? The Assault on a Biblical Text.* Collegeville, MN: Liturgical Press, 2005.

Bauckham, Richard. *God Crucified: Monotheism and Christology in the New Testament.* Grand Rapids: Eerdmans, 1998.

Bauckham, Richard J. *Climax of Prophecy: Studies on the Book of Revelation.* Edinburgh: T & T Clark, 1993.

Bauman, Clarence. *The Sermon on the Mount: The Modern Quest for Its Meaning.* Macon, GA: Mercer University Press, 1985.

Bauman, Elizabeth Hershberger. *Coals of Fire.* Scottdale, PA: Herald Press, 1954.

Bishop, Peter D. *A Technique for Loving: Non-Violence in Indian and Christian Traditions*. London: SCM Press, 1981.

Boobyer, G. H. "Galilee and Galileans in St. Mark's Gospel," *Bulletin of John Rylands Library* 35 (1953): 334-38.

Bonhoeffer, Dietrich. *A Testament to Freedom: The Essential Writings of Dietrich Bonhoeffer*. HarperSanFrancisco, 1990.

Boyarin, Daniel. *Borderlines: The Partition of Judeo-Christianity*. Philadelphia: University of Pennsylvania Press, 2004.

———. *Dying for God: Martyrdom and the Making of Christianity and Judaism*. Stanford, CA: Stanford University Press, 1999.

_____. "Judaism as a Free Church: Footnotes to John Howard Yoder's *The Jewish-Christian Schism Revisited*." *CrossCurrents* 56 (2007): 6-21.

———. *A Radical Jew: Paul and the Politics of Identity*. Berkeley: University of California Press, 1994.

Boyd, Gregory A. *God at War: The Bible and Spiritual Conflict*. Downers Grove, IL: InterVarsity Press, 1997.

Braaten Carl E. and Robert W. Jenson, eds. *Jews and Christians: People of God*. Grand Rapids: Eerdmans, 2003.

Brandon, S. G. F. *Jesus and the Zealots*. New York: Scribner, 1967.

Brenneman, Laura L. "Further Footnotes on Paul, Yoder, and Boyarin." *CrossCurrents* 56 (2007): 60-69.

Brown, Dale W. *Biblical Pacifism*. Rev. ed. Nappanee, IN: Evangel Publishing House; Scottdale, PA: Herald Press, 2003.

Bruce, F. F. *The Spreading Flame: The Rise and Progress of Christianity*. Grand Rapids: Eerdmans, 1953.

Burkill, T. A. "Galilee and Jerusalem." In *Mysterious Revelation*. Ithaca, 252-57. NY: Cornell University Press, 1963.

Burkholder, J. R. "The Politics of Jesus." 32-37, in *A Peace Reader*, ed. E. Morris Sider and Luke Keefer Jr. Nappanee, IN: Evangel Publishing House, 2002.

Burge, Gary. "Theological and Biblical Assumptions of Christian Zionism." In *Challenging Christian Zionism*, ed. Ateek, et al., 45-58.

Byler, Daryl J., and Lisa Schirch. "Becoming Strategic Doves in a Land of Hawks: Alternative Security Through an Anabaptist Lens." In *At Peace and Unafraid*, ed. Friesen and Schlabach, 179-94.

Cadoux, C. J. *The Early Church and the World*. Edinburgh: T&T Clark, 1925.

Chilton, Bruce. *A Galilean Rabbi and His Bible: Jesus' Use of the Interpreted Scripture of His Time*. Wilmington, DE: Michael Glazier, 1984.

———. *The Kingdom of God in the Teachings of Jesus*. Philadelphia: Fortress, 1984.

———. "Regnum Dei Deus Est." *Scottish Journal of Theology* 31 (1978): 261-70.

Clemens, James E. "The Prince of Peace: A Song Cycle on the Words of Menno Simons." *A Field of Voices: Hymns for Worship*, by James E. Clemens and David Wright. Table Round Press, 2007.

Connick, C. Milo. *Jesus: The Man, the Mission, and the Message*. Rev. ed. Englewood Cliffs, NJ: Prentice-Hall, 1973.

Corson, Sarah. "Welcoming the Enemy: A Missionary Fights Violence with Love." *Sojourners* 12 (April 1983): 29-31(http://www.sifat.org/about_us/True%20Stories/welcoming%20the%20enemy.htm).

Cullmann, Oscar. *The State in the New Testament*. New York: Scribner, 1956.

Davids, Peter. *The First Epistle of Peter*, NICNT. Grand Rapids: Eerdmans, 1990.

Dinkler, Erich. "*Eirēnē*—the Early Christian Concept of Peace." In *The Meaning of Peace*, ed. P. B. Yoder and W. M. Swartley, 99-101.

Dintaman, Stephen. "The Spiritual Poverty of the Anabaptist Vision." *Conrad Grebel Review* 10 (Spring 1992): 205-8. Cf. follow-up essays in *CGR* 13 (Winter 1995): 2-22.

Dodd, C. H. *According to the Scriptures: The Sub-Structure of New Testament Theology*. London: Nisbet, 1952.

Driedger, Leo, and Donald B. Kraybill. *Mennonite Peacemaking: From Quietism to Activism*. Scottdale, PA: Herald Press, 1994.

Driver, John. "The Kingdom of God: Goal of Messianic Mission." In *The Transfiguration of Mission*, ed. Wilbert R. Shenk, 83-105. Scottdale, PA: Herald Press, 1993.

Dunn, James D. G. "The New Perspective on Paul." In *Jesus, Paul, and the Law*, 183-215. Louisville: Westminster John Knox, 1990.

Durnbaugh, Donald F., ed. *On Earth Peace: Discussions on War/Peace Issues Between Friends, Mennonites, Brethren, and European Churches, 1935-1975*. Elgin, IL: Brethren Press, 1978.

Egan, Eileen. *Peace Be with You: Justified Warfare or the Way of Nonviolence*. Maryknoll, N.Y.: Orbis Books, 1999.

Eller, Vernard. *War and Peace from Genesis to Revelation: King Jesus' Manual of Arms for the 'Armless*. Scottdale, PA: Herald Press, 1981.

Enns, Fernando. "Public Peace, Justice, and Order in Ecumenical Conversation." In *At Peace and Unafraid*, ed. Duane Friesen and Gerald Schlabach, 241-59. Scottdale, PA: Herald Press, 2005.

Enz, Jacob. "Judaism and Jews." In *Mennonite Encyclopedia*, vol. 5, ed. C. J. Dyck and D. D. Martin, 469. Scottdale, PA: Herald Press, 1990.

Epp Weaver, Alain. "Further Footnotes on Zionism, Yoder, and Boyarin." *CrossCurrents* 56 (2007): 41-51.

______ . "The Power of Diaspora: Seeking the Peace of Palestine-Israel." In *At Peace and Unafraid*, ed. Friesen and Schlabach, 275-89.

______, ed. *Under Vine and Fig Tree: Biblical Theologies of Land and the Palestinian-Israeli Conflict*. Forthcoming.

Farmer, William R. *Jesus and the Gospel: Tradition, Scripture, and Canon*. Philadelphia: Fortress, 1982.

Farmer, William R., and Denis M. Farkasfalvy. *The Formation of the New Testament Canon: An Ecumenical Approach*. New York: Paulist Press, 1983.

Ferguson, John. *The Politics of Love: The New Testament and Nonviolent Revolution*. Cambridge: James Clarke, 1970; Nyack, NY: Fellowship Publications, 1979; Greenwood, SC: Attic Press. n.d.

Finger, Thomas N. *Christian Theology: An Eschatological Approach*. Vol. 1, Nashville: Thomas Nelson, 1985. Vol. 2, Scottdale, PA: Herald Press, 1989.

Flusser, David. *Jesus*. Jerusalem: Magnes Press, 1998.

Frankemölle, Hubert. "Jesus als deuterojesajanische Freudenbote? Zur Rezeption von Jes 52,7 und 61,1 im Neuen Testament, durch Jesus und in den Targumim." In *Vom Christentum zu Jesus* (FS Joachim Gnilka), ed. Hubert Frankemölle, 34-67. Freiberg: Herder, 1989.

Friedrich, J., W. Pohlmann, and P. Stuhlmacher. "Zur historischen Situation and Intention von Rom 13.1-7." *Zeitschrift für Theologie and Kirche* 73 (1967): 131-66.

Friesen, Duane. "In Search of Security: A Theology and Ethic of Peace and Public Order." In *At Peace and Unafraid*, ed. Friesen and Schlabach, 37-82.

Friesen, Duane, and Gerald Schlabach, ed. *At Peace and Unafraid: Public Order, Security, and the Wisdom of the Cross*. Scottdale, PA: Herald Press, 2005.

Fry, A. Ruth. *Victories Without Violence*. London: Dennis Dobson, 1957.

Furnish, Victor Paul. *The Moral Teaching of Paul*. Nashville: Abingdon, 1979.

Gardner, Clinton. *The Church as a Prophetic Community*. Philadelphia: Westminster, 1967.

Garrett, Susan. R. *The Temptations of Jesus in Mark's Gospel*. Grand Rapids: Eerdmans, 1998.

Gibson, Jeffrey B. "Jesus' Wilderness Temptation According to Mark." *JSNT* 53 (1994): 3-34.

———. *The Temptations of Jesus in Early Christianity*. JSNTSup 112; Sheffield: Sheffield Academic Press, 1995.

Gingerich, Ray, and Ted Grimsrud, ed. *Transforming the Powers: Peace, Justice, and the Domination System*. Minneapolis: Fortress, 2006.

Gorman, Michael J. *Cruciformity: Paul's Narrative Spirituality of the Cross*. Grand Rapids: Eerdmans, 2001.

Gowan, Donald E., ed. *The Westminster Theological Wordbook of the Bible*. Louisville: Westminster John Knox, 2003.

Grannis, Christopher, Arthur Laffin, and Elin Schade. *The Risk of the Cross: Christian Discipleship in the Nuclear Age*. New York: Seabury, 1981.

Grassi, Joseph A. *Informing the Future: Social Justice in the New Testament*. New York: Paulist Press, 2003.

———. *Peace on Earth: Roots and Practices from Luke's Gospel*. Collegeville, MN: Liturgical Press, 2004.

Hallie, Philip. *Lest Innocent Blood Be Shed*. New York: Harper & Row, 1979.

Harder, Lydia. "Seeking Wisdom in the Face of Foolishness: Toward a Robust Peace Theology." In *At Peace and Unafraid*, ed. Friesen and Schlabach, 117-52.

Hays, Richard B. "Anti-Judaism and Ethnic Conflict." In *The Moral Vision*, 407-43.

______. *The Moral Vision of the New Testament*. San Francisco: HarperSanFrancisco, 1996.

Herberg, Will. *Faith Enacted as History: Essays in Biblical Theology*. Philadelphia: Westminster, 1976.

Hershberger, Guy F. *War, Peace, and Nonresistance*. Scottdale, PA: Herald Press, 1944. Rev. ed., 1953. 3rd ed., 1969.

Heschel, Abraham J. *The Prophets*. New York: Harper & Row, 1962.

Holwerda, David E. *Jesus and Israel: One Covenant or Two?* Grand Rapids: Eerdmans, 1995.

Hornus, Jean-Michel. *It Is Not Lawful for Me to Fight.* Translated by Alan Kreider and Oliver Coburn. Scottdale, PA: Herald Press, 1980.

Horsley, Richard A. *Jesus and the Spiral of Violence: Popular Jewish Resistance in Roman Palestine.* San Francisco: Harper & Row, 1987.

Hurtado, Larry W. *How on Earth Did Jesus Become a God? Historical Questions About Earliest Devotion to Jesus.* Grand Rapids: Eerdmans, 2005.

———. *Lord Jesus Christ: Devotion to Jesus in Earliest Christianity.* Grand Rapids: Eerdmans, 2003.

Jackson, David. *Dial 911: Peaceful Christians and Urban Violence.* Scottdale, PA: Herald Press, 1981.

Jenson, Robert W. "Toward a Christian Theology of Judaism," 1-13, in *Jews and Christians: People of God*, ed. by Carl E. Braaten and Robert W. Jenson. Grand Rapids: Eerdmans, 2003.

Jeschke, Marlin. *Rethinking Holy Land: A Study in Salvation Geography.* Scottdale, PA: Herald Press, 2005.

Johns, Loren L. *The Lamb Christology of the Book of Revelation: An Investigation into Its Origins and Rhetorical Force.* WUNT[2] 167. Tübingen: Mohr Siebeck, 2003.

Johns, Loren L., and James R. Krabill, eds. *Even the Demons Submit: Continuing Jesus' Ministry of Deliverance.* Elkhart, IN: Institute of Mennonite Studies; Scottdale, PA: Herald Press, 2006.

Juel, Donald. *Messiah and Temple.* Missoula, MT: Society of Biblical Literature, 1977.

Kaufman, Donald D. *The Tax Dilemma: Praying for Peace, Paying for War.* Scottdale, PA: Herald Press, 1978. Rev. ed., Eugene, OR: Wipf & Stock, 2006.

———. *What Belongs to Caesar? A Discussion on the Christian Response to Payment of War Taxes.*

Scottdale, PA: Herald Press, 1969. Rev. ed., Eugene, OR: Wipf & Stock, 2006.

Kaufman, Gordon, D. *Nonresistance and Responsibility and Other Mennonite Essays*. Newton, KS: Faith & Life Press, 1979.

Kirk, Alan. "'Love Your Enemies,' the Golden Rule, and Ancient Reciprocity." *JBL* 122 (2003): 677-86.

Klassen, William. "'Love Your Enemies': Some Reflections on the Current Status of Research." In *The Love of Enemy and Nonretaliation*, edited by W. M. Swartley, 1-31.

———. "Love Your Enemy: A Study of New Testament Teaching on Coping with an Enemy." *Biblical Realism Confronts the Nation: Ten Christian Scholars Summon the Church to the Discipleship of Peace*, edited by Paul Peachey, 153-83. Scottdale, PA: Herald Press distributing for Church Peace Mission / Fellowship Publications, 1963.

———. "The Novel Element in the Love Commandment of Jesus." In *The New Way of Jesus: Essays Presented to Howard Charles*, edited by William Klassen, 100-114. Newton, KS: Faith & Life Press, 1980.

Klassen Wiebe, Sheila. Uniform Series: *Adult Bible Study*, December 3, Winter 2006–7. Scottdale, PA: Faith & Life Resources, 2006.

Koester, Helmut, "Jesus the Victim," *JBL* 111 (1992): 2-15.

Krabill, James R., Walter Sawatsky, and Charles E. Van Engen, eds. *Evangelical, Ecumenical, and Anabaptist Missiologies in Conversation: In Honor of Wilbert R. Shenk*. Maryknoll, NY: Orbis Press, 2006.

Kraybill, Donald B. *The Upside-Down Kingdom*. Scottdale, PA: Herald Press, 1978. Rev. 3rd ed., 2003.

Kraybill, J. Nelson. *Imperial Cult and Commerce in John's Apocalypse*. JSNTSup 132. Sheffield: Sheffield Academic Press, 1996.

Krehbiel, June. "Focus on Jesus: Pentecostal Pacifist to Speak for Joint Worship at San José Mennonite Convention." *The Mennonite*, May 15, 2007, 14-15.

Kreider, Alan. *Journey Toward Holiness: A Way of Living for God's Nation*. Scottdale, PA: Herald Press, 1987.

———. "Light." *The Third Way* 11 (October 1988): 14-16.

———. "Pacifist Christianity." See W. M. Swartley and A. Kreider.

———. "Salt and Light." *The Third Way* 11 (September 1988): 14-16.

———. "Salty Discipleship." *The Other Side* 25 (March-April 1989): 34-37.

Kreider, Roy. *The Land of Revelation: A Reconciling Presence in Israel*. Scottdale, PA: Herald Press, 2004.

Kremer, Jacob. "Peace—God's Gift: Biblical-Theological Considerations." In *The Meaning of Peace*, edited by P. B. Yoder and W. M. Swartley, 21-35.

Lane, William. *Commentary on the Gospel of Mark*. Grand Rapids: Eerdmans, 1974.

Lapp, John A., ed. *Peacemakers in a Broken World*. Scottdale, PA: Herald Press, 1969.

Lapp, John E. *Studies in Nonresistance: An Outline for Study and Reference*. Scottdale, PA: Peace Problems Committee of the Mennonite General Conference, 1948.

Lehn, Cornelia. *Peace Be with You*. Newton, KS: Faith & Life Press, 1980.

Leivestad, Ragner. *Christ the Conqueror: Ideas of Conflict and Victory in the New Testament*. London: SPCK, 1954.

Lind, Millard. *Yahweh Is a Warrior*. Scottdale, PA: Herald Press, 1980.

Marshall, Chris. *The Little Book of Biblical Justice*. Intercourse, PA: Good Books, 2005.

Martin, Ernest D. *Colossians and Philemon*. BCBC. Scottdale, PA: Herald Press, 1993.

Mauser, Ulrich. *The Gospel of Peace: A Scriptural Message for Today's World*. SPS 1. Louisville: Westminster/John Knox, 1992.

McAlpine, Thomas H. *Facing the Powers: What Are the Options?* Monrovia, CA: MARC, 1991.

McClain, George. *Claiming All Things for God.* Nashville: Abingdon, 1998.

Meier, John P. *The Vision Of Matthew : Christ, Church, And Morality In The First Gospel.* New York: Paulist Press, 1979.

Meggitt, Justin J. "The Social Status of Erastus (Rom 16:23)." *Novum Testamentum* 38 (1996): 218-23.

Miller, Marlin E. "Gospel of Peace." *Mission Focus* 6 (September 1977): 1-5. See next entry.

———. "He Came Preaching Peace." *Gospel Herald* 76 (August 30, 1983): 593-96. "Gospel of Peace" and "He Came Preaching Peace" reprinted in *Theology of the Church: Writings by Marlin E. Miller*, edited by Richard A. Kauffman and Gayle Gerber Koontz, 3-20. Text-Reader Series no. 7. Elkhart, IN: Institute of Mennonite Studies, 1997.

Miranda, José. *Marx and the Bible: A Critique of the Philosophy of Oppression.* Translated by John Eagleson. Maryknoll, NY: Orbis Books, 1974.

Nation, Mark Thiessen. "Toward a Theology for Conflict Transformation: Learnings from John Howard Yoder." *MQR* 80 (2006): 43-60.

Neuhaus, Richard John. "Salvation Is from the Jews." In *Jews and Christians: People of God*, edited by Carl E. Braaten and Robert W. Jenson, 65-77. Grand Rapids: Eerdmans, 2003.

Neville, David J. "Toward a Teleology of Peace: Contesting Matthew's Violent Eschatology." *JSNT* 70 (2007), forthcoming.

Nouwen, Henri. "Letting Go of All Things." *Sojourners* 8 (March 1979): 5-6.

Novak, David. "From Supersessionism to Parallelism in Jewish-Christian Dialogue." In *Jews and Christians*, ed. Braaten and Jenson, 95-113.

O'Donovan, Oliver. *In Pursuit of a Christian View on War.* Bramcote, UK: Grove Books, 1977.

Ollenburger, Ben C. *Zion, City of the Great King: A Theological Symbol of the Jerusalem Cult.* Sheffield: Sheffield Academic Press, 1987.

Pilgrim, Walter. *Uneasy Neighbors: Church and State in the New Testament.* Minneapolis: Fortress, 1999.

Prior, Michael. *The Bible and Colonialism: A Moral Critique.* Sheffield, UK: Sheffield Academic Press, 1997.

Rossing, Barbara R. *The Rapture Exposed: The Message of Hope in the Book of Revelation.* Boulder, CO: Westview Press, 2004.

Roth, John D. *Choosing Against War: A Christian View; A Love Stronger Than Our Fears.* Intercourse, PA: Good Books, 2002.

Rutenber, Culbert G. *The Dagger and the Cross: An Examination of Pacifism.* Nyack, NY: Fellowship Publications, 1950.

Ruth, John L. *'Twas Seeding Time: A Mennonite View of the American Revolution.* Scottdale, PA: Herald Press, 1976.

Sattler, Michael. "On Two Kinds of Obedience." In *The Legacy of Michael Sattler,* trans. and ed. John H. Yoder, 121-25. Classics of the Radical Reformation Series 1. Scottdale, PA: Herald Press, 1973.

Schertz, Mary H., and Ivan Friesen, eds. *Beautiful Upon the Mountains: Biblical Essays on Mission, Peace, and the Reign of God.* Elkhart, IN: Institute of Mennonite Studies; Scottdale, PA: Herald Press, 2004.

Schirch, Lisa, and Daryl J. Byler. "Effective and Faithful Security Strategies." In *At Peace and Unafraid*, ed. Friesen and Schlabach, 423-44.

Schlabach, Gerald. "Just Policing and the Christian Call to Nonviolence." In *At Peace and Unafraid*, ed. Friesen and Schlabach, 405-21.

Schmidt, Daryl. "Luke's 'Innocent' Jesus: A Scriptural Apologetic." In *Political Issues in Luke-Acts*, edited by Richard J. Cassidy and Philip Scharper, 111-21. Maryknoll, NY: Orbis Press, 1983.

Schottroff, Luise. "'Give to Caesar What Belongs to Caesar and to God What Belongs to God': A Theological Response of the Early Christian Church to Its Social and Political Environment." In *Love of Enemy and Nonretaliation*, ed. W. M. Swartley, 223-57.

Segal, Alan F. *Paul the Convert: The Apostolate and Apostasy of Saul the Pharisee*. New Haven: Yale University Press, 1990.

Shank, David A. "Jesus the Messiah: Messianic Foundation of Mission." In *The Transfiguration of Mission*, ed. Shenk, 83-105.

Shenk Wilbert R. ed. *The Transfiguration of Mission*. Scottdale, PA: Herald Press, 1993.

Shillington, George. *2 Corinthians*. BCBC. Scottdale, PA: Herald Press, 1999.

Sider, Ronald J. *Christ and Violence*. Scottdale, PA: Herald Press, 1979.

Sizer, Stephen. "The Historical Roots of Christian Zionism from Irving to Balfour: Christian Zionism in the United Kingdom (1820-1918)." In *Challenging Christian Zionism*, ed. Ateek. *et al.*, 20-31.

———. *Zion's Christian Soldiers: The Bible, Israel, and the Church*. Nottingham, UK: InterVarsity Press, 2007.

Smith, Morton. "Zealots and Sicarii: Their Origins and Relation." *Harvard Theological Review* 64 (1971): 1-19.

Stassen, Glen H. "The Fourteen Triads of the Sermon on the Mount." *JBL* 122 (2003): 267-308.

———. *Just Peacemaking: Transforming Initiatives for Justice and Peace*. Louisville: Westminster/John Knox, 1992.

Stassen, Glen H., and David P. Gushee. *Kingdom Ethics:*

Following Jesus in Contemporary Context. Downers Grove, IL: InterVarsity Press, 2003.

Stauffer, Ethelbert. *Christ and the Caesars*. London: SCM Press, 1955.

Stendahl, Krister. *Paul Among Jew and Gentile*. Philadelphia: Fortress, 1976.

Stuhlmacher, Peter. *The Gospel and the Gospels*. Grand Rapids: Eerdmans, 1991.

Sugden, Chris. *A Different Dream: Non-violence as Practical Politics*. Bramcote, UK: Grove Books, 1976.

Swartley, Jacob. "Letter to Bishop John Herr in 1819." *Pennsylvania Mennonite Heritage* 30 (January 2007): 20-22.

Swartley, Willard M. "Biblical Faith Confronts Evil Spiritual Realities," 24-40, and "Reflections on Deliverance Ministry," 108-13. In *Even the Demons Submit: Continuing Jesus' Ministry of Deliverance*, edited by Loren L. Johns and James R. Krabill. Elkhart, IN: Institute of Mennonite Studies; Scottdale, PA: Herald Press, 2006.

———. "Biblical Sources of Stewardship." In *The Earth Is the Lord's: Essays on Stewardship*, edited by Mary Evelyn Jegen and Bruno Manno, 22-43. New York: Paulist Press, 1978.

______. "Bosch and Beyond: Biblical Issues in Mission," *Mission Focus* 11 Supplement (2003): 77-105.

———. *Covenant of Peace: The Missing Peace in New Testament Theology and Ethics*. Grand Rapids: Eerdmans, 2006.

———. "Exorcism," 285-87, and "Satan," 791-94. In *The Mennonite Encyclopedia*, vol. 5, edited by C. J. Dyck and D. D. Martin. Scottdale, PA: Herald Press, 1990.

———. "How to Interpret the Bible: A Case Study of Romans 13:1-7 and the Payment of Taxes Used for War." *Seeds* 3, no. 4 (June 1984): 28-31.

———. *Israel's Scripture Traditions and the Synoptic*

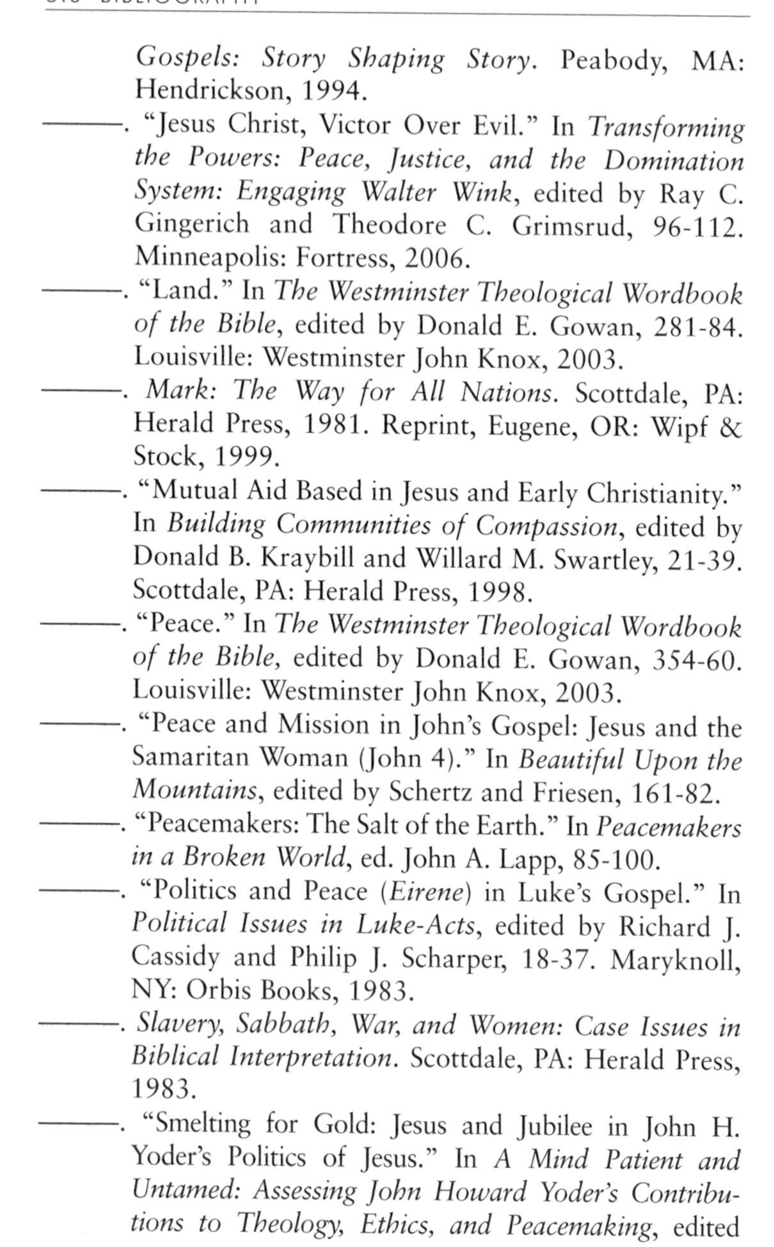

Gospels: Story Shaping Story. Peabody, MA: Hendrickson, 1994.

———. "Jesus Christ, Victor Over Evil." In *Transforming the Powers: Peace, Justice, and the Domination System: Engaging Walter Wink*, edited by Ray C. Gingerich and Theodore C. Grimsrud, 96-112. Minneapolis: Fortress, 2006.

———. "Land." In *The Westminster Theological Wordbook of the Bible*, edited by Donald E. Gowan, 281-84. Louisville: Westminster John Knox, 2003.

———. *Mark: The Way for All Nations*. Scottdale, PA: Herald Press, 1981. Reprint, Eugene, OR: Wipf & Stock, 1999.

———. "Mutual Aid Based in Jesus and Early Christianity." In *Building Communities of Compassion*, edited by Donald B. Kraybill and Willard M. Swartley, 21-39. Scottdale, PA: Herald Press, 1998.

———. "Peace." In *The Westminster Theological Wordbook of the Bible,* edited by Donald E. Gowan, 354-60. Louisville: Westminster John Knox, 2003.

———. "Peace and Mission in John's Gospel: Jesus and the Samaritan Woman (John 4)." In *Beautiful Upon the Mountains*, edited by Schertz and Friesen, 161-82.

———. "Peacemakers: The Salt of the Earth." In *Peacemakers in a Broken World*, ed. John A. Lapp, 85-100.

———. "Politics and Peace (*Eirene*) in Luke's Gospel." In *Political Issues in Luke-Acts*, edited by Richard J. Cassidy and Philip J. Scharper, 18-37. Maryknoll, NY: Orbis Books, 1983.

———. *Slavery, Sabbath, War, and Women: Case Issues in Biblical Interpretation*. Scottdale, PA: Herald Press, 1983.

———. "Smelting for Gold: Jesus and Jubilee in John H. Yoder's Politics of Jesus." In *A Mind Patient and Untamed: Assessing John Howard Yoder's Contributions to Theology, Ethics, and Peacemaking*, edited by Gayle Gerber Koontz and Ben C. Ollenburger, 288-301. Telford, PA: Cascadia Publishing House; Scottdale, PA: Herald Press, 2004.

———, ed. *The Love of Enemy and Nonretaliation in the New Testament*. Chap. 10 trans. by Gerhard Reimer. Louisville: Westminster/John Knox, 1992.

———, ed. *The Meaning of Peace*. See Yoder, Perry B., and Willard M. Swartley.

———, ed. *Politics of Discipleship and Discipleship in Politics: Jürgen Moltmann Lectures in Dialogue with Mennonite Scholars*. Eugene, OR: Cascade Books / Wipf & Stock, 2006.

Swartley, Willard M., and Alan Kreider. "Pacifist Christianity: The Kingdom Way." In *War and Pacifism: When Christians Disagree*, edited by Oliver Barclay, 38-60. Leicester, UK: Inter-Varsity Press, 1984.

Swartley, Willard M., and Thomas Finger. "Bondage and Deliverance: Biblical and Theological Perspectives." In *Essays on Spiritual Bondage and Deliverance*, edited by Willard M. Swartley, 10-38. Occasional Papers 11. Elkhart, IN: Institute of Mennonite Studies, 1988.

Tambasco, Anthony J. "Principalities, Powers, and Peace." In *Blessed Are the Peacemakers: Biblical Perspectives on Peace and Its Social Foundations*, edited by Anthony J. Tambasco, 116-33. New York: Paulist Press, 1989.

Taylor, Richard K. *Blockade: A Guide to Non-Violent Intervention*. Maryknoll, NY: Orbis Books, 1977.

Toews, John E. *Romans*. BCBC. Scottdale, PA: Herald Press, 2004.

Van Braght, Thieleman J., compiler. *Martyrs Mirror*. 1660. Translated from the original Dutch by Joseph F. Sohm. 2nd English ed., Elkhart, IN, 1886. Reprint, Scottdale, PA: Mennonite Publishing House, 1950.

Von Rad, Gerhard. " שלמ in the Old Testament." *TDNT* 2: 402-6.

Wagner, Donald. "From Blackstone to Bush: Christian Zionism

in the United States (1890-2004)." In *Challenging Christian Zionism,* Ateek *et al.*, ed., 32-44.

Wallis, Jim. "The Work of Prayer." *Sojourners* 8 (March 1979): 3-5.

Weaver, Dorothy Jean. *Matthew's Missionary Discourse: A Literary-Critical Analysis.* JSNTSup 38. Sheffield: JSOT Press, 1990.

Williams, George Hunston, and Angel M. Mergal, eds. *Spiritual and Anabaptist Writers: Documents Illustrative of the Radical Reformation and Evangelical Catholicism as Represented by Juan de Valdés.* Philadelphia: Westminster Press, 1957.

Willimon, William, and Stanley Hauerwas. *Lord Teach Us: The Lord's Prayer and the Christian Life.* Nashville: Abingdon, 1996.

Wink, Walter. *Engaging the Powers: Discernment and Resistance in a World of Domination.* Minneapolis: Fortress, 1992.

———. *Naming the Powers.* Philadelphia: Fortress, 1984.

———. "Neither Passivity nor Violence: Jesus' Third Way." In *SBL Seminar Papers*, 210-24. Atlanta: Scholars Press, 1988. Revised, in *Love of Enemy and Nonretaliation*, edited by W. M. Swartley, 102-25.

———. *Unmasking the Powers: The Invisible Forces That Determine Human Existence.* Philadelphia: Fortress, 1986.

———. *When the Powers Fall: Reconciliation in the Healing of the Nations.* Minneapolis: Fortress, 1998.

Westermann, Claus. "Peace [Shalom] in the Old Testament." In *The Meaning of Peace*, edited by Perry B. Yoder and Willard M. Swartley, 37-70.

Wright, N. T. *Jesus and the Victory of God.* Minneapolis: Fortress, 1996.

Yaguchi, Yorifumi. *The Poetry of Yorifumi Yaguchi: A Japanese Voice in English.* Edited by Wilbur J. Birky. Intercourse, PA: Good Books, 2006.

Yancey, Philip. "Exploring a Parallel Universe." *Christianity Today*, November 2005, 128.

Yoder, John Howard. *Body Politics: Five Practices of the Christian Community Before the Watching World.* Scottdale, PA: Herald Press, 2001.

———. *The Christian Witness to the State.* Elkhart, IN: Institute of Mennonite Studies; Newton, KS: Faith & Life Press, 1964. 3rd printing with updated notes, Faith & Life Press, 1977. 2nd ed., Scottdale, PA: Herald Press, 2002.

———. *He Came Preaching Peace.* Scottdale, PA: Herald Press, 1985.

———. "'It Did Not Have to Be.'" In *The Jewish-Christian Schism Revisited*, edited by Michael C. Cartwright and Peter Ochs, 43-68. Grand Rapids: Eerdmans, 2003.

———. *The Original Revolution.* Scottdale, PA: Herald Press, 1972.

———. *The Politics of Jesus: Vicit Agnus Noster.* Grand Rapids: Eerdmans, 1972. Rev. ed., 1994.

———. *Reinhold Niebuhr and Christian Pacifism.* Heerewegen Pamphlet 1. Zeist, Netherlands: [Mennonite Conference and Peace Center], 1954. Reprint as article, *MQR* 29 (April 1955): 101-17. Reprint as booklet, Scottdale, PA: Herald Press, 1968.

———. *What Would You Do? A Serious Answer to a Standard Question.* Expanded edition with Joan Baez, Tom Skinner, Leo Tolstoy, and others. Scottdale, PA: Herald Press, 1992.

Yoder Neufeld, Thomas. *Ephesians.* BCBC. Scottdale, PA: Herald Press, 2002.

———. *"Put on the Armour of God": The Divine Warrior from Isaiah to Ephesians.* JSNTSup 140. Sheffield: Sheffield Academic Press, 1997.

Yoder, Perry B. *From Word to Life: A Guide to the Art of Bible Study*. Scottdale, PA: Herald Press, 1982.

———. *Shalom: The Bible's Word for Salvation, Peace, and*

Justice. Newton, KS: Faith & Life Press, 1988. Reprint, Nappanee, IN: Evangel Press, 1997.

———. "Shalom Revisited." AMBS Library: Unpublished manuscript, 1984.

Yoder, Perry B., and Willard M. Swartley, eds. *The Meaning of Peace: Biblical Studies.* Translated by Walter Sawatsky. SPS 2. Louisville: Westminster/John Knox, 1992. Rev. ed., Elkhart, IN: Institute of Mennonite Studies, 2001.

Zehr, Howard. *Changing Lenses: A New Focus for Crime and Justice.* Scottdale, PA: Herald Press, 1990.

SCRIPTURE INDEX

Old Testament

AUTHOR AND NAMES INDEX

SUBJECT INDEX

THE AUTHOR

Willard M. Swartley is professor emeritus of New Testament at Associated Mennonite Biblical Seminary. He has served as dean of the seminary and director of the Institute of Mennonite Studies, and New Testament editor of the Believers Church Bible Commentary series. Among other titles, he is author of *Covenant of Peace: The Missing Peace in New Testament Theology and Ethics*, *Homosexuality: Biblical Interpretation and Moral Discernment*, *Slavery, Sabbath, War, and Women: Case Studies in Biblical Interpretation*, editor of *The Love of Enemy and Nonretaliation in the New Testament*, and co-editor (with Perry Yoder) of *The Meaning of Peace.*